POLICE IN URBAN SOCIETY

Police in Urban Society

Edited with an introduction by

HARLAN HAHN

S SAGE PUBLICATIONS / Beverly Hills   London

Portions of this volume appeared in the May—August, 1970 issue of The American Behavioral Scientist *(Volume 13, Numbers 5 and 6), published by Sage Publications, Inc.*

For information address:

SAGE PUBLICATIONS, INC.
275 South Beverly Drive
Beverly Hills, California 90212

Printed in United States of America

International Standard Book Number 0-8039-0082-1

Library of Congress Catalog Card No. 77-127986

FIRST PRINTING

Contents

Acknowledgments

In recent years, popular concern about the conduct of police officers has increased dramatically. As America became aroused by a mounting fear of crime, protest demonstrations, and urban violence, many citizens began to regard the police as the only arm of government that stood between the maintenance of public order and the danger of massive social upheavals. At the same time, law enforcement agencies were confronted by opposing demands to stop "crime in the streets" and to end "police brutality." The role of policemen in an urbanized society, therefore, emerged as one of the nation's most pressing social and political issues.

This volume represents an effort by twenty social scientists to grapple with some basic questions in this controversy. It is based, in part, on a special issue of the *American Behavioral Scientist* on police and society. All of the contributions are original either to that issue or to this book.

The editor would like to take this opportunity to express his appreciation to the contributors for their excellent cooperation and assistance in this project. Although many of the authors may not agree with all of the analyses presented in the introductions or the chapters of the book, they might—if they were assembled—support the need to raise many of the issues and problems discussed on these pages. Thanks also must be extended to the publishers for their patience and understanding in the preparation of this volume.

—HARLAN HAHN
University of California
Riverside

The Public and the Police

A Theoretical Perspective

HARLAN HAHN
University of California, Riverside

Although the study of law enforcement long has formed a neglected area of research, there have been growing indications that police forces are becoming a major subject of interest both to social scientists and to the general public. In part, this mounting concern has been prompted by the involvement of police officers in pressing social and political controversies. As extensive anxiety about crime, protests, demonstrations, and violence began to emerge as salient national issues, serious consideration of the role of policemen in those events seemed inescapable. Moreover, the increasing attention that has been devoted to police practices appeared to reflect the social concerns of behavioral scientists, as well as other observers. The growth of research on law enforcement apparently has signified a desire not only to gain an improved understanding of the difficulties confronting police officers but also to employ that information in the solution of some of the country's most critical social problems.

In addition, however, the study of the police seems to raise some fundamental issues in social and political theory. While the routine actions of patrolmen on city streets might appear to be relatively mundane and unexceptional, they also seem to represent an important means by which many of a nation's highest values are transmitted to the public. Concepts such as law, order, authority, and justice might convey the appearance of remote abstractions, but in modern society perhaps the principal public official who is authorized to apply those standards to social conduct is the policeman. Law enforcement officers may play a crucial role in the relationship between ordinary citizens and the awesome principles that sustain an organized society.

The study of police activities, therefore, must encompass the examination of relatively broad philosophical issues concerning law enforcement responsibilities, as well as efforts to secure increased information about police practices and to assist in resolving major social crises. While the need to devise appropriate remedies for police problems represents an important objective, the fulfillment of that task also may depend upon an ability to answer several prior questions. How can policemen contribute to the maintenance of the rule of law and to the preservation of public order? What is the role of law enforcement officers in curbing antisocial behavior and in dispensing justice? What is the relationship between police officers, public authorities, and the people? The purposes of this essay are to examine several different theoretical approaches to the assessment of police duties and to explore the impact of those concepts upon the association between policemen, political leaders, and the public.

THE FUNCTIONS OF POLICE FORCES

Although a close relationship seems to exist between police activities and broad theoretical issues, relatively few efforts have been made to identify the major functions of law enforcement officers. Many statements of police responsibilities have seemed either too descriptive and detailed or too ambiguous and vague (see, for example, Lohman and Misner, 1966: 25-26; Niederhoffer, 1967: 11). The former type of declarations often has defined the tasks of law enforcement officers as the specific orders and assignments given them by their organizational superiors; the latter assertions frequently have characterized the police mandate in overly broad or equivocal phrases such as the prevention and control of crime, the protection of life and property, and similar terms. Neither formulation has appeared to provide an especially useful perspective for the study of police practices. While the explicit description of police routines has yielded an unwieldy number of categories for analysis, explanations of the police mission in diffuse or ambivalent terms frequently have produced classifications that seem to be devoid of content or meaning.

Perhaps more importantly, however, both types of statements usually have failed to relate police behavior to the general principles that form the basis of law enforcement operations. As a public agency that has developed more contact with citizens than nearly any other government bureau, perhaps the police have had a greater direct impact upon the association between personal conduct and abstract social standards than many other political leaders. Attempts to discover the contemporary meaning of such basic values as law and order or authority and justice, therefore, have seemed to require a careful examination of interactions between police officers and members of society.

Perhaps the most significant features of police duties emerge from their encounters with the public. The principal activities of policemen are not conducted in isolation, but they arise from direct confrontations and close interpersonal relations with civilians. In fact, the major province of police responsibility may be located at the precise intersection of public authority and social behavior. As long as persons engage in conduct that is unrelated to the regulations which the state has defined as essential for the maintenance of orderly social life, the actions of private citizens usually are not regarded as matters of legitimate police interest or concern. Similarly, individual activities that are consistent with the law may be viewed as outside the scope of law enforcement duties, except insofar as they require police supervision or protection. Interference with behavior that is either irrelevant to or compatible with the legal requirements created by the state might be perceived as unwarranted police intrusion in private affairs. As public conduct begins to approach legal or social boundaries, however, a growing demand may develop for police intervention to curtail the behavior and to enforce the rules that normally sustain personal relations in society.

The proper jurisdiction of police officers, therefore, may be confined to the thin barrier that separates permissible social conduct and legal prohibitions. Personal behavior may become police business only when these two points are joined, that is, when public activities begin to trespass upon the legal preserves established by government officials. Perhaps the chief problem of police work is the task of ascertaining whether or not the particular conduct of an individual represents a form of behavior that the society, acting through its political leaders, has classified as inimical to its fundamental interests. Although this issue may be subjected to extensive subsequent litigation and controversy, it is the policeman who, in the first instance, must make this critical and often instantaneous decision. Moreover, in the minds of many citizens, it is the policeman who may symbolize and personify external public authority.

The actions of police officers in securing the border between social conduct and the legal obligations erected by the state, therefore, represent a vital relationship between the behavior of individuals and the principles that comprise the foundations of organized society. In fact, the juxtaposition of public conduct and abstract social or political doctrines may be not only the characteristic that determines police responsibilities, but police forces also might be *the* institutions that most clearly exemplify this juncture. The presence of police officers in almost all communities seems to bear implicit testimony to the proposition that apparently remote social standards do exist and that they are relevant to the everyday activities of ordinary citizens. Although the punitive duties of law enforcement officers frequently have failed to arouse strong public sympathy or support, few of even their most severe critics would contend that police forces could be totally abolished. In the absence of a public agency to supervise the division between personal actions and political authority, the task of relating governmental regulations to individual behavior would be nearly impossible.

Fundamentally, the police seem to form a crucial linkage between public officials empowered to make decisions on behalf of society and the people whose lives may be governed by those decisions. Since policemen are authorized to invoke the powers of the state in specific social situations, the actions of law enforcement officers not only reflect an important means by which personal conduct is related to abstract social values, but they also may signify a direct connection between the public and political leaders. Thus the examination of police practices, in part, seems to provide another approach to the perennial political problem of identifying the relationship between elites and masses. Although social and political scientists have explored many facets of the interaction between citizens and government leaders, they have often appeared to neglect the role of police officers in this relationship.

THE SOCIAL CONTROL PERSPECTIVE

Perhaps one of the most common descriptions of law enforcement duties is encompassed by the concept of social control. Policemen often are regarded primarily as officials who administer significant restrictions upon human behavior. As a result, major emphasis is placed upon the coercive impact of police operations. According to this view, the task of imposing authoritative limitations upon public activities may be the principal function and the defining characteristic of police practices.

Actually, however, the actions of police officers reflect only one of three apparent methods by which social control is applied to public behavior. Initially, social conduct frequently is guided or restrained by *personal discipline.* The individual may exert limitations upon his own actions that ultimately contribute to the perpetuation of orderly and predictable social life. In general, those internal restraints are regarded as *psychological* forms of social control. Secondly, personal interactions may be governed by often subtle and sometimes unspoken *social conventions.* Those rules may include established traditions, as well as norms or mores. Although the total range of such customs may not even be fully identified or enumerated as yet, there is little doubt that they exert a strong influence upon human behavior. The efforts to isolate and to discover those social controls usually are contained in *sociological* or *anthropological* research. Finally, there are regulations that emanate from the major sources of public authority in society. The primary obligation to administer the *laws* that are originated by government leaders is bestowed upon policemen. Hence, both the enactment and the enforcement of laws seem to represent an essentially *political* form of social control. While this assessment of social control mechanisms may reflect a severe oversimplification of the complex processes by which social relations are regulated, it appears to illustrate the political significance of the forms of social control exercised by police officers. Unlike the restrictions that arise from psychological or sociological origins, the rules that are enforced by policemen seem to be closely related to major political institutions and principles.

The social controls imposed by law enforcement officers, therefore, appear to denote a distinctively political component of the broad range of influences that may guide or direct social activity. Although the operation of psychological and sociological as well as political restraints may constitute the basic prerequisites for a viable political community, the authoritative regulations upon human conduct administered by the police seem to be especially critical for the survival of the state. Perhaps the basic framework of any society can be found in the provisions of its criminal code. The definition of types of behavior that are to be proscribed as well as those that are to be regarded as tolerable or appropriate may be one of the most fundamental prerogatives of the body politic.

The judgments implied in outlawing specified activities not only constitute highly salient political decisions, but also may provide an indication of the political influence wielded by various groups in the country. From this perspective, the political impact of persons engaged in commercial exaggeration or misrepresentation—the despoliation of the environment, or warfare, for example—might be adjudged to exceed the political strength of thieves, arsonists, or murderers. Although relatively few attempts have been made to employ the criminal statutes as direct indices of political power, it is difficult to escape the conclusion, as Holden (1970: 240) notes, that "the behaviors defined as criminal are more likely than not the behaviors of the poorer and politically less skillful members of the polity." The act of labeling a form of behavior as illegal or contrary to the interests of the entire society embodies an unusually critical political evaluation that is closely related to the foundations of the social order.

While the decisions of legislators and judges in shaping the criminal law appear to represent an especially significant type of political activity, the practices of police officers in enforcing those decisions seem to reflect an even more fundamental form of political action. Since the statutes cannot encompass all of the complex circumstances in which they might be applied, perhaps the basic responsibility for determining the legal propriety of personal conduct is vested in police officers. In making a decision about invoking the penalties of the criminal code, policemen exercise enormous power and broad discretion. Ultimately, some of the tangled problems of applying legal stipulations to the varied events that arise in human affairs must be resolved by the courts or by legislatures. Without police enforcement, however, the policies adopted by judges and lawmakers might be ineffective and meaningless. The functions of law enforcement officers, therefore, seem to rest at the base of the broader legislative and judicial process that is responsible for defining the standards of acceptable social conduct.

The social controls imposed by police officers seem to represent a highly political means of regulating public behavior. In fact, growing public demands for the control of "crime in the streets" might even be interpreted as an indication that the restraints exerted by individual discipline or by social conventions are no longer capable of providing adequate coordination or direction for social relations. Perhaps many would argue that the emergence of the police as a target of mounting popular controversy reflects a major decline in personal ethics or commonly held moral values. As a result, the state is compelled to intervene in a broad variety of social circumstances to preserve those principles incorporated in the criminal law that are essential to the maintenance of an organized society. The supervision of personal conduct thus may be regarded as an increased governmental responsibility when other forms of social control have collapsed.

Perhaps the growth of popular concern about the social control functions of law enforcement agencies, however, has been promoted primarily by a pervasive misconception regarding the nature of crime and police duties. In general, public assessments of unlawful behavior seemingly have been shaped by a fear of the unknown, the deviant, or the stranger who may perpetrate his crimes by stealth and under the cover of darkness. This prevalent image of illegality, with its strong connotations of mystery and evil, has become a salient threat in the everyday activities of many citizens. Public opinion surveys have revealed that the fear of criminal attack has prompted a large proportion of Americans to state that they are reluctant to walk alone in public at night (Reiss, 1967: 102-109; Ennis, 1967: 72-79). As a result, increasing numbers of persons have turned to the police—often in desperation or panic—for protection from this menace to their lives and property.

Several studies (see, for example, President's Commission on Law Enforcement and Administration of Justice, 1967a: 17-53), however, indicate that a high proportion of violent crimes occur in private dwellings rather than in public places, and that they are most frequently committed by friends, relatives, or acquaintances of the victim. The probability that a major crime will be perpetrated by a stranger, or a person who is not known to the victim, is extremely low, except for certain offenses such as robbery and burglary. Moreover, the police are least successful in solving those crimes that are generally committed by strangers. If they do succeed in making an arrest in a criminal case, it is usually made on the basis of information supplied by the victim or one of his acquaintances. The facts of crime, therefore, yield the ironic conclusion that a person may have less to fear from strangers than from his friends and relatives.

Since few persons normally are willing to support increased social controls that may be imposed primarily upon themselves or their friends, fear of the strange and alien forces of crime also has seemed to form the basis of an intriguing dualism that has pervaded the thinking of most Americans. Public perceptions of crime and police problems often have appeared to reflect an implicit distinction between "criminal elements" in society and supposedly "law-abiding" segments of the population. Perhaps this dichotomy has been fostered, in part, by the high rates of recidivism recorded in the penal system and by the fact that a large proportion of crimes undoubtedly are attributable to a comparatively small group of habitual offenders. Even though it is extremely difficult to estimate either the total amount of crime or the actual levels of law observance in the country, the commission of crimes probably has been differentially distributed in various sectors of society. Some persons—especially those who have engaged in similar acts previously—may have committed a disproportionate number of crimes, while others have accounted for a relatively small percentage of illegal acts.

The propensity to draw a clear distinction between supposedly "criminal" and "law-abiding" citizens, however, may contribute little to an understanding of the problem of crime. Efforts to classify the population according to the amount of crime committed cannot produce iron-clad or airtight compartments; they are flexible and porous. Persons who may commit crimes—on occasions when they are not engaged in illegal conduct—tend to act in ways that are indistinguishable from the behavior of others; and people who are usually regarded as upright and "law-abiding" also may be capable of committing serious crimes. The rigid categories implied by phrases such as "law-abiding" and "criminal" not only might undermine respected legal principles by presuming guilt without sufficient proof, but they also may assume an inordinate or undue measure of innocence on the part of the allegedly "law-abiding." Perhaps the use of this dichotomy by many citizens actually reflects an implicit division between people who are unfamiliar and somewhat threatening and persons such as themselves or their friends and relatives. As a result, the demand for the increased control of crime seldom is perceived as having direct or personal effects.

In addition, however, contact between police officers and the public is not uniformly distributed throughout society. The types of offenses that normally require police intervention are crimes that are most prevalent among lower-class sectors of the population. To the extent that the law reflects the distribution of political influence within society, this pattern may represent the ability of high-status groups to protect themselves both from the stringent restrictions of the criminal code and from demeaning encounters with policemen who may occupy an inferior social position. As Sutherland (1949) pointed out in his classic treatise on "white-collar crime," the definition of many acts of corporate illegality as matters encompassed by the civil rather than the criminal law has a major impact upon prevailing concepts of crime and police duties. Many violations of the law in which middle-class people tend to indulge, such as the absence of total veracity in commercial transactions or in the completion of income tax returns, usually do not entail police intervention or enforcement. The provisions of the criminal law seemingly have been structured so that most law enforcement practices, with the exception of traffic regulation, are directed at relatively low-status segments of the population.

Many citizens probably tend to identify the primary targets of the social controls imposed by policemen as persons with whom they are unfamiliar and those who possess less social prestige than themselves. As a result, the development of plans to combat crime based upon the fear of threatening strangers and upon the false dichotomy between "criminals" and the "law-abiding" appears to be highly dangerous. The tendency of many persons to view the problems of crime as a conflict between "law-abiding" and "criminal" segments of the population—because they seldom identify with the latter group—could provide the impetus for a righteous crusade that might be prepared to quash established civil liberties in an effort to detect and eliminate so-called "criminals." Police involvement in any popular movement that fails to respect traditional guarantees of individual rights might compel police officers to become violators rather than enforcers of the law. Public policies founded upon the perception of policemen solely as agents of social control, therefore, seem to contain some frightening implications for the social order.

Although perspectives based upon the concept of social control appear to recognize the essentially political nature of police duties, they also seem to rest upon some intrinsically hostile assumptions regarding both politics and human nature. Not only is the interference of government apparently perceived as an unwelcome intrusion in private affairs that may be necessary only when other forms of restraint have proven to be inadequate, but man is also viewed as a creature whose normal instincts might lead him to inflict serious injuries upon others if they were not governed by a firmly instilled sense of self-discipline, strong social conventions, and detailed legal restrictions. The basic motives of human beings are regarded as reflecting an inclination toward anarchy and irresponsibility that must be restrained by the intervention of the state. While the assumptions that form the basis of the appraisal of police officers as agents of social control have gained extensive currency, they also seem to represent a somewhat limited view of human behavior. At times, man has displayed a propensity toward social disorganization that may necessitate the application of strict limitations upon his conduct, but, on other occasions, he has appeared to exhibit a basic impulse toward mutual accommodation and cooperation that might contribute to the perpetuation of organized society. Approaches to social issues that are based upon the assumption that human conduct is inherently immoral or anarchical without devoting equivalent or corresponding attention to the more constructive aspects of man's nature may fail to offer a sufficiently comprehensive orientation for the study of police practices.

In addition, the social control perspective may reflect an excessively formal appraisal of police responsibilities. The notion of social control seems to imply that police activities are confined almost exclusively to law enforcement duties or to the detection and apprehension of criminal suspects. In a manner analogous to an early doctrine of constitutional interpretation, the principal obligation of police officers apparently is to lay the criminal statutes beside specific forms of public behavior to see whether the latter squares with the former. While this image of police practices is widely disseminated by the mass media, it represents a highly limited and relatively inaccurate perception. This viewpoint not only fails to convey the variability or discretion that is characteristic of police behavior, but police functions also encompass a large number of acts that are not implied by this restricted perspective. Perhaps the basic flaw in the concept of social control is that it is simply incomplete. Policemen are involved in a broader range of social circumstances than are contained in the duties of law enforcement. The investigation of police conduct solely from the perspective of social control, therefore, may fail to provide an adequate means of assessing their activities.

THE LAW AND ORDER PERSPECTIVE

Perhaps the most popular approach to the study of police functions has been founded upon an examination of the concepts of both law and order. This perspective has been based upon the principle that police activities might be divided into two relatively distinct tasks that could be described as "enforcing the law" and "maintaining order." While policemen commonly have been expected to administer the regulations that are contained in criminal statutes, they also have been granted the responsibility of enforcing the implicit norms and mores that facilitate social interaction. As a result, several investigators (see, for example, Barth, 1961: 19-34; Skolnick, 1966: 6-9; Wilson, 1968a, 1968b) have sought to approach the study of police conduct by distinguishing between behavior that represents an effort to apply the authority of legal codes and those actions simply designed to support social customs or conventions existing apart from the law.

Moreover, in many studies of police practices, the concepts of law and order have been considered opposing principles that may subject law enforcement officers to serious occupational strains. Problems arising in the performance of police duties frequently have been attributed to an inherent contradiction between the objectives of law and those of order.

In fact, the apparent conflict between law and order usually is ascribed to two distinct, though somewhat overlapping, sources. Initially, the clash between law and order often is equated with a basic incompatibility between substantive and procedural law. Policemen not only are assigned the responsibility of enforcing the statutes that regulate public conduct, but they also are required to respect the rights of those who have violated the rules. The obligation to maintain law and order, in part, appears to reflect a fundamental tension between what Packer (1964) has termed the "crime control" and "due process" models of law enforcement. While police must assume the duty of imposing penalties upon legally proscribed forms of conduct, they also are compelled to observe practices that may impede them from accomplishing that mission. As Skolnick (1966: 9) notes, " 'law' and 'order' are frequently found to be in opposition, because law implies rational restraint upon the rules and procedures utilized to achieve order." The necessity of following legal guidelines that could conceivably result in the release or escape of a suspect from apprehension seems to be a primary source of frustration for many police officers.

There is, however, a second, closely related, meaning that is attributed to the dilemma of law and order. The alleged inconsistency of law and order also appears to imply an intrinsic contradiction between individual liberties and the rights of society. Just as procedural guarantees are considered equivalent to "law," while substantive rules are viewed as the basis of "order," personal liberties frequently are identified with "law," and the rights of the public are translated as "order." The individual freedoms afforded all citizens by the law may be depicted as antithetical to the interests of the broader community in preserving public order. As a result, the duties of police officers sometimes require them to guard the privileges granted each person from the animosity of the larger society and, on other occasions, to protect the common rights of all from the attacks of isolated individuals.

Depending upon one's viewpoint, however, the use of the phrase "law and order" may be either redundant or contradictory. If "order" is defined as a pattern of social conduct based upon principles embodied in the law, the concept of "law and order" probably is tautological or repetitious. Order merely means adherence to the procedures and regulations contained in the law, and the second term in the expression "law and order" adds little to the meaning of the phrase that is not implied by the first word. Law is the foundation of social life, and order may be simply superfluous verbiage. On the other hand, if order means a type of discipline or regimentation that exceeds the constraints required by law, then "order" may become, at best, extralegal or, at worst, illegal. "Order" is thus distinguishable from or a substitute for law. Although few would deny that the responsibilities of policemen include many duties that are not contained in the written statutes, the description of law and order as opposing principles may inspire demands for regulations upon public behavior that contradict or supersede the requirements of the law.

There is, of course, another highly ideological or partisan meaning that has been attached to the phrase "law and order." In this usage, "law and order" is employed less as a perspective for examining police functions and objectives than as a propagandistic symbol for promoting the particular type of social order its proponents desire. The exponents of "law and order" in political campaigns often seem to appeal to voters who are desperately seeking to preserve the somewhat limited status that they have managed to acquire and who view any disruption of the existing social system that they have mastered—and with which they have become familiar—as a direct and personal menace. The advocacy of "law and order" frequently appears to imply a desire to punish the persons or groups that threaten their perquisites through the denial of equal protection of the laws, the application of separate standards of conduct to different segments of society, or other practices that could be regarded as illegal or that would require the repeal of present laws to legitimate them. What those voters apparently have in mind, therefore, may actually be a kind of "law-'n-order" in which the meaning of the phrase is skipped over through its rapid repetition and in which the understanding of law becomes so inextricably joined with a particular definition of order that the content of law is obscured and made subservient to order. Order thus becomes the operative principle of society, and a particular kind of order at that—one that eliminates all threats to personal security and that sanctions many expedients for preserving security including methods contrary to existing law.

The evaluation of the political slogan, "law-'n-order," therefore, must include a searching assessment of the type of order that one wishes to achieve. To paraphrase the widely quoted comment of Paul Freund (1961: 44) regarding constitutional standards for freedom of speech, "No matter how rapidly we utter the phrase . . . or how closely we hyphenate the words, they are not a substitute for the weighing of values." Unfortunately, in the context of much political rhetoric, the phrase seems to connote a radical change in the kinds of regulations that policemen would be required to administer, as well as in the destruction or the repeal of established legal guarantees. Hence, the use of "law-'n-order" as a hyphenated slogan might impose additional burdens upon police officers by asking them to defy the law for the sake of public order.

Although the paradox of law and order might appear to offer a useful perspective for examining the conflicting forces that impinge upon police duties, the distinction seems to rest upon a false and relatively misleading dichotomy. In fact, interpretations of the alleged tension between law and order may contribute to the confusion rather than to the clarification of the police mission. Initially, the perceived opposition of the two concepts appears to reflect an erroneous assumption that the legal regulation of public conduct is inconsistent with the protection of civil liberties. The fundamental premise of civil liberties, however, is that the failure to respect the rights of the lowliest member of society may be just as costly to the entire society as it is to the recipient of such action. Without the existence of explicit processes for ascertaining the legality of personal conduct, the application of the law to human affairs would become arbitrary and capricious. The failure to observe traditional methods of adjudicating guilt or innocence—tested in the crucible of human experience—ultimately may redound to the disadvantage of all citizens by depriving them of clearly defined standards of conduct. A society that is willing to neglect its legal guarantees in an effort to eradicate crime eventually could become a society so confused and uncertain about its methods of evaluating human behavior that it may degenerate into chaos. Legal provisions designed to protect the civil liberties of the accused and to impose penalties upon proscribed forms of conduct, therefore, exist in a complementary and mutually supportive rather than in an antagonistic or competitive relationship to each other.

Perhaps the most serious implication of the perceived conflict between law and order, however, is the possibility that it might be employed to legitimize the enforcement of a particular definition of public order. Although the existence of an order that is not based upon law seems undeniable, a serious question might be raised about whether or not policemen should be allowed—let alone encouraged—to enforce that type of order. In fact, many policemen undoubtedly do issue commands and administer rules vis-à-vis the public that could not be found in legal codes. Law enforcement officers tend to be highly suspicious of unconventional or deviant behavior. Yet, the official mandate of police officers is confined to the imposition of social controls upon activity that is obviously at variance with legal restrictions rather than upon behavior that simply reflects a departure from established social norms. Although the enforcement of pervasive notions of order instead of the complicated provisions of the law would diminish the difficulties confronting police officers, it also might yield a society in which limitations upon human conduct are fixed not by the law, but by prevailing—and especially police—definitions of what behavior contributes to the preservation of their concept of the social order. One of the major responsibilities of both the public and the political leaders, therefore, is to ensure that the duties of police officers are not expanded to include the administration of rules of behavior that lack the imprimatur of law.

Although approaches to the study of police conduct based upon the dilemma of law and order appear to be more comprehensive than the concept of social control, both perspectives seem to yield some potentially dangerous policy implications. Just as the appraisal of police duties solely as the application of social controls might embroil the police in a moralistic crusade of "law-abiding" citizens against the "criminal" elements in society, interpretations of the supposed conflict between law and order could be translated into a growing demand for "law-'n-order" that might require the enforcement of social rules not contained in the law.

Perhaps the basic difficulty with the law and order approach, however, is that it seems to rest upon the assumption that order is distinct from or superior to the law. Although law is perceived as a necessary instrument for curbing human behavior, it is also viewed simply as a means by which order might be attained. The ultimate objective appears to be a society in which coercion may no longer be required or in which public conduct might be governed by the informal norms that sustain social interaction rather than by the legal restrictions that emanate from public officials. Order thus may supersede or even supplant the law. While some might argue that social conventions might form a more accurate representation of the common interests of society than the principles that are recorded in the statutes after they have been filtered through the political process, police forces operate essentially at the behest of the public and in accordance with directives issued by political authorities. The concepts of law and order, therefore, appear to place relatively little emphasis upon the political origins or content of law enforcement duties. Not only is "the law" frequently viewed as a body of rules that seems to develop apart from the exercise of political preferences, but order is also portrayed as an intrinsically social commodity that does not require political authority for its existence and administration.

The use of the notion of law and order often appears to be both elusive and deceptive. Frequently, for example, the critical concept of "order" even remains essentially undefined. While few would deny the existence of a regularity or a pattern in human affairs that may not be explicitly embodied or recognized in law, extensive research has failed to codify or even to isolate all of the subtle and intricate social norms or mores of which order might consist. "Order" is no more susceptible to definition than "disorder." Although "disorderly conduct" is one of the most common causes for arrest, almost no legal or pragmatic criteria exist for identifying "disorderly" forms of behavior. In addition, the concepts of law and order also form a relatively limited description of police functions. The notion of "order" does add at least one component of police activities that is not implied by social control, but police officers also engage in many duties that are not directly related to "enforcing the law" or to "maintaining order." The somewhat restricted scope of the terms law and order, as well as the essentially indefinable and amorphous nature of "order," therefore, seem to restrict the utility of both concepts for the examination of police practices.

POLICING AS AN EXTENSION OF PUBLIC AUTHORITY

The rationale for the functions of police forces does not appear to depend solely upon the premise that men must be constantly exposed to the threat of punishment to deter them from antisocial conduct. Nor is it based upon the assumption that the presence of police officers is a necessary—though perhaps not a sufficient—condition for ensuring that people respect the values sustaining orderly and predictable social life. Even if men could learn to live by either the legal regulations promulgated by the state or the implicit norms and conventions that guide much social interaction, the existence of local police forces still might be needed to manage, direct, and superintend the affairs of the community. Perhaps most importantly, policemen may be required simply to fill the void that would otherwise exist between public authority and the citizens of a nation. In the absence of police organizations, a serious social and political vacuum might develop within society. Perhaps the critical issue in the investigation of police practices, therefore, is how do police officers act as intermediaries between political decision makers and the public?

Fundamentally, police functions seem to comprise an extension of political authority. Political decisions concerning basic regulations of public behavior eventually are transmitted from executive, legislative, and judicial bodies through policemen to the public. Law enforcement officers, therefore, constitute the extended arm of the polity and a crucial link between ordinary social conduct and the rules devised by duly constituted public officials. In fact, policemen may be the principal representatives of public authority at the grass-roots level.

The role of police officers in exerting public authority, or in relating social conduct to the standards emanating from political institutions, however, raises some fundamental issues affecting the theoretical foundations of the state. The ability of law enforcement officers to perform their duties ultimately rests upon the authority of government agencies and officials. The authority of the state, in turn, is based upon several philosophical premises that constitute some of the most critical problems in political thought. Perhaps the first prerequisite for political authority is the ability to command; hence, sovereignty is an essential attribute of any government. Not only must the state establish its capability of controlling a geographic territory, but it also must exercise supreme, uncontested power to enact and administer the laws within that area. The existence of political sovereignty is closely related to Weber's definition of the state as an institution that preserves a legitimate monopoly on the use of physical force. Although modern democratic societies seldom are plagued by the problems of competing political institutions and rival police forces, the history of America also encompasses several attempts by private vigilante groups to challenge established law enforcement agencies. Perhaps the two principal types of law that policemen are required to enforce include rules intended to outlaw behavior that could damage the social order and regulations designed to prohibit conduct that might imperil the survival of the state. Policemen are authorized to prevent members of the public from usurping police prerogatives and from substituting their own definitions of legality for the criteria adopted by the state. Political agencies, therefore, continually employ police forces to protect themselves from actions by private citizens that might threaten governmental sovereignty.

Political authority also is dependent upon the equally complex and fundamental concept of legitimacy. Not only must a government possess the capability of formulating and enforcing laws for the residents who live within its borders, but the ability to issue and impose those rules also must be perceived as justifiable and acceptable. The capacity of police officers, as agents of the government, to administer the laws may be determined by public assessments of the moral rectitude of executive, legislative, and judicial institutions. If a prevalent belief develops among the citizenry that political bodies lack the appropriate credentials for enacting legislation, then the propriety of police officers, acting in behalf of the state, in enforcing those laws might be seriously questioned. Police powers, therefore, are closely related to public appraisals of political legitimacy.

This relationship may have both favorable and disadvantageous consequences for police officers. On the one hand, police activities often are cloaked with the awesome sanctity and majesty of the law and of the political institutions from which it emanates. One of the principal resources of police officers may consist of the deference usually inspired by the state. By invoking the symbols and esteem of the government, policemen might acquire a nearly insurmountable advantage in their encounters with the public. On the other hand, members of society may not universally share or subscribe to a faith in the political legitimacy of the state. Persons who do not regard the government agencies that are the source of a policeman's directives as legitimate would not be inclined to honor his commands. As a result, police officers must assume the problems that arise when major segments of the population lose their faith and confidence in the moral ascendancy of established political institutions. In fact, the loss of a sense of legitimacy may have a greater effect upon policemen who must continually confront groups that have become distrustful and suspicious of governmental power than upon political officeholders who are relatively insulated from those sentiments.

The public authority exerted by police officers also is closely related to another basic concept that has been a source of controversy and concern among social and political theorists for centuries. Central to the duties of law enforcement officers is the principle of political obligation. Without a pervasive popular sentiment that a society's laws are worthy of respect and fealty, a nation might not be considered a genuine political community. Ultimately, moreover, the impact of a decline in the willingness of persons to obey the law might be experienced primarily by police officers. If private citizens lack a sense of allegiance to the political institutions that comprise the polity, they are unlikely to respect the position of policemen who personify those institutions. Perhaps the basic task of a police officer is to secure public compliance with his directives. Law enforcement agencies probably would be incapable of policing a society in which persons felt no compelling reason or need to observe the laws. The ability of police officers to intervene effectively in diverse social circumstances may depend upon the loyalties that people attach to broader and more encompassing political symbols and institutions. The performance of police duties, therefore, seems to be closely related to some of the most fundamental philosophical premises upon which the state is founded. The loss of the moral basis of political authority could have serious—and damaging—repercussions for the activities of policemen. As a result, the investigation of police conduct might be approached from a perspective that recognizes the intimate association between police action and major issues in social and political theory.

The perspective of police duties as an extension of public authority not only illustrates the close relationship between police practices and fundamental principles of society, but it also seems to demonstrate the essentially political nature of law enforcement activities. In fact, in some unusually crucial circumstances, police work often might begin where the functions of political executives end. During major civil disturbances or insurrections, the willingness of public officials to summon large numbers of police officers to the scene of the disorders may signal the collapse of normal political processes. Law enforcement officers often are requested to intervene in a dispute after social conflict has advanced to the point at which traditional channels for negotiation and the redress of grievances cannot contain the opposing forces. When all other avenues of conciliation have been thoroughly tested and found to be incapable of resolving the differences, policemen may be called upon to solve the problem. Police operations, therefore, not only form an indispensable means of sustaining the foundations of political leadership, but they also may play a critical role in supporting public leaders in the event that the leaders should fail to fulfill their responsibilities.

The examination of police practices as an extension of public authority also delineates the significant relationship that exists between police officers and the public. In a democratic society, the public is usually regarded as the ultimate foundation of political action. According to much classical theory, sovereignty is retained by the people, even though it may be exercised by constitutionally selected political representatives. Moreover, political legitimacy and obligations are based upon popular perceptions. The development of a widespread belief that governmental institutions are not politically legitimate or that they are undeserving of loyalty could prevent law enforcement officers from accomplishing their mission. Since police functions are closely related to fundamental questions of political authority, policemen—as well as other governmental officials—must depend upon extensive civic support not only to gain compliance with their directives but also to secure general public approval of their activities.

PUBLIC SUPPORT FOR POLICE FUNCTIONS

Despite the critical role of police officers in the performance of awe-inspiring political responsibilities, the basis of public support for police functions may be more restricted and transitory than has been commonly recognized. The difficulties that confront policemen in attempting to develop a favorable climate of opinion for their activities may arise from two problems that are intrinsic to law enforcement duties. Initially, police officers serve the public collectively rather than distributively. Unlike many other government agencies whose programs may bestow major benefits upon specific segments of the population that can be depended upon to provide energetic political support for their activities, police forces are unable to develop an identifiable constituency that enjoys the advantages of their services and that will become politically active in promoting the value of their work. In fact, the only distinct clientele that occupies a special relationship to police forces are violators of the law, who are essentially hostile to law enforcement officers and who may possess the least political influence of any group in the society.

In addition, law enforcement functions may not appear to confer direct or visible rewards upon the public. In patrolling community neighborhoods, policemen actually do offer a vital service by providing protection for lives and property. Yet, the residents seldom recognize—or, in the minds of many police officers, appreciate—the advantages of patrolling. The average citizen may become aware of the value of police practices only after he has been the victim of a crime. By this time, the importance of police patrolling is no longer salient and the commission of the crime seems to demonstrate that police operations are inadequate to prevent such occurrences. Persons may learn of their dependence upon police protection simultaneously with the realization that police security might not be absolute. As a result, the awareness of police actions frequently coincides with strong public criticism of their activities. In addition to the understandable reluctance of persons to sympathize with the punitive nature of police duties, law enforcement officers are deprived of a special clientele that receives tangible benefits from their work and that can be relied upon to support the police politically.

The effective performance of law enforcement functions, however, may depend upon extensive public confidence and support. Just as the law—which defines and guides police activities—must rest upon the consent of the governed, the administration or enforcement of the law also must be based upon public trust and approval. Police officers are under a basic obligation not only to serve but also to earn the respect of all sectors of the population. In fact, it even might be argued that, if there were two distinct subgroups in society, as most persons probably believe, it may be more important for policemen to secure the cooperation of habitual offenders or persons who come into frequent conflict with the law than to gain the praise of higher-status and supposedly "law-abiding" groups which enjoy superior political power. Since police practices are designed essentially to obtain the compliance of persons at whom they are directed, police officers must receive at least a minimal amount of cooperation and respect from their principal "clients." The refusal of a single criminal suspect to obey the commands of a policeman might be overcome by physical force, but the development of this type of encounter as a pervasive pattern could produce a major social crisis. While a loss of confidence among high-status segments of the community might deprive the police of a valuable source of political influence, a sharp decline in public trust, even among criminal suspects, also may have a direct and potentially disastrous impact upon the performance of police work.

To accomplish their objectives, police departments may require not only a general reservoir of popular acceptance and goodwill, but they also may need active public approval and support. In order to garner necessary public confidence, therefore, policemen might be compelled to engage in activities that would offer direct and tangible rather than broad and amorphous social benefits. Perhaps police work must be designed to assist individual citizens, as well as the society at-large. Law enforcement agencies might be required to perform functions analogous to the services provided by other government bureaus if they are to acquire comparable levels of political support.

A careful examination of police practices, however, reveals that police officers already are conducting numerous tasks that confer personal benefits upon the public and that are relatively unrelated to their law enforcement responsibilities. Perhaps the greatest volume of public requests for police action and the largest share of active police duty are focused upon activities that could be classified as community services. As the sole agents of local government that constantly circulate throughout the community, policemen are perhaps the only public officials available to respond to many problems and emergencies such as sickness or injury, family or marital troubles, disturbing neighborhood incidents, and other occurrences that necessitate prompt intervention by outside sources of assistance. As events that require greater resources than the average citizen is capable of mobilizing himself, those needs seem to merit instantaneous attention by government institutions.

Moreover, calls for such services are most likely to originate in segments of the community—such as low-income families, minority groups, and young people—that tend to be most critical of police behavior. Unlike relatively affluent residents, those groups may lack the necessary means of obtaining private professional help from clergymen, physicians, lawyers, and psychiatrists to meet personal needs and emergencies. As a result, policemen have been granted a rare opportunity to render invaluable aid or comfort to those specific sectors of the population in which they have encountered the greatest resistance and hostility. In addition, the provision of vital services such as transporting a sick person to the hospital, resolving family problems, or other action in a crisis often is the type of aid that may yield enduring gratitude and respect. Law enforcement officers, therefore, have been provided with a highly effective means of acquiring needed public support without significantly altering their existing routines and responsibilities.

Perhaps a major factor in the emerging crisis of public confidence in police authority has resulted from their failure to seize the advantages afforded them through the performance of community service activities. Even though those functions account for a large proportion of the time spent by law enforcement officers in the community, policemen often have considered this type of work as an unwarranted interference with their principal mission of controlling crime. Many police officers have regarded service functions as inappropriate or demeaning, and they have sought to avoid those duties. By stressing the punitive aspects of their jobs, however, police forces probably have increased their sense of estrangement from the community.

The subordination of service activities to law enforcement duties also might be difficult to justify. The moral criterion that assigns a higher priority to the detection and apprehension of criminal suspects than to the offering of community services may not be as clear as many policemen have assumed. The question of whether the solution of crimes should be accorded greater value than, for example, transporting an injured person to a hospital or even resolving family difficulties raises ethical issues that are not susceptible to facile answers. Although communities eventually might conclude that law enforcement agencies should devote their primary attention to crime-related problems rather than to the provision of service activities, this judgment at least might be made as an explicit policy decision after a careful weighing of the alternatives by representatives of the public and political leaders, as well as by police officers.

There would appear to be compelling reasons, however, to halt the continued downgrading of the service functions that presently consume a large amount of police time and energy. Perhaps the community services performed by policemen should be granted explicit recognition and value as well as coequal status with their law enforcement responsibilities. In fact, prevailing concepts of police duties could be expanded to redefine— and perhaps even to retitle—police departments as community service organizations rather than simply as law enforcement agencies. Although this reorganization merely would sanction the predominant activities of police officers, it may contribute to an increased public understanding and appreciation of police responsibilities.

The proposal to reorient police duties within the broad context of community services could have far-ranging implications not only for police departments but also for political institutions generally. By explicitly recognizing the responsibility of a public agency to respond immediately to the varied personal emergencies that arise in everyday life, political officials might be required to accept a much more expansive definition of the role of government than has prevailed in most countries of the world. Even if the proposal is perceived as politically feasible, however, some persons might contend that public requests for services should be answered by trained professionals in fields such as medicine, counseling, or social work rather than by police officers. However, two attributes of police officers—namely, their accessibility and their availability—might be cited in support of the continued performance of those duties by policemen or community service officers—who might possess different occupational training and specialties—rather than by other public or private organizations. Unlike many other service personnel, law enforcement officers spend their working days mingling with members of the community rather than within the confines of an office. Policemen go into the community rather than imposing upon residents to visit them. As a result, police officers are apt to be—at any given moment—within a short distance of the location where their services are required, and they can be dispatched almost instantaneously to that address. In addition, policemen are among few public employees that are available on a 24-hour-a-day basis. For highly pragmatic reasons, therefore, police departments or community service organizations might be in a better position to respond to citizen requests for public services than might other governmental agencies.

POLICEMEN AND THE POLITICAL PROCESS

A major reorganization of law enforcement agencies might provide policemen with the active public support that they need for the effective performance of their duties. To successfully fulfill their responsibilities, police forces may be required to place increasing emphasis upon community service activities rather than to launch isolated or limited departmental programs for improving police-community relations. Similarly, however, police officers cannot depend solely upon a general climate of favorable perceptions; they must also gain public respect and confidence.

Unlike the tasks of many governmental bureaus, the law enforcement functions of police departments cannot be directly and immediately "responsive" to public opinion. Perhaps neither the basic tenets of the law nor its enforcement and administration should be subjected to the variable mood of the public and to the possibility that the standards regulating social conduct might be periodically revised by shifting popular attitudes without a thorough review by other institutions of government. Although police practices might not be made directly *responsive* to changing community opinions, however, they can be *responsible* to public sentiments. In other words, police departments—like all other political agencies—must be accountable to the public for their policies and actions. Police officers must be both amenable to public scrutiny and susceptible to the impact and direction of the people acting through their elected representatives.

The development of increased community support for law enforcement operations, therefore, does not imply that attempts should be made to persuade citizens to adopt a "police point of view." Public confidence cannot be founded upon a blind approval of whatever policemen should decide to do. In fact, the growth of genuine popular faith in law enforcement agencies may entail a merger of public and police sentiments. People often are skeptical of agencies that demand trust solely on the basis of their allegedly superior knowledge and expertise. The type of support that policemen increasingly may require is a form that encompasses criticism as well as praise, censure as well as loyalty, and surveillance or supervision rather than subservience or repression.

Ultimately, the regulations that policemen administer are based upon the decisions of elected public officeholders. Policemen cannot be expected or required to impose personal restraints that do not reflect—or that are at variance with—official government policies. Law enforcement officers must not be allowed to substitute either their own policy preferences or the partisan positions urged upon them by political enthusiasts for the moral values embodied in legal codes. Fundamentally, police departments are a local extension of relatively remote political institutions, and even though their responsibilities cannot be precisely limited to the duties outlined for them in the statutes, they must be guided and controlled by responsible political leadership.

As an extended arm of governmental authority, police forces are an integral and vital part of the political system. Although many attempts have been made to divorce the police from other political institutions, the functions of police departments seem to be more clearly political than the duties of many other municipal agencies such as sanitation bureaus, public utilities, and similar government bodies. Perhaps the only effective means of ensuring that police forces will be responsible to the people, therefore, is through the political process. One important method of increasing the accountability of police departments is by expanding their accessibility to public desires and requests for community services. In addition, however, efforts might be launched to lower the rigid wall that has separated politics and the police.

Basically, police departments exist primarily to communicate the decisions of public leaders to ordinary citizens and to provide a mechanism by which police officers can observe and report changing patterns of social conduct to higher political authorities. Although the former responsibility usually receives more emphasis than the latter function, the lines of transaction between policemen and the public cannot be an exclusively one-way flow. In fact, the frequently unrecognized and nearly invisible process by which policemen adapt the static requirements of the legal code to public behavior—often by withholding penalties in circumstances where they no longer seem appropriate—may be one of the principal means by which a necessary element of flexibility and discretion is injected into the law. Patrolmen, however, often fail to report either major changes in the social behavior that they encounter on the streets or the methods by which they accommodate legal requirements concerning new forms of social organization and interaction to their political superiors. As a result, government leaders may be deprived of a crucial source of information not only about emerging trends in social relations but also about the conduct of police officers and their law enforcement duties. Improving the lines of transmission that extend upward from police officers to political leaders, therefore, may be an essential means of enhancing the public responsibility of police departments.

There is, however, an implicit danger that increased public support could become the basis of a movement for an expansion rather than a limitation of social control or law enforcement functions. Since many persons apparently subscribe to a rigidly dualistic perspective of crime in which they identify themselves with supposedly "law-abiding" segments of the community, the public might be mobilized to wage an overly zealous crusade that could undermine fundamental legal safeguards in seeking to eradicate the anonymous forces of crime that allegedly haunt society. The basic problem of law enforcement, therefore, may not be protecting the police from the public, or even protecting the public from the police, but, ultimately, it may be protecting the public from itself.

Perhaps the major guarantee that increased public support for police activities will not degenerate into irresponsible demands for expanded law enforcement powers, however, is suggested by the empirical results of police work. Most crimes are not committed by faceless strangers, but are perpetrated by friends, relatives, or acquaintances of the victim. Moreover, laws are not designed for alien and distant segments of society, but apply equally to all persons, and each man may be exposed to the risk of violating the law. In fact, some studies indicate that large proportions of the population have, at some time during their lives, committed an act that could be classified as a serious crime (for a brief review of this literature, see President's Commission on Law Enforcement and Administration of Justice, 1967b: 77). In addition, policemen frequently are perceived as the enforcers of laws governing minor infractions that affect everyone, including traffic ordinances, as well as of major offenses. Many citizens probably would raise defensive objections to the claim that people such as themselves have engaged in conduct that could be interpreted as criminal. Without probing the motives or the psychological dimensions of those rebuttals, however, even persons who firmly insist that they have never participated in a serious breach of the law might find it impossible to claim that they have succeeded in living their lives without running afoul of some statutory regulation. Many policemen, as well as members of the public, undoubtedly are aware that the absolute, undeviating, and full enforcement of the law would leave the records of few Americans unblemished by legal charges. Public demands for increasing police powers, therefore, might be restrained by a common recognition that, even though many persons are anxious to project an image of infallibility in the eyes of the law, they are also simply human beings who may discover that it is difficult to lead totally blameless or irreproachable lives.

Efforts to resolve the mounting problems that afflict police forces, however, not only may require enhanced popular support for police activities, as well as a major reorganization of law enforcement agencies, but they also may necessitate increased public understanding of police duties. The duties of policemen are not confined to the application of social controls or coercion. Nor do they necessarily reflect an inherent tension between the conflicting principles of law and order. The examination of police conduct as an extension of political authority seems to yield a broader conception of their functions than either of those perspectives. Among such functions might be included protection from crime, or the imposition of social controls; the maintenance of order, or the enforcement of basic social norms and values; authority, or the supervision of public behavior; and service, or the willingness to respond to personal needs and emergencies. Furthermore, and perhaps most importantly, an emphasis on the close association between police practices and public authority might prevent police forces from being captured by transitory movements that would attempt to promote either a moralistic crusade against so-called "criminal" elements in the population or to impose a highly partisan definition of "law-'n-order" upon society. To perform their duties effectively, police operations must be based upon firm public support that encompasses demonstrable responsibility as well as tacit approval. By seeking to encourage a close relationship of mutual cooperation and respect, rather than of opposition and antagonism between the police and the public, police officers might find that they will be able to cope with the increasing problems that may be imposed upon them in the future.

REFERENCES

BARTH, A. (1961) The Price of Liberty. New York: Viking.

ENNIS, P. H. (1967) Criminal Victimization in the United States: A Report of a National Survey. Washington D.C.: Government Printing Office.

FREUND, P. A. (1961) The Supreme Court of the United States. Cleveland: Meridian.

HOLDEN, M., Jr. (1970) "Politics, public order and pluralism," pp. 238-255 in J. R. Klonoski and R. I. Mendelsohn (eds.) The Politics of Local Justice. Boston: Little, Brown.

LOHMAN, J. D. and G. E. MISNER (1966) The Police and the Community. Washington, D.C.: Government Printing Office.

NIEDERHOFFER, A. (1967) Behind the Shield. Garden City, N.Y.: Doubleday.

PACKER, H. L. (1964) "Two models of the criminal process." Univ. of Pennsylvania Law Rev. 113 (November): 1-68.

President's Commission on Law Enforcement and Administration of Justice (1967a) The Challenge of Crime in a Free Society. Washington, D.C.: Government Printing Office.

——— (1967b) Task Force Report: Crime and Its Impact—An Assessment. Washington, D.C.: Government Printing Office.

REISS, A. J., Jr. (1967) "Public perceptions and recollections about crime, law enforcement, and criminal justice," pp. 1-114 in Studies in Crime and Law Enforcement in Major Metropolitan Areas. Volume 1. Washington, D.C.: Government Printing Office.

SKOLNICK, J. H. (1966) Justice Without Trial. New York: John Wiley.

SUTHERLAND, E. H. (1949) White Collar Crime. New York: Holt, Rinehart & Winston.

WILSON, J. Q. (1968a) Varieties of Police Behavior. Cambridge, Mass.: Harvard Univ. Press.

——— (1968b) "Dilemmas of police administration." Public Adminstration Rev. 28 (September-October): 407-417.

PART ONE

The Growth of Police Problems

The Growth of Police Problems

Since the mid-nineteenth century, when police departments were established in major American cities, the problems encountered by law enforcement officers have undergone marked changes. Many conditions of modern life such as urbanization, improved systems of communication and transportation, and the escalation of social conflict have appeared to impose new and unusual responsibilities upon policemen. Yet, those duties were not totally unprecedented; they were also the products of prior tradition and experience. The examination of trends affecting police functions, therefore, has provided a valuable perspective for understanding the increased challenges that confront law enforcement agencies.

The nature of police work has long been shaped by the political forces that swept metropolitan areas. During much of American history, for example, urban police departments were closely linked to big-city political machines that sought to serve the needs of immigrant groups in exchange for electoral support. Perhaps a justification for this relationship between the police and the machines was offered by Martin Lomansy, the political boss of Boston, who told muckraker Lincoln Steffens in 1915, "I think that there's got to be in every ward somebody that any bloke can come to—no matter what he's done—and get help. Help, you understand; none of your law and justice, but help." Although the evils of crime and corruption aroused the ire of municipal reformers, the latter problem produced little basis for agreement between the reformers and police forces associated with the machines. As Mark H. Haller notes, however, police officials and reformers did discover that they shared a common desire to control crimes against property. As a result, numerous technical and administrative changes were adopted to improve the crime-fighting capabilities of policemen. Subsequently, the impact of the reform movement upon police departments not only was evident in the increased crime rates that resulted from improved methods of keeping records, but it also might have been instrumental in diverting police attention from the needs of ethnic neighborhoods. In addition, those reforms may have formed the basis of the movement toward police professionalism. The principal mission of the police was defined as combatting crime rather than providing community services.

Although the reform movement in American cities destroyed the relationship between police forces and urban machines, it did not appear to yield increased government support for law enforcement programs. Despite the mounting public concern about crime that emerged during the twentieth century, David J. Bordua and Edward W. Haurek demonstrate that local expenditures for police agencies have not increased since 1902 when other factors such as population growth, inflation, urbanization, and the use of motor vehicles were taken into account. The implications of this finding appear to suggest that police efforts to acquire increased political support were not strikingly successful. Since law enforcement officials are dependent upon appropriations that emanate from the political process, police departments in the future may be compelled to gain expanded backing from the public as well as from government leaders for the resources necessary to fulfill their mandate of controlling crime.

The effects of growing urbanization and an apparent increase in crime rates, however, have prompted a searching examination of law enforcement problems by national as well as by local governments. As Robert W. Clawson and David L. Norrgard observe, the development of this political movement in America has not been unique. In England and the Soviet Union as well as in the United States, mounting anxiety about "crime in the streets" has provoked similar political responses and comparable proposals to centralize law enforcement functions, to improve police-community relations, and to adopt repressive tactics. As the experience of a "police state" has demonstrated, however, the policy of repression has not been effective in reducing the types of crimes that are the major sources of public concern. The emergence of increasing public controversy, therefore, has seemed to produce a need for an improved understanding of police functions and for new solutions to the problems confronting law enforcement officers.

Civic Reformers and Police Leadership

Chicago, 1905-1935

MARK H. HALLER
Temple University

From 1905 to 1935 civic reformers in Chicago undertook a number of ongoing and overlapping campaigns to reform the city's police. The men and women who led the campaigns commanded the advantages of wealth, social prestige, and scholarly expertise. In occupation they were bankers and merchants, corporation lawyers active in the Chicago Bar Association, respected ministers, professors of law and social science at the better universities, members of elite women's clubs, and nationally known social settlement workers. In background, they were native born and overwhelmingly Protestant (see Johnson, 1966; Miller, 1966: 23-28). Their values and goals were generally shared by editors of the city's major newspapers. Despite these advantages, the civic leaders had only a limited impact upon the administration and operations of the police department. The degree of success of different reform organizations was related to the specific strategies and goals that guided the organization. In order to understand the relationship of civic reformers and the police, it is necessary to examine the strategies and goals of the various reform organizations and the police leadership.

POLICE AND POLITICS

The civic reformers stood outside of the political factions that were rooted in the ethnic neighborhoods and competed for office and influence in the city; the police, on the other hand, were deeply involved with the political factions. The police were themselves recruited from the ethnic neighborhoods, so that in 1930, some seventy-six percent of the police captains were of Irish background (see Ogburn and Tibbits, 1930). Among the lower levels of the department, the belief was widespread that, while police promotions were under civil service, in fact politicians exercised influence over both promotions and assignments. At the top, the police chief was chosen by the mayor, usually from among the police captains. (From 1905 to 1935, police chiefs had remarkably short tenure, serving an average of about two years each.) Not only was promotion to chief a political decision, but other top officers were often assigned to please powerful ward leaders in the areas in which they served. Successful leadership in the department, then, required that the top officers be partisans of particular political factions or else men with friendly links to several factions.[1]

The police acted under the further constraint that some of the regularized criminal activity in the city operated with close ties to politics. Those who ran prostitution and gambling, as well as saloon keepers, and, in the 1920s, bootleggers—all had ties to politicians through friendship, money, and political services. Even many pickpockets, burglars, and other professional thieves were associated with political factions. Hence policemen had to learn which criminals, for political reasons, could not be seriously pursued. In rare cases, a policeman might risk his own career by making arrests; in other cases, an arrest was futile since the criminal would escape conviction through contacts in the State's Attorney's office or from among judges and other court personnel.[2] Throughout the police force, then, there was a cynical understanding that one of the functions of the department was to provide favors that helped to maintain political factions.

While political constraints often contributed to cynicism, the constraints did not always violate seriously the police view of the proper functions of a police department. On the whole, the police acted more to regulate than to eliminate professional criminal activity. Detectives, as well as patrolmen, maintained extensive and sometimes friendly contacts with the professional thieves and criminal fixers of the city and participated in the determination of which gangs would operate in what parts of the city. Then, if there was pressure on the police to recover property after a theft, the police had the contacts to make good the recovery.[3] As far as prostitution was concerned, the police generally believed that vice should be restricted to segregated red-light districts so that the police could better control abuses. Chicago had its famous Levee district during the first decade of the century; but every major city in the United States, from the Barbary Coast of San Francisco to the Tenderloin of New York, had its segregated vice area. Although prostitution was illegal in Illinois, the written Chicago police regulations in 1910 stated that "no house of ill-fame shall be permitted outside of certain restricted districts, or to be established within two blocks of any school, church, hospital, or public institution or upon any street car line." The regulations further prescribed that children over age three should not be allowed in the districts, that girls should not be held against their wills, and that "short skirts, transparent gowns or other improper attire shall not be permitted in the parlors, or public rooms."[4]

In Chicago, as in other cities, the extensive relations of police and criminals were cemented by systems of pay-offs and shakedowns. Before World War I, regularized pay-offs to the police in order to operate vice resorts ranged as high as $25.00 per week per prostitute; by the early 1920s, partly because pressure from reformers had destroyed the safety of the arrangements, weekly pay-offs of $50.00 per prostitute were collected by the police on Chicago's Near North Side.[5] From saloonkeepers, restaurant owners, and other businessmen in the ethnic neighborhoods the police accepted gifts ranging from occasional free drinks to regular payments of money. Some police also shared, regularly or irregularly, in the profits of the city's thieves. A 1914 Chicago City Council Committee on Crime (1915: 185-186), under the chairmanship of reform alderman Charles E. Merriam, hired three investigators to pose as pickpockets in order to study the interaction of police and criminals. The assumed pickpockets soon made contact with police detectives, who informed them concerning the best places to operate, protected them from arrest while working, and accepted fifty percent of the proceeds.

DIVISION AMONG REFORMERS
CONCERNING POLICE PRIORITIES

The operation of Chicago's police force was, of course, deeply shocking to the city's civic reformers. The reformers believed that laws should be enforced rigorously and impartially. Not only should corruption and political influence be eliminated from law enforcement but the police department should seek ways to achieve administrative and technological efficiency. The purpose of the police, in short, was to arrest and convict criminals.

Yet, despite their agreement upon common values, elite reformers were on occasion divided, especially during the 1920s, concerning the main priorities for police enforcement. Some reformers—including social workers, ministers, and prohibitionists—were concerned with the moral quality of neighborhood life in the city. For such reformers, a major problem of urban life was that temptations lay in wait to victimize the poor and to corrupt the young into lives of crime and dissolution. In 1916, the Chicago Committee of Fifteen complained, for instance:

> The decent people of Chicago are alarmed at the marked increase of vice in dance halls and cabarets, two institutions which have become veritable traps for the unwary, where young girls are lured to prostitute life and young men and boys are started on the road to ruin. When policemen, with and without uniform, calmly watch the vicious orgies take place in these amusement centers without interfering, the neglect of duty is painfully evident.

The moral reformers, then, advocated that police resources be mobilized against gambling, prostitution, obscenity, and liquor law violation—activities concentrated in the poor neighborhoods and appearing to victimize primarily the poor (see Addams, 1912; Wilson, n.d.; Chicago Juvenile Protective Association, n.d.). Other members of the civic elite—especially business leaders, lawyers, and the city's newspapers—believed that the police should be concerned chiefly with crimes against persons and property: assault, shoplifting, burglary, and robbery. As one newspaper pointed out:

> The decent citizens can avoid bootleggers and poolrooms and bad women. All he has to do is to mind his own business. But he can't avoid being stuck-up or shot; he can't avoid the burglary of his house by being a good husband and father; his wife and daughters can't avoid deadly fear even while walking down their own home street.[6]

Some aspects of the civic leaders' expectations were more compatible with police expectations than were other aspects. When civic leaders urged that the department be administered efficiently in order to protect the public from crimes against persons and property, police and reformers could sometimes work together to secure common goals. But when reformers insisted upon the elimination of corruption and political influence so that the police might undertake vigorous and impartial enforcement of laws against gambling, vice, and liquor, then they faced entrenched interests that made mutual cooperation nearly impossible. Thus, an examination of the pressures from reformers must be sensitive to the nature of the demands being made. In fact, elite reformers had some impact upon the Chicago police department, but primarily in those areas in which the demands of reformers were most in keeping with police interests and least upsetting to entrenched relationships.

ANTI-VICE CAMPAIGN

The campaign against commercialized vice in the early twentieth century provides a case study of the difficulty that reformers faced when trying to loosen the close relations between police, politicians, and vice. The campaign represented a broad coalition of civic reformers. By 1908, as a result of several highly publicized prosecutions of white slavers and a growing national concern with the white slave traffic, reformers in Chicago had organized at all levels to fight vice. In many neighborhoods, church and business groups organized to drive vice out of the neighborhoods. At the same time the Illinois Vigilance Association, the Chicago Law and Order League, and other formal and informal groups focused upon the problem at a citywide level. In October 1909, Gipsy Smith, an evangelist, led a parade of thousands of decent citizens through the Levee district in protest. The next year, the Church Federation of Chicago asked the mayor to appoint a vice commission to investigate the problem. In 1911 the commission, representing both political and civic leaders, brought in a detailed report that, in brief, demanded a policy of law enforcement in order to root out commercialized vice. In the same year a number of business and other civic leaders established a Committee of Fifteen to lead a permanent campaign. The Committee of Fifteen hired a staff of investigators who, for the next twenty years, roamed about the city getting themselves solicited and preparing daily reports on vice activities (see Brooks, 1928; Reckless, 1929: ch. 18; Washburn, 1954: chs. 17-20; Landesco, 1968: ch.2; Roe, 1911).

Despite prosecutions of white slavers, highly publicized police raids, and the closing by Mayor Carter H. Harrison of the world-famous house of the Everleigh sisters in October 1911, the Levee district continued relatively unchanged into 1912. Civic leaders did exert enough pressure, however, to force a civil service investigation of the police in 1911. The investigation resulted in charges being placed against three inspectors, five captains, seven lieutenants, and forty-one plainclothesmen. The report of the investigation, issued in 1912, placed the number of prostitutes in the city at 20,000. The report also noted that segregated vice districts had been tolerated in Chicago "from time immemorial" and that the police were failing even to enforce the police regulations for the district (Chicago Civil Service Commission, n.d.: 9).

By late 1912, however, the days of the Levee were numbered. In October the state's attorney, goaded by reformers, undertook a series of raids and prosecutions. By this time, Mayor Harrison had reluctantly decided that the district would have to be reduced or eliminated. In March 1913 he appointed Major Metellus L. C. Funkhouser to the new position of second deputy police commissioner and gave him control of the vice squad. Funkhouser had the confidence of reformers and worked with the reform organizations. Then, in the summer of 1914, two vice squad detectives were killed while operating in the vice district. For weeks thereafter the police had orders to arrest known criminals on sight, and much of the criminal activity in the area came to a halt. By the end of the year, the Chicago Committee of Fifteen (1914) could declare, optimistically and perhaps prematurely, that "it is admitted by all who are in a position to know the facts that the old vice district on the south side is practically closed" (see Brooks, 1928; Reckless, 1929; Washburn, 1954; Landesco, 1968; Roe, 1911).

Then in 1915 William Hale (Big Bill) Thompson won his first of three terms as Republican mayor of Chicago. His terms in office were generally characterized by a wide-open policy. He soon undermined Funkhouser's position in the police department and in 1918 had him removed from the force. Within a year after Thompson took office, the Chicago Committee of Fifteen (1916) was complaining:

> We have found policemen going personally and collecting tribute from women, and giving evidence of their willingness to protect vicious resorts by taking keepers to the Morals Court to point out certain officers of the law against whom the women were to be on guard. We have dictagraph records of conversations and records of telephonic communications which reveal facts indicating that this system of graft is in vogue in all sections of the city where vice is prevalent.

Soon, too, the Democratic state's attorney undertook investigations, culminating in the indictment of Thompson's chief of police. The investigators uncovered a notebook of a police lieutenant, in which were two lists of gambling houses and shady hotels—one headed "Can be raided," the other headed "Can't be raided." The notebook listed prices for protection, ranging from $40.00 to $150.00 per week. For division of the protection money, some resorts were "the chief's places," others were labelled "three ways" (see Landesco, 1968: 35). As a result of the indictment, Big Bill Thompson lost the first of the seven police chiefs who served under him during his twelve years as mayor.

In succeeding years, newspaper exposés, grand jury investigations, and reports by reformers uncovered the continuing association of the police with vice activities. The old Levee district, with its famous parlor houses, ceased to have the commanding importance that it had once enjoyed. The center of vice moved deeper into the black ghetto on the South Side. But in many parts of the city, prostitutes continued to operate by street soliciting, by working in rooms behind or over bars, by operating from hotels and flats, as well as by the continuance of a few fine old parlor houses. The structure of vice changed; gradually vice itself became less important as a source of income within organized crime; but the relationship of vice, politicians, and the police remained in effect.[7]

From 1923 to 1927, moral reformers were briefly encouraged by the policies of Mayor William E. Dever and Morgan Collins, his police chief. Early in Dever's administration, in response to pleas by social workers and ministers, the police made raids designed to break up vice and gambling in the South Side black ghetto. Although Dever believed that prohibition was destroying good government through corruption, he nevertheless ordered the police to enforce prohibition laws. Morgan Collins periodically summoned the police captains to his office and threatened them with suspension if they were unwilling to follow his policy of vigorous enforcement. As a result, his men closed the breweries in the city, the mayor revoked licenses of more than one thousand businesses that were fronts for liquor sales, and prostitution became more covert and limited.[8]

Yet, from another point of view, Dever's administration ushered in the period of open gang warfare that made Chicago—and Al Capone—notorious through the world. And Collins, in fact, was not entirely successful in controlling the police. This was seen, for instance, in Collins' plaintive order to the police in 1923 that police flivvers were not to be used to escort beer trucks; or in the discovery in 1925 that eleven police officers were selling booze in one of the stations; or the discovery that the notorious Genna brothers, bootlegging rivals of Capone, had hundreds of policemen on their payrolls.[9] By his efforts to enforce the laws against vice and alcohol, Dever made his administration sufficiently unpopular so that Big Bill Thompson won the mayoralty election in 1927 and returned to office. For reformers who wished to sever the relationships by which police and politicians became associated with vice activities, the battle was a disappointing one.

THE CHICAGO CRIME COMMISSION

While the moral reformers were generally unable to change police practices, some of the business elite were more successful in their contacts with the police. In the early 1920s, their contacts were chiefly through the Chicago Crime Commission, organized in 1919 by the Chicago Association of Commerce to wage a continuing war against crime and against the corruption and inefficiency of the criminal justice system that, so the business leaders believed, made crime possible. Henry Barrett Chamberlin, a crusading newspaper man, was operating director and soon became a leading figure in the reform of the criminal justice system in Chicago and in the rest of Illinois. In general, the Crime Commission sought to make criminal justice more punitive and deterrent: it vigorously supported the death penalty, attacked the courts for the inefficiencies and technicalities that allowed criminals to escape conviction, and sought to limit the availability of parole and probation (see Chicago Association of Commerce, 1918, 1919; Bulletin of the Chicago Crime Commission, 1919-1926; Roberts, 1927: 45 ff.). The punitive outlook was often shared by the police leadership.

When the Crime Commission was first formed, its leaders were appalled by the corruption and demoralization of the police force. But when Mayor Thompson appointed Charles C. Fitzmorris, a former newspaper reporter, chief of police in November 1920, the Crime Commission began a close working relationship with the department. Upon taking office, Fitzmorris shook up the department by transferring 712 police officers. He expressed a determination to improve the administrative efficiency of the department, although he generally ignored the growing corruption of the police by bootleggers and vice interests. And he turned to the Crime Commission for advice.[10]

The chief focus for cooperation between business leaders and Fitzmorris was a joint drive to increase the city's police force by one thousand men. Such an increase had long been advocated. The grand jury that investigated the bloody Chicago race riots of 1919, for instance, had strongly recommended an increase of one thousand men. The police chief had taken the same position in 1920. But the City Council resisted out of a firm commitment to avoid higher taxes. By working with the Crime Commission, Fitzmorris could hope to neutralize the usual opposition of the business community to increased taxes (see Waskow, 1967: 51-52).[11]

In early 1922, Chamberlin established a committee consisting of prominent civic leaders. These included Colonel Robert McCormick of the Chicago *Tribune* and the presidents of Marshall Field and Company and Carson, Pirie, Scott and Company, two of the city's major department stores. This committee met on May 19 with the chairman of the City Council finance committee to urge that the police force be increased. When two of the city's newspapers opposed the move, the Crime

Commission organized delegations of businessmen, worried about holdups and shoplifting, to visit the editors in order to persuade them to change their stand. On May 24, an ordinance adding one thousand men passed the City Council by a vote of fifty-five to five.[1][2]

What is interesting about this example of cooperation between civic leaders and the police is that the civic leaders ignored almost completely the corrupt relationships that the police had with vice and gambling, ignored the growing and open corruption of the police by bootleggers, and defined the police problem chiefly in terms of preventing crimes against property and persons.

With the inauguration of Dever as Mayor and the appointment of former police captain Morgan Collins as police superintendent, the close cooperation between the Crime Commission and police leadership ceased for four years. One reason, perhaps, was that by 1920 the Crime Commission had a confidential report that Collins, as a police captain, was less than honest. The chief reason, however, was that the Crime Commission, unlike the moral reformers, lacked interest in the efforts by Dever and Collins to enforce the laws against liquor, vice, and gambling. Such a use of police resources was not high on the priority list of the business leaders who supported the Crime Commission.[1][3]

During the mayoral election of 1927, Big Bill Thompson, seeking his third term, concentrated upon denouncing Dever as a tool of King George of England. To some extent, however, his campaign was concerned with the functions of the police. He promised a wide-open town (see Pasley, 1931: 148) and also promised to drive the criminals from the city: "Elect me and I'll turn the police from sneaking under the mattresses of your homes, looking for a little evidence of a minor infraction of the Volstead Act, to driving the crooks out" (see Wendt and Kogan, 1953: ch. 22; Stuart, 1935: 310 ff.). Some idea of Thompson's enforcement policy can be gotten from an incident that occurred in early 1928, less than a year after his election to a third term. When the newspapers exposed a large policy racket flourishing openly in the black ghetto, police captain William F. Russell (see Chicago Daily News, 1928), who had charge of the district, declared:

Mayor Thompson was elected on the "open-town" platform. I assume the people knew what they wanted when they voted for him . . . I haven't had any orders from downtown to interfere in the policy racket, and until I do get such orders you can bet I'm going to keep my hands off . . . Personally, I don't propose to get mixed up in any jam that will send me to the sticks.

The statement made sense in Chicago.

Then in April of 1928, the so-called "Pineapple Primary," in which bombs were used against Thompson's political enemies, brought repudiation of the Thompson machine. In the aftermath of the primary, Thompson removed his police commissioner and appointed Captain William F. Russell to the post. With this appointment came a period of remarkable cooperation between some civic leaders and the police department.

CITIZENS' POLICE COMMITTEE

By means of the Citizens' Police Committee, established in early 1929 with the approval of Russell, the business and academic elite assisted in a thorough administrative reorganization of the police department. The immediate occasion for the formation of the Citizens' Police Committee came when Henry B. Chamberlin, operating director of the Crime Commission, charged in August 1928 that the police department consistently suppressed reports of crimes. (The department, he declared [see Criminal Justice, 1929], finds it "easier to suppress complaints than to suppress crime.") Chamberlin demanded an impartial study and complete reform of the department. Publicly, Russell denied the charges, but privately he met with Chamberlin to explore a solution. By autumn, representatives of the University of Chicago, Northwestern University, and the Institute of Criminal Law and Criminology had joined the discussions. By January an eight-member Citizens' Police Committee had been established.[14]

The committee included such men as John H. Wigmore, dean of the Northwestern University Law School; Leonard D. White, professor of political science at the University of Chicago; Andrew A. Bruce of the American Institute of Criminal Law and Criminology; Ernest W. Burgess, a sociologist at the University of Chicago; Ernst W. Puttkammer, professor of criminal law at the University of Chicago Law School; and Henry B. Chamberlin of the Chicago Crime Commission. After consulting with Raymond Fosdick and other experts on police administration, the committee chose Bruce Smith to direct a thorough study of the Chicago police department. Financial support for the study came from the University of Chicago, Northwestern University, the Rosenwald Fund, and the city's business community.[15]

In order to understand the relative success of the committee, it is necessary to understand the expectations that guided members of the committee and the police leadership. Commissioner Russell could hope to gain support for his plans to increase the number of policemen and to replace the inadequate physical plant. He could also hope to insulate himself from some of the inevitable attacks upon the police by civic leaders and newspapers. The civic leaders, on the other hand, could expect that, by working with the police commissioner, they could achieve some significant reforms that would otherwise be impossible to achieve. Yet, by working with the commissioner, they placed limits upon the types of investigations and recommendations that they might make. As Professor Leonard D. White admitted privately: "The view of the committee is that it is not their business to search out police malefactors, but rather to assist the commissioner in the proper organization and management of the police force by making constructive suggestions based on the best police practice."[16] Commissioner Russell, in a speech to the committee in May, was perhaps more frank. "We have government by politics, and that is all there is to it," he warned, and added:

> We will have to keep our feet on the ground, and remember that that is so, and that you, I, or all of us combined, with a hundred thousand others, cannot change the situation at this time. People say that the police department is hampered by politics. I grant you that it is, and always has been and probably always will be, while we have our present form of government . . . So the only thing that is possible for any and all of us to do, is to do the best we can, and guide this particular inquiry along lines that will be constructive and helpful to the people of the City of Chicago.[17]

The ground rules of the study, then, were that it would deal with administrative reforms and would not expose corruption nor directly threaten entrenched political relationships. The emphasis upon administrative efficiency became, in short, a way to "reform" the police without raising questions of who could control the police and for what purposes.

Beginning in June 1929, Bruce Smith and his five research assistants compiled information and recommendations which were submitted periodically to Commissioner Russell. Relations between Russell and the Citizens' Police Committee were sufficiently close so that on occasion Russell would accept the recommendation immediately and then call upon the committee to assist him in implementation.[18]

One area of cooperation, for instance, was in the training of police recruits. In 1929, there was a four-week training course. Some idea of its worth can be gathered from the fact that one-fourth of the training consisted of close-order drill, that the trainees were expected to memorize the definitions of crimes in alphabetical order, and that no recruit had been known to fail the course. Under the direction of Ernst W. Puttkammer, a member of the Citizens' Police Committee and of the University of Chicago Law School, a three-month course was provided to train police instructors so that they in turn might operate a better police training program. Furthermore, the Citizens' Police Committee prepared a syllabus for the police instructors, covering important aspects of criminal law and legal procedures.[19]

COMMUNICATIONS AND RECORDS REFORM

More important was the cooperation of the Citizens' Police Committee and the department in a reform of the records and communications system of the department. Citizen complaints were often made to local police stations; only a portion of such complaints were then reported by the local police stations to the central office. Indeed, for certain major crimes, only seven percent were reported to the central station in 1926, only eighteen percent in 1927. As a result, the Detective Bureau, unable to use the central records, established its own major crimes bureau in late 1928 in order to collect information concerning robbery and burglary. Thus, the department had two central bureaus collecting crime information. The decentralized and inaccurate records system was nicely matched by an inadequate communications system. The police teletype was located at some distance from the records division. At the time of the survey, the police did not have its own radio communications system. Instead, the Chicago *Tribune,* as a public service, had installed radios in several police cars and broadcast police bulletins over its commercial radio station WGN (standing for World's Greatest Newspaper). Police efficiency, then, was seriously hampered by lack of control over the records and communications that should be the heart of modern police operations (see Chicago Citizens' Police Committee, 1931: ch. 9).

The Citizens' Police Committee recommended that the department should have a central complaint room to which the public and the police would report all crimes. The central complaint room would be the communications center for the department. Adjacent to the complaint room should be the central records bureau. In October of 1929, the Citizens' Police Committee sent its recommendations to Commissioner Russell; in November, Russell accepted the recommendations and requested the committee's aid in establishing the new system. During the next few months, the members and staff of the Citizens' Police Committee devoted much of their efforts to this important reform. On May 1, 1930, the central complaint room, minus radio transmission, went into effect. A month later the Chicago police department was operating its own radio transmitter. Thus the cooperation of the department and of civic leaders produced a major reorganization of police administration.[20]

ADMINISTRATIVE REFORMS

In addition to these and other administrative changes, the Citizens' Police Committee formulated a plan for the reorganization of the lines of authority within the department. At the time of the survey, the Police Commissioner had nineteen subordinate administrators who reported directly to him, including five deputy commissioners in charge of the five police districts into which the forty-one police precincts were divided, a first deputy commissioner in charge of miscellaneous activities, a deputy commissioner in charge of the various detective activities, plus the officers in charge of such functions as movie censorship, the signal section, and property section. This meant that the commissioner was necessarily burdened with many detailed decisions that detracted from his ability to devote time to major policy matters. His inability to exercise overall supervision of the department was further undermined by the fact that his office was in city hall, a mile from the central police headquarters. To reformers, of course, the city hall office was a symbol of political control of the police (see Chicago Citizens' Police Committee, 1931: ch. 2).

Under a reorganization proposed by the Citizens' Police Committee, the number of persons reporting to the police commissioner would have been reduced to eight, and the various sections of the department would have been regrouped so that similar services would fall within the same office. As a result there would be clear lines of responsibility and authority. Furthermore, the reorganization called for the commissioner to move his office out of city hall and into the central police station. In early January of 1930 Bruce Smith forwarded the reorganization proposal to Commissioner Russell. The plan soon had the support of the Chicago Association of Commerce, the Crime Commission, several aldermen, and Russell himself.[21]

Then on June 9, 1930, Jake Lingle, a Chicago *Tribune* police reporter, was killed in a gangland slaying in the heart of the city. In the aftermath of the slaying, Lingle was found to have had extensive underworld contacts, including a warm and continuing friendship with Al Capone (see Pasley, 1931: pt. 6). He was also found to be a friend and secret business partner of Russell, both of them having income considerably in excess of their salaries. Many citizens were convinced that Lingle's association with Russell had allowed him to play a central role in arranging for police promotions and for the protection of criminal activities. Russell, the reform commissioner, went the way of most Chicago police commissioners.

With the resignation of Russell in June 1930, John Alcock, the second in command, became acting commissioner and remained in that position throughout the remainder of Big Bill Thompson's mayoralty and into the early weeks of Anton Cermak's administration. Alcock terminated the cooperation with the Citizens' Police Committee.

The climax to police reform came with the election of Anton Cermak as mayor of Chicago in 1931. In October, several months after his inauguration, Cermak named James F. Allman police commissioner. Greeting the appointment with approval, civic leaders declared that he was the best choice for commissioner from among the many men who had been promoted from the force. (One sign of his excellence was that he had been transferred fourteen times in his thirteen years as captain.) Allman's first act was to announce that he would reorganize the department as recommended by the Citizens' Police Committee. Bruce Smith and his staff were recalled to Chicago and spent the next twenty-seven months overhauling the department. They put into effect the organizational reform that had been shelved by the previous commissioner. They also introduced a new system of property control, improved the technology of police communications, further revised the training and recruitment system, and made other changes within the department. Thus, within four years after formation of the Citizens' Police Committee, civic leaders completed a major reform of the administrative structure of the Chicago police department (see Smith, 1934; New York Times, 1932; Chicago Tribune, 1932).[22]

CONCLUSION

There were two models by which reform might be attempted during the period under discussion. Under one model, the reformers defined their goal to be administrative and technological efficiency of the police. They could then, on occasion, join with the police leadership in investigations of the department, in framing recommendations, and in implementation of the recommendations. Those reform groups that wished to see police resources used to combat crimes against property and persons were most able to define the problem to be one of efficiency and to work with the police.

Under the second model, reformers defined corruption and political control of the police to be the major problem. Far from cooperating in investigations, the police became the objects of investigations whose purpose was to uncover scandal that could be used to embarrass the police and shock the public. Such reform campaigns made good newspaper material, arousing strong moral passions, but—by guaranteeing the enmity of police leadership and of many leading politicians—could achieve only gradual and limited changes. The moral reformers, concerned with vice, gambling, and liquor, were most likely to make police corruption the major target.

Most movements for police reform, of course, involved some aspects of both models. Furthermore, the threat of investigations that would embarrass the police was an important factor that inclined police leadership to cooperate with reformers in administrative reforms and thereby attempt to coopt crucial elements from among the civic reformers. The attempted cooptation was never entirely successful, however. After all, at any given time an individual civic leader might belong to one organization that cooperated with police officials for reform and to another organization that investigated police or political corruption. Tensions between police officials and civic reformers remained constant.

NOTES

1. For a discussion of political influence on promotion, see a letter from an agent to Henry B. Chamberlin, September 22, 1920 and the report of a police officer to Chamberlin in 1919, in the Chicago Crime Commission file 600-9. For general discussions of political influence at all levels, see the informants' reports in the Charles E. Merriam papers, University of Chicago Library, boxes 87 and 88. The author is now completing a book on crime and criminal justice in Chicago, 1900-1935, in which the relations of politicians, police, and criminals will be treated in considerable detail. This paper is concerned mostly with the relations of reformers to the police leadership.

2. Studies of ties between criminals and politicians are voluminous. See, for instance, the informants' reports in the Merriam papers, University of Chicago Library; Landesco (1935, 1968: chs. 2, 8 especially); Wendt and Kogan (1943); and the copies of *Lightnin'*, an occasional newspaper edited by Elmer L. Williams in the 1920s and 1930s.

3. Informants' reports in the Merriam papers, University of Chicago Library.

4. See the Vice Commission of Chicago (1911: 329-330). Mayor Harrison also believed in a segregated and regulated red-light district; see Harrison (1935: 308-314).

5. See the handwritten notes of October 7, 1914 in the Merriam papers, University of Chicago Library, box 88, folder 1; the "Statement of Mrs. Maud Banks" (1922 or 1923), Juvenile Protective Association papers, Library of the University of Illinois at Chicago Circle, folder 96; the report, "Commercialized Prostitution," December 10, 1922, Juvenile Protective Association papers, folder 92; and the investigator's report, "Law Enforcement and Police," December 5, 1922, Juvenile Protective Association papers, folder 94.

6. See the Chicago *Herald and Examiner*, January 12, 1925; see also the Chicago *Tribune*, January 11, 1925 and September 21, 1929.

7. On the changing structure of vice, see Reckless (1929); the voluminous investigators' reports in the files of the Committee of Fifteen, University of Chicago Library; the typewritten "Vice Investigation," August 1 through September 11, 1920, Juvenile Protective Association papers, folder 108; the report, "Commercialized Prostitution," December 10, 1922, Juvenile Protective Association papers, folder 92; and "Commercialized Prostitution," May 6 through May 26, 1933, in Juvenile Protective Association papers, folder 97.

8. See correspondence of Dever with his police chief in William E. Dever papers, Chicago Historical Society, folders 24 through 26. Also see the news clippings and reports in the Chicago Crime Commission files 600-9 and 550-1.

9. See the newspaper clippings in the Chicago Crime Commission file 600-9.

10. See the reports in the Chicago Crime Commission file 600-9; the *Bulletin of the Chicago Crime Commission* (1921); Sims (1920); and the *Greater Chicago Magazine* (1922).

11. See also John J. Garrity to Henry B. Chamberlin, January 19, 1920 in the Chicago Crime Commission file 600-9.

12. See the correspondence and news clippings in the Chicago Crime Commission file 600-9. In 1911 the department had 4,437 men; in 1920, 5,152 men; in 1922, 6,184 men. See Chicago Police Department (1930: 13).

13. See the confidential report dated September 22, 1920 in the Chicago Crime Commission file 600-9. The split between the commission and Collins is discussed in the Chicago *Tribune*, January 9 and 11, 1925; see also the memo of January 10, 1925 in the Chicago Crime Commission file 600-9.

14. The public controversy can be followed in the Chicago *Tribune*, August 15, 1928 and other Chicago papers for that date. The negotiations can be followed in the memos and correspondence in the Chicago Crime Commission file 600-33.

15. See the correspondence, minutes of meetings, and news clippings in the Chicago Crime Commission file 600-33; see also the correspondence in the Julius Rosenwald papers, University of Chicago Library, box 13.

16. Letter of White to Julius Rosenwald, February 23, 1929, in the Rosenwald papers, University of Chicago Library, box 13.

17. See the minutes of the Citizens' Police Committee, May 13, 1929 in the Chicago Crime Commission file 600-33.

18. The minutes, correspondence, and interim reports of the Citizens' Police Committee after July 1929 may be found both in the Chicago Crime Commission file 600-33 and in the Ernest W. Burgess papers, University of Chicago Library.

19. See the Chicago Citizens' Police Committee (1931: 79-84); the minutes of the Citizens' Police Committee for November 18, 1929 and May 14, 1930 in the Chicago Crime Commission file 600-33.

20. See the Chicago Citizens' Police Committee (1931: ch. 9) and the minutes and memos of the Citizens' Police Committee from October 1929 to June 1930 in the Chicago Crime Commission files 600-9 and 600-33.

21. See the minutes, memos, and correspondence of the Citizens' Police Committee after January 8, 1930 in the Chicago Crime Commission file 600-33.

22. Not until the early 1960s, when Orlando Wilson became police commissioner, did the commissioner finally move his office from City Hall to the police headquarters.

REFERENCES

ADDAMS, J. (1912) A New Conscience and an Ancient Evil. New York: Macmillan.
BROOKS, F. O. (1928) "Crime in 1908." Term paper in E. W. Burgess papers, University of Chicago Library (Winter).
Bulletin of the Chicago Crime Commission (1919-1926) Chicago.
––– (1921) "Report of committee on police." (January 31): 7-12.
Chicago Association of Commerce (1919) Annual Reports.
––– (1918) Annual Reports.
Chicago Citizens' Police Committee (1931) Chicago Police Problems. Chicago.
Chicago City Council Committee on Crime (1915) Report of the City Council Committee on Crime. Chicago.
Chicago Civil Service Commission (n.d.) Final Report, Police Investigations, 1911-1912. Chicago.
Chicago Committee of Fifteen (1916) Annual Report. Chicago.
––– (1914) Annual Report. Chicago.
Chicago Daily News (1928) March 15.
Chicago Juvenile Protective Association (n.d.) Annual Reports. Chicago.
Chicago Police Department (1930) Annual Report. Chicago.
Chicago Tribune (1932) November 27.
Criminal Justice (1929) March.
Greater Chicago Magazine (1922) "Why crime is decreasing in the city of Chicago." 2 (November): 3-9.
HARRISON, C. H. (1935) Stormy Years: The Autobiography of Carter H. Harrison, Five Times Mayor of Chicago. Indianapolis: Bobbs-Merrill.
JOHNSON, D. R. (1966) "Crime fighting reform in Chicago, an analysis of its leadership, 1919-1927." M.A. thesis. University of Chicago.
LANDESCO, J. (1968) Organized Crime in Chicago. Chicago: Univ. of Chicago Press.
––– (1935) "Chicago's criminal underworld of the '80's and '90's." J. of Criminal Law & Criminology 25 (March): 928-940.
MILLER, J. S. (1966) "The politics of municipal reform in Chicago during the progressive era: the municipal voters' league as a test case, 1896-1920." M.A. thesis. Roosevelt University.
New York Times (1932) June 5.
OGBURN, W. F. and C. TIBBITS (1930) "A memorandum on the nativity of certain criminal classes engaged in organized crime, and of certain related criminal and non-criminal groups," pp. 42-43 in C. E. Merriam papers, University of Chicago Library (July 30).

PASLEY, F. D. (1931) Al Capone: The Biography of a Self-Made Man. Chicago: Ives Washburn.

RECKLESS, W. C. (1929) Vice in Chicago. Reprint series in Criminology, Law Enforcement and Social Problems. New York: Patterson Smith.

ROBERTS, K. L. (1927) "Watchdogs of crime." Saturday Evening Post (October 8).

ROE, C. G. (1911) The Prodigal Daughter: The White Slave Evil and the Remedy. Chicago: Callaghan.

SIMS, E. W. (1920) Statement in the Bulletin of the Chicago Crime Commission (December 23): 9-10.

SMITH, B. (1934) Chicago Police Problems: An Approach to Their Solution. New York: Harper.

STUART, W. H. (1935) The Twenty Incredible Years. Chicago: Henry Regnery.

Vice Commission of Chicago (1911) The Social Evil in Chicago. Chicago: Open Court.

WASHBURN, C. (1954) Come into my Parlor: A Biography of the Aristocratic Everleigh Sisters of Chicago. New York: Little, Brown.

WASKOW, A. I. (1967) From Race Riot to Sit-In. Garden City, N.Y.: Doubleday.

WENDT, L. and H. KOGAN (1953) Big Bill of Chicago. Indianapolis: Bobbs-Merrill.

––– (1943) Lords of the Levee: The Story of Bathhouse John and Hinky Dink. Indianapolis: Bobbs-Merrill.

WILSON, S. P. (n.d.) Chicago and Its Cess-Pools of Infamy. Chicago: Oceana.

The Police Budget's Lot

Components of the Increase in Local Police Expenditures, 1902-1960

DAVID J. BORDUA
University of Illinois, Urbana-Champaign

EDWARD W. HAUREK
University of Minnesota

From 1902 to 1960, annual local police expenditures in the United States went from $50,000,000 to $1,612,000,000 (U.S. Bureau of the Census, 1960; 1965). This is a spectacular increase of $1,562,000,000 or 31.24 times the amount spent in 1902. The initial impression from these data is that the increased expenditure for local police activities reflects a very large increment in public investment in the traditional police function of criminal law enforcement. Such an impression can lead to the conclusion that the dramatic expenditure increase provides the local police with much greater financial resources that they can translate into more effective law enforcement. A more ominous interpretation of rising police expenditures has been that this increase is the necessary response to a rise in national crime rates. Thus, it has been argued that increasing police expenditures are one of the "costs" of rising crime rates (President's Commission on Law Enforcement, 1967: 53).

Authors' Note: *The authors wish to thank Otis Dudley Duncan, Robert E. Kennedy, Jr., and Gene F. Summers for critical comments on earlier drafts of this paper.*

MAJOR PREMISES

This paper will attempt to demonstrate that the expenditure change is not due to a real increase in resources available to improve the quality of police efforts in the area of criminal law enforcement, and that it is due to the joint effect of components which are largely independent of changes in crime rates. These components are population growth, inflation, urbanization, and motor vehicle increase. The preceding statement can be considered the major hypothesis of the paper.

A second purpose of the authors is to illustrate that the use of fiscal data and analysis with relatively simple control and standardization techniques is a useful approach to understanding social phenomena of this type (see, for example, Barclay, 1958: 161-162). In a market economy, fiscal expenditures are excellent indicators of the process of societal resource allocation. More importantly, these data often are readily available, and yet they have been largely ignored by sociologists.

It is apparent that if expenditures increased simply to cope with a larger crime problem due to population growth, the *quality* of law enforcement as measured by per capita expenditure would not have increased. A second possible component of the increase in expenditure is inflation. Police expenditures are especially susceptible to the effects of inflation because a very large proportion is for wages and salaries, and it is the rising cost of labor that has mainly contributed to inflation.[1] The third possible component of the expenditures increase is the change since 1902 of the proportion of population residing in urban areas. This component is independent of population growth. The size-of-place distribution of the population is important for analysis of police expenditures because it has been consistent through time that expenditures for police services are a function of size of place.

This may be illustrated with ratios of police employees to population. In 1907, cities with over 300,000 population had 19.4 officers, detectives, and patrolmen per 10,000 inhabitants while cities with 30,000 to 50,000 inhabitants had 10.5 per 10,000 inhabitants (U.S. Bureau of the Census, 1907: 394). In 1960 this differential still exists. Cities over 500,000 population had a median of 24.9 police employees per 10,000 population, and cities with population of 25,000 to 50,000 had 13.8 police employees per 10,000 population (International City Manager's Association, 1961: 396). The increased use of police personnel as city size increases reflects the greater expenditure for law enforcement in urban areas.

The fourth component of expenditure increases studied is the growth of motor vehicle use and the concomitantly higher proportion of police resources devoted to traffic control. Data necessary for computing the effects of this last component are very limited. However, a reasonable approximation can be made for the expected police expenditure in 1960 if per capita motor vehicle registration had not increased since 1902.

FINDINGS

To improve the clarity of presentation of the central argument, details of computations, assumptions, and data sources are presented in the Appendix. Table 1 summarizes the findings. The joint effect of population growth, inflation, urbanization, and motor vehicle increase was determined by calculating the expected expenditures in 1960 if none of the four had occurred since 1902. These expected expenditures are $44 million which is *less* than the $50 million which was actually expended in 1902. The net decrease may be interpreted as signifying that the nominal increases since 1902 in local police expenditures have been explained by the operation of the 4 components studied. Of much greater significance is the interpretation that the local police have not received increases in resources that have kept pace with the increased demands that social changes have placed upon them and the input of resources available for criminal law enforcement into the police function is *less today* than at the turn of the century. Some implications of this finding are discussed in the conclusions.

Subtracting the $44 million expected 1960 expenditure from the unadjusted 1960 total of $1,612 million leaves $1,568 million of nominal

TABLE 1

COMPONENTS OF INCREASE IN LOCAL POLICE EXPENDITURES: 1902-1960

| | | Effect of Single Components | |
Item	Amount (millions)	Percentage of Increase	Multiple of Urbanization
1960 Unadjusted expenditures	$1,612	–	–
1960 Expected expenditures	44	–	–
1960 Expenditures due to components jointly	1,568	100	–
Due to inflation	718	46	5.52
Due to population growth	453	29	3.48
Due to motor vehicles	267	17	2.05
Due to urbanization	130	8	1.00

increase accounted for by the 4 components jointly. The relative weight of each component in contributing to the increase from 1902 to 1960 when all components are jointly operating is expressed in percentages of the total increase accounted for and in multiples of the least important component—urbanization.

CONCLUSIONS

The implications suggested by the analysis are numerous, but the authors will limit themselves to a few. After the four components of increase are taken into account, it appears that local police departments have not made any gains since 1902 in terms of societal resources (as measured by expenditures) available to them. Therefore, any conclusions that local police must be more effective today than at the turn of the century, because of a large increase in financial resources available to them, are unwarranted. This is not to deny the possibility that the police may have become more effective. However, the source of such increased effectiveness would be, not greater financial resources, but increased administrative and technological efficiency. The potential of increased police productivity through investment of a larger proportion of their financial resources in technological development has the seeming limit that policing is fundamentally a labor-intensive activity. Both at the turn of the century and in 1960, the percentage of police expenditures that was consumed by wages and salaries was about ninety percent. This allows only ten percent of expenditures to be invested in capital equipment which is a major source of increased technological productivity. The productivity benefits of patrol cars, two-way radios, computerization, and the like, cannot be denied. However, the potential of productivity increases from technological innovations appears more limited for policing than for other societal activities which are less labor intensive and are continually becoming less so.

LABOR

Two examples, although not entirely comparable, suffice to point out the gross contrast between the greater labor intensity of policing and other societal activities. In 1960, the total expenditure for salaries of the instructional staffs of public elementary and secondary schools was forty-nine percent of the total expenditures in this area of education. National defense provides a more extreme contrast. In 1965, the federal budget expenditure for military personnel was thirty-two percent of the total budget of the Department of Defense. Even more pertinent, the cost category of "research, development, test and evaluation" was fourteen percent of the total defense budget (U.S. Bureau of the Census, 1966: tables 164, 353). The fourteen percent of the total defense budget consumed by this item alone is greater than the ten percent of police expenditures that must cover all nonsalary costs.

The labor-intensive character of police work coupled with a lack of gain in financial resources makes the efforts of the police "professionalizers" more understandable. Technical development and administrative reorganization become the main foci of efforts to increase effective police resources because those changes seem the major sources of increased police labor productivity. One may speculatively suggest that if the police are even as effective today as in 1902, it is only because they have incorporated administrative and technological innovations which have offset the net decrease of financial resources.

The hypothesis of this paper was in part that the increases in police expenditures were largely independent of any rise in crime rates, and, therefore, the increasing police expenditures could not be legitimately considered a "cost" of rising crime rates. Inflation and traffic control are clearly independent of crime rates in the standardization technique utilized. Population growth would not in itself result in an increase in *per capita* crime rates. These three components alone account for more than ninety percent of the increase without reference to changing crime rates, and the hypothesis is considered confirmed at this point.

URBANIZATION

The control for urbanization did eliminate the effects on police expenditures due to rising national crime rates which might result from a larger proportion of the population living in urban areas which are in turn assumed to have higher crime rates. Even if the crime rates specific to size of place remained the same in 1960 as in 1902, the national crime rate would have risen if the 1902 urban crime rates were higher than the rural rates. Therefore, urbanization is not entirely independent of changing national crime rates. However, it should be noted that urbanization accounted for only eight percent of the expenditure increases and was the least important of the four components. Moreover, whether to attribute this proportion entirely to higher urban than rural crime rates is a moot question.

The authors can only state with any certitude that this proportion of explained expenditure increase is due to the traditionally higher per capita police expenditures in urban areas. It is also reasonable to assume that this higher per capita expenditure partially reflects a higher urban crime rate. To maintain that the higher urban expenditure *only* reflects higher urban crime rates is, however, very dubious. Urban life differs from rural life in many more dimensions which could influence police expenditures than just in crime rates, though the analysis does not identify or control the effects of these dimensions upon expenditures. Therefore, only a part of the already small proportion of expenditure increases accounted for by urbanization can be safely attributed to increasing national crime rates, assuming size-of-place specific rates remain constant over the period.

The control for urbanization as operationalized in this paper did *not* eliminate the possible effects that any assumed increases in size-of-place specific crime rates have upon police expenditures. Such effects would therefore be included in the remaining $44 million expended in 1960. Data necessary for the analysis of the effects of possible changes in urban crime rates since 1902 are not available. However, if increases in urban crime rates were added to the four components, such increases could only approach the explanatory power of population growth, inflation and motor vehicles if the expected amount of resources remaining to the police were far less in 1960 than the already low figure of $44 million. Yet, these far fewer remaining resources would still have to cope with law enforcement problems of the same magnitude as 1902, because the model utilized here standardizes upon 1902 conditions.

This additional hypothetical decrease in resources, while coping with the same magnitude problem, at the 1902 level of effectiveness, would have had to be absorbed by a remarkable increase in police efficiency or by some sort of "surplus" available to police. A "surplus" would be available if the police had been able to eliminate some responsibilities which are costly but unrelated to law enforcement. If one assumes that increased efficiency or an available surplus are not adequate to absorb a further reduction in "net" resources, one is tempted to speculate that local policing in 1960 was "underfinanced" by 1902 standards or was less effective than in 1902. The authors forego this temptation and suggest instead that increases in crime rates have been unduly emphasized as a major component of increasing police costs.

Moreover, it seems appropriate to question any scheme of social accounting that allocates the growth in local police expenditures as an increase in the cost of crime. Given the results of our analysis, it is much more sensible to say that as far as local law enforcement costs are concerned, the per capita, deflated "cost" of the average crime may well have decreased since 1902—a result which should redound to the credit of the police professionalization movement.

We may draw out one final implication of the analysis. Faced with the real budgetary limitations documented in this paper, it is not surprising, as we have mentioned, that police reformers have turned to organizational modernization—technological innovation and managerial sophistication—as cost-reducing devices. Such devices have had—in the minds of some observers at least—the consequence of making police work less personal, more withdrawn from parts of the community, and less sensitive to the variety of human situations (Bordua, 1968; Tifft and Bordua, 1969; Wilson, 1968: ch. 9 esp.).

Suggestions for dealing with these consequences of modernization all seem to involve more manpower used less "efficiently" from a cost viewpoint. Clearly, developments in this direction will require substantial changes in the pattern of investment in police service that has prevailed thus far in this century.

APPENDIX
COMPUTATIONAL PROCEDURES

CONTROLLING FOR INFLATION

The 1960 expenditures were divided into two parts. Ninety percent of the $1,612 million expenditures in 1960, or $1,451 million, was classified as police salaries and wages and the remaining $161 million as expenditures for all other police purchases of goods and services. This 90% estimate of expenditures for salaries is based upon the total police expenditure of 1,303 cities with over 10,000 population in 1960 of which 90% was for salaries and wages (International City Manager's Association, 1961: 400). This division of 1960 expenditures was made in order that a deflator index geared specifically to police salaries could be applied to this most important component of the expenditures. The 90% estimate for the salary proportion appears to be relatively constant through time. A gross estimate of this proportion for the turn of the century is that in 1907 the average patrolman's salary ($1,052) divided by the 1907 average annual departmental expenditure per police employee equaled .87 or 87% (U.S. Bureau of Census, 1907: 394, 407). These two separate components were simply added together again after each was separately deflated to 1902 dollars by different indexes.

Salary expenditures or 90% of the 1960 expenditures were deflated as follows:

$$\left(1960 \text{ salary expenditures} \right) \left(\frac{1907 \text{ patrolman's annual salary}}{1960 \text{ patrolman's annual salary}} \right) \text{ x}$$

$$\left(\frac{1960 \text{ annual policemen working days}}{1913 \text{ annual policemen working days}} \right) \left(\frac{1960 \text{ police hours per day}}{1907 \text{ police hours per day}} \right) \text{ x}$$

$$\left(\frac{\text{Value of 1907 dollars in constant dollars}}{\text{Value of 1902 dollars in constant dollars}} \right) = \begin{array}{l} 1960 \text{ salary expenditures} \\ \text{in 1902 dollars.} \end{array}$$

The logic of this formula and its possible shortcomings will be spelled out here because inflation is by far the most important component of expenditure increase. The second factor (annual salary ratio) is a coefficient of reduction which eliminates the effect of salary increases since 1907. The year 1907 was used instead of 1902 because this was the earliest source of usable data. Data for 1960 are more complete, but the 1960 data that could be utilized were limited by the available 1907 data since information had to be comparable for both years. The best available 1907 datum on annual police salaries was the mean salary of patrolmen in cities with more than 30,000 population (U.S. Bureau of the Census, 1907: 394). The 1960 datum used was the mean salary of patrolmen in cities over 25,000 (Fraternal Order of Police, 1961).[2]

Salary increases alone are an inadequate deflator because a concomitant decrease in annual working days has occurred. The third factor (annual working days ratio) deflates for this. The earliest usable source for this datum was from 1913 (Milwaukee Municipal Reference Library, 1913). Thus, any decrease in annual working days from 1907 to 1913 is not included in the deflator, and this contributes to a slight underestimate of the effects of inflation. The 1913 source provided a mean number of annual working days based upon 29 police departments in cities with more than 100,000 population. The computed mean was weighted by the number of patrolmen in each city in 1907. Similarly, the 1960 mean was weighted and was based upon cities over 100,000 population although the sample of cities used was much larger (Fraternal Order of Police, 1961).

The fourth factor (working hours ratio) deflates for the decrease in the working day length. The 1907 datum was a mean based upon 75 cities with over 35,000 population weighted by the number of patrolmen in each city (Fuld, 1909: 122-123). The 1960 datum was based upon a 1956 survey of 122 cities of which 120 had exactly 8-hour working days

(American Federation of State, County and Municipal Employees, 1956). The remaining 2 had reduced their weekly hours to 40 and 40.5 by 1960 (Fraternal Order of Police, 1961). Therefore, the figure of 8 hours was utilized for 1960.

Finally, the fifth factor (1902/1907 constant dollar ratio) serves to deflate the product of the other four factors. The product of the first four factors is the 1960 salary expenditure in 1907 dollars. The final factor is the price deflator for the gross national product (U.S. Bureau of the census, 1960). The gross national product price index was the only deflator available for this period and it converts the current 1902 and 1907 dollars into 1929 dollars.

In addition to the underestimation of inflation effects due to use of 1913 data for annual number of working days, none of the costs of 1960 salary expenditures due to increased fringe benefits such as pensions are included in the formula. Vacations and holidays are included in the working-days factor. However, the amount of underestimation due to using 1913 data and excluding fringe benefits is slight. The final figures used in the salary deflation computation are as follows:

$$\left(\$1{,}451\text{ million}\right)\left(\frac{\$1{,}052}{\$5{,}681}\right)\left(\frac{243.4}{344.2}\right)\left(\frac{8.0}{9.4}\right)\left(\frac{100/54.5}{100/49.5}\right) = \$146.84\text{ million.}$$

The remaining 10% of the 1960 expenditures ($161 million) was deflated by the utilization of 2 price indices. The 1960 expenditure for goods and services was converted into constant 1929 dollars by using the price index for state and local government purchases of goods and services (U.S. Department of Commerce, 1959: 2-3; 1963: 4, 6). Because this goods and services price index was only available back to 1929, the expenditures expressed in 1929 dollars were then converted into 1902 dollars by the price index for gross national product (U.S. Bureau of the Census, 1960). This resulted in the figure of $29.72 million. The sum of the two deflated components of 1960 expenditures thus was $176.56 million.

CONTROLLING FOR POPULATION GROWTH

"Expected" expenditures in 1960 with 1902 population $= \left(\dfrac{E}{P}\right) p = \$706$ million

Where E = 1960 Police Expenditure, P = 1960 Population,
  p = 1902 Population (U.S. Bureau of the Census, 1965).

CONTROLLING FOR URBANIZATION

"Expected" expenditures in
   1960 with 1902 Urban $= \sum_i$ (Ai) (Bi) (C) = \$1,353 million
   Population Distribution

Where i = size of place: 7 categories in thousands of population;
   500+, 250-500, 100-250, 50-100, 25-50, 10-25, below 10.

A = Per Capita Expenditure in 1960 (International City Manager's Association, 1961: 400).

B = Proportion of Population in 1902 (U.S. Bureau of the Census, 1960, 1965).

C = 1960 Population (U.S. Bureau of the Census, 1965).

CONTROLLING FOR MOTOR VEHICLE INCREASE

In 1902, there were 23,000 motor vehicles registered and per capita motor vehicle registration was .0002905 (U.S. Bureau of the Census, 1960). Multiplying this per capita rate by the 1960 population as follows:

$$180,684,000 \times .0002905 = 52,489$$

provides the number of motor vehicles in 1960 that could be expected if only population growth had contributed to this increase. However, in 1960 there were 73,768,565 motor vehicles registered (U.S. Bureau of the Census, 1965). This is an increase of 73,716,076 (73,768,565 - 52,489) motor vehicles beyond that expected from population growth alone.

It is necessary to have an estimate of the cost per registered motor vehicle of police traffic control. Data of this nature are extremely limited, but one study based upon budget analyses of 9 cities enabled us to make an estimate of \$7.23 per vehicle in 1960 (Seburn and Marsh, 1959: 77).

This study was based on the year 1957, and the mean cost weighted by number of vehicles of the 9 cities was \$6.52 per vehicle. Because this was the only source the authors found, this estimate was assumed to also hold in 1960, and with a correction for inflation, the figure is \$7.23 in 1960 dollars.[3]

The smallest city in this study had a population of 85,000. However, this figure of \$7.23 does not appear biased in the direction of a high estimate when used as a national estimate by the general trend of higher general police expenditures in large urban areas because the per vehicle rate increased as size decreased. If a national estimate is extrapolated from these data, the conclusion would be that inclusion of smaller cities in these data would have *increased* the estimate of $7.23 as a national estimate.

This figure may appear too high if only the percentage of police personnel assigned to traffic division is considered. The $7.23 estimate multiplied by the total number of registered vehicles in 1960 provides a total of $533 million as the national cost of local police traffic control. This is $\frac{\$533 \text{ million}}{\$1,612 \text{ million}}$ or 33% of the total local police expenditure in 1960. Percentages based upon data from the 1940s indicate that the percentages of police personnel assigned to traffic divisions range from 11 to 23%, depending on city size (Smith, 1946: 32; Smith, 1949: 131).

It should be noted here that proportion of police assigned to traffic divisions in the 1940s appears to increase as city size decreases, which is somewhat consistent with the previous observation that if smaller cities were included in this paper's source of data, the national estimate of $533 million would perhaps be higher. Nevertheless, this percentage range of 11-23% is less than 33%. However, large proportions of the traffic control function are handled also by police not assigned to the traffic division. For example, in 43% of cities in the Wilbur Smith study, street patrol personnel investigated minor accidents and in 38% of the cities, street patrol personnel enforced parking regulations and in the same percentage of cities, handled traffic control at intersections. Thus, the total proportion of police resources utilized in traffic control can be reasonably expected to be appreciably higher than the 11-23% estimate provided by personnel assignment to traffic divisions. Another factor that should be emphasized is the 11-23% estimate occurs with the lower per capita automobile registration of the 1940s. In 1945, per capita motor vehicle registration was .219 while in 1960 it was .408. With the increase in per capita motor vehicle registration since 1945, it may be expected that the proportion of police resources utilized in traffic control would have also increased.

Multiplying the $7.23 per vehicle cost by the 73,716,076 vehicle increase not due to population growth gives the figure of $533 million. Thus, if this $533 million is subtracted from the $1,612 million expenditures in 1960, it provides us with an estimate of the police expenditure that would have occurred in 1960 if per capita motor vehicle registration had not increased since 1902. This estimated expenditure is $1,079 million.

The above calculation assumes a per vehicle national estimate which is a constant over different size-of-place groups. The discussion indicates that this is probably not the case, but adequate size-of-place specific data on costs of traffic control and per capita vehicle registration are not available.

Moreover, the only data available for size-of-place specific per capita police expenditures do not report separate traffic and nontraffic expenditures.

Had such data been available, urbanization would be expected to account for more of the increase in nontraffic expenditures than it did of traffic and nontraffic combined expenditures since the ratio of nontraffic to total expenditures presumably increases with size of place. At the same time, expected 1960 traffic expenditures also would be greater if urban population proportions had not changed since 1902 because the smaller size-of-place groupings have higher per vehicle traffic control costs. This latter statement assumes per capita motor vehicle registration is constant across all size-of-place groupings. The effect of standardizing traffic and nontraffic expenditures separately upon the 1902 urban population distribution would have further reduced the remaining $44 million, although the additional reduction is expected to be slight.

JOINT EFFECT OF ALL COMPONENTS AND THEIR RELATIVE CONTRIBUTIONS

Expected 1960 expenditures produced by controlling each component separately are summarized in Table 2 and each expected value given a symbol for further computation.

Because these components are conceptually independent, their joint effect may be conceived of as analogous to the probability of joint events occurring. The 1960 expected expenditures when any *one* component, such as inflation, is held constant since 1902 are a proportion of the total unadjusted expenditures (A 1960). Thus, the proportion for inflation is $\frac{\text{B } 1960}{\text{A } 1960}$ or $\frac{\$ 177,000,000}{\$1,612,000,000}$. This proportion can provide the expected

TABLE 2
EXPECTED 1960 LOCAL POLICE EXPENDITURES

Component Controlled	Expected Amount (millions)	Symbol
Inflation	$ 177	B 1960
Population	706	C 1960
Motor vehicle increase	1,079	D 1960
Urbanization	1,353	E 1960

expenditures in dollars simply by multiplying it by A 1960 (the total 1960 unadjusted expenditures) as follows:

$$\left(\frac{B\ 1960}{A\ 1960}\right) \quad x \quad A\ 1960\ =\ B\ 1960$$

This formula can be expanded to compute the joint effect of the 4 components by incorporating the expected expenditures when the components are each controlled separately as below.

$$\left(\frac{B\ 1960}{A\ 1960}\right) \left(\frac{C\ 1960}{A\ 1960}\right) \left(\frac{D\ 1960}{A\ 1960}\right) \left(\frac{E\ 1960}{A\ 1960}\right) \quad (A\ 1960)\ =\ \$44\ \text{million.}$$

The figure of $44 million (F 1960) represents the expected expenditure in 1960 if population growth, inflation, urbanization, and motor vehicle increase taken jointly had not occurred since 1902.

The amount of expenditure increase that each component has contributed from 1902 to 1960 when all four components operate *jointly* can be derived as follows. The amount that each component contributes to the increases from 1902 to 1960 when computed *separately* provides a measure of the relative importance of each component. This amount is the unadjusted total 1960 expenditures minus the adjusted or "expected" 1960 expenditures for a component. The following formula utilizes these relative increase contributions that each component accounts for when analyzed separately and provides the amount of increase each has contributed when the four components operate jointly.

$$(A\ 1960 - B\ 1960)\ Z + (A\ 1960 - C\ 1960)\ Z + (A\ 1960 - D\ 1960)\ Z$$
$$+ (A\ 1960 - E\ 1960)\ Z + F\ 1960 = A\ 1960$$

Solving for the constant Z (Z = .50047) and multiplying by Z the increase amount that each component accounts for when analyzed separately, provides the amount of increase in 1960 dollars due to each component when all are operating. These amounts and the percentage of the total increase each has contributed are reported in Table 1.

NOTES

1. For example, in 1960 among 1,303 cities with populations over ten thousand, ninety percent of police department expenditures were for salaries and wages (International City Manager's Association, 1961: 400).

2. The specific publication date, is March 15, and because of this early 1961 date, this source was considered a better source for 1960 data than the equivalent 1960 publication. The 1961 publication data must have been collected at the end of 1960 or very early in 1961.

3. The $6.52 figure was inflated as follows: The salary proportion ($6.52 x .9 = $5.87) was inflated by an inflation index for police patrolmen (U.S. Bureau of Labor Statistics, 1962: 20). The other proportion was inflated by a price index for local government purchases of goods and services (U.S. Department of Commerce, 1963: 4, 6).

REFERENCES

American Federation of State, County and Municipal Employees (1956) Employment Conditions for Police Officers. October 18 (mimeo).

BARCLAY, G.W. (1958) Techniques of Population Analysis. New York: John Wiley.

BORDUA, D. J. (1968) "Comments on police-community relations," pp. 204-221 in S. I. Cohn (ed.) Law Enforcement Science and Technology II. Chicago: ITT Research Center.

Fraternal Order of Police (1961) A Survey of 1961 Salaries and Working Conditions of the Police Departments in the United States (March 15).

FULD, L. F. (1909) Police Administration. New York: G. P. Putnam's Sons.

International City Manager's Association (1961) The Municipal Year Book. Chicago.

Milwaukee Municipal Reference Library (1913) Schedule of Salaries, Hours, Vacations, and Costs of Uniforms of Patrolmen in Various Cities.

President's Commission on Law Enforcement and Administration of Justice (1967) Task Force Report: Crime and Its Impact—An Assessment. Washington, D.C.: U.S. Government Printing Office.

SEBURN, T. J. and B. L. MARSH (1959) Urban Transportation Administration. New Haven: Yale University.

SMITH, B. (1949) Police Systems in the United States. New York: Harper & Brothers.

SMITH, W.S. (1946) The Organization of Official Traffic Agencies in Cities and States. New York: Eno Foundation for Highway Traffic Control.

TIFFT, L. L. and D. J. BORDUA (1969) "Police organization and future research." J. of Research on Crime & Delinquency.

U.S. Bureau of Labor Statistics (1962) Salary Trends; Firemen and Policemen, 1924-1961, Report 233. Washington, D.C.: U.S. Government Printing Office.

U.S. Bureau of the Census (1966) Statistical Abstract of the United States. Washington, D.C.: U.S. Government Printing Office.

——— (1965) Historical Statistics of the United States from Colonial Times to 1957: Continuation to 1962 and Revisions. Washington, D.C.: U.S. Government Printing Office.

——— (1960) Historical Statistics of the United States from Colonial Times to 1957. Washington, D.C.: U.S. Government Printing Office.

——— (1907) Statistics of Cities Having Population of Over 30,000: Special Reports. Washington, D.C.: U.S. Government Printing Office.

U.S. Department of Commerce (1963) Business Statistics. Washington, D.C.: U.S. Government Printing Office.

——— (1959) Business Statistics. Washington, D.C.: U.S. Government Printing Office.

WILSON, J. Q. (1968) Varieties of Police Behavior. Cambridge: Harvard Univ. Press.

National Responses to Urban Crime

The Soviet Union, the United Kingdom, and the United States

ROBERT W. CLAWSON
Kent State University

DAVID L. NORRGARD
University of Minnesota

Accelerated urbanization is a dynamic phenomenon today whether one is discussing characteristics of Pakistan, Morocco, Poland, Venezuela, or nearly any of the some 130 nation-states now in existence. Accompanying accelerated urbanization is a variety of symbiotic problems clearly not confined to a single state or geographical area: inadequate housing and transportation, insufficient water and sewer facilities, air and water pollution, and substandard educational programs. Also among these are what are widely recognized as significant deficiencies in law enforcement practices (Walsh, 1969: 7).

Meeting demands imposed upon a political system by urbanization is increasingly a public responsibility and, more importantly, a responsibility met by the central rather than a decentralized segment of the governmental structure. In some nations (e.g., United States) this represents a departure from traditional decentralized action of local or state governmental units. In others (e.g., United Kingdom) already existing central involvement (although not direct control) has been recognized as essential. In still others (e.g., USSR) it represents another shift in a policy which vacillates between central and decentralized control.

The Soviet Union, the United Kingdom, and the United States appear to share a recognition of the linkage between rapid urbanization and a marked increase in urban crime. National political leaders, perceiving this linkage, have reevaluated national policy concerning law enforcement.[1] It is suggested here that a significant change in policy has been taking place. New input data affecting leadership perception of urban crime has produced new policy outputs: increased national involvement in law enforcement activities which heretofore, in varying degrees, have been decentralized. The purpose of this study is to explore leadership perceptions of urban crime and relate these perceptions to new policy outputs in each of these countries.

Before proceeding, however, mention should be made of the use of comparative crime statistical data. There are significant cultural variations in definitions of crime, degrees of responsibility, types and severity of penalities, probabilities of discovery, and especially methods of data collection (Wolfgang, 1967: 65). For our purposes, national crime rate comparisons need not be made. Rather, our concern is with the perception of urban crime by the political leadership within a given country and the varying policy outputs related to such perception. Any crime rate data utilized in this study therefore applies only to a specific country, and no effort has been made to determine levels of urban crime as such.

POLICY INPUTS AND INITIAL RESPONSES

Law enforcement in the United States has been the province of state and local units, although the federal government exempts certain areas (e.g., bank robbery).[2] The federal government of the Soviet Union[3] has responded to various exigencies in law enforcement by stressing strong central control during Stalin's regime, then a degree of decentralized control by the republics, and more recently greater federal control once again. As a consequence of the United Kingdom's unitary system, a degree of central government involvement in law enforcement has long been the rule. Nonetheless, a searching inquiry in the early 1960s resulted in national legislation which, among other things, urged the consolidation of the numerous locally subordinated police forces and the further solidification of control over such forces by the appropriate cabinet level Secretaries of State.[4] Each of the nations under consideration has in fact launched such a national inquiry in response to a growing perception of urban crime. The inquiry was made by a royal commission in Britain, a presidential commission in the United States, and a series of high-level conferences in the USSR.

Two problem areas were largely responsible for bringing the issue of urban crime control to national attention: (1) enforcement difficulties resulting from seemingly unnecessary fragmentation of authority, and (2) abusive police tactics having marginal impact on crime rate reduction while serving to alienate portions of the polity. Each country has made policy changes in response to these two problems. This section will describe the two areas of difficulty as well as a more extensive treatment of the initial policy changes. As a consequence of responding to specific problems, however, new comprehensive national policies have emerged stressing centralization or recentralization of law enforcement activities. This result will be treated in the third section of this analysis accompanied by some assessments and conclusions regarding the three seemingly disparate political systems and their respective efforts to cope with the demands of urban crime.

BEGINNINGS OF NATIONAL AWARENESS

"Law and order" in the United States was first raised as a national campaign issue in the 1964 presidential race (and discussed even more vigorously in 1968). This stimulus led to the formation of the President's Crime Commission in 1965 (Executive Order 11236). Ostensibly focusing on all aspects of the criminal justice system, most of the 200 recommendations of the commission were concerned in fact with police practices at the state and local levels. Moreover, this commission, the National Advisory Commission on Civil Disorders (1967), and the National Commission on the Causes and Prevention of Violence (1969) covered similar terrain.

As noted previously, law enforcement has been traditionally an exception to the American concept of shared functions. Outside of a few Federal Bureau of Investigation activities which stress cooperative action, state and local control and responsibility have been the rule. Now the national political leadership has begun to deviate from this principle.

Increasing federal preoccupation with problems related to the criminal justice system in the United States is reflected best in two recent messages from President Richard M. Nixon—namely, the State of the Union Message[5] and the Executive Budget for Fiscal Year 1971. In his annual message to Congress the President said:

> If there is one area where the word war is appropriate it is in the fight against crime. We must declare and win the war against the criminal elements which increasingly threaten our cities, our homes and our lives. . . . That is why 1971 Federal spending for local law enforcement will double that budgeted for 1970.

The Nixon administration budget proposal suggests an even more significant change. None of the 1963 federal government's budget allocation to the Department of Justice was for local law enforcement and only a modest amount in 1965. By 1971, federal expenditures for Justice Department activities are expected to have increased nearly 500%, a major portion being devoted to local law enforcement—this in less than a decade. These two dates define the period in which "law and order" and urban crime became a national political issue. Actual federal law enforcement operations are being directed toward the kinds of crime identified with urbanization which are as much federal problems as state and local ones. Typical is the use of the 1964 Civil Rights Act which has been interpreted to allow federal investigation and prosecution for many crimes of personal violence. A significant percentage of the total Justice Department budget is now allotted for programs virtually nonexistent a few years ago, such as grants-in-aid to state and local law enforcement agencies and programs. Moreover, the grants-in-aid budget now exceeds the budget of the FBI, suggesting that the political leadership perceives federal-state-local cooperation, as exemplified by the FBI, as less effective than actual federal involvement in state and local law enforcement activities (Bureau of Budget, 1970a: 25-26; 1970b: 146). In short, the Nixon administration, through its budget and other actions, has taken significant notice of what it perceives as a well-articulated public concern, the rapid increase in urban crime.

Somewhat before the U.S. study, Britain had launched a wide-ranging investigation of police affairs throughout the United Kingdom, highlighted by the 1962 report of the Royal Commission on the Police. This inquiry constituted the first substantive review of all police forces in Great Britain since the mid-1830s; other reviews had had more limited objectives. It is significant, too, that a "Royal Commission" conducted the inquiry, rather than the less prestigious "committee" which appears to investigate matters of less pervasive importance. Indeed, only three other Royal Commissions have explored questions directly relevant to police affairs (1836-1838, 1908, and 1929), but in each instance the scope of inquiry was more limited than that of 1960-1962.

The Royal Commission on the Police (1962: iv) was charged mainly with evaluating the structure and functioning of local police authorities and investigating the accountability of police forces to chiefs of police. The commission recommended reducing the number of police units through countrywide consolidation and urged greater uniformity in recruitment, police force composition, and functioning. It noted the pressing need for employing modern technology, particularly in increased automobile patrol and more effective communications systems. This document, like its counterpart in the United States, now serves as an impetus to increasing central involvement in local police affairs.

The British report, however, has not as yet resulted in any major departures from accepted policy, although the recommendations were made early in the 1960s. Slow to carry out major policy alterations, the British required several years, for example, to implement socialized medicine once the issue had been decided, and even that decision came nearly 25 years after a Royal Commission recommendation. It is assumed that, as the British public attaches increasing importance to the urban crime rate, major changes in accord with the commission recommendations will occur.

In July, 1966, a Union-Republic MOOP was created in the Soviet Union, reestablishing a centrally coordinated ministry after an experimentation with republic or decentralized control. This policy change resulted from high-level meetings, held between late-1964 and mid-1966, in which Brezhnev himself participated (Yegorichev, 1965; Smirnov, 1966). The Soviet leadership was then beginning to perceive urban crime as an anachronism in the Soviet system, and impatient with its existence, was attempting to eradicate it by any means possible, harsh as they might be. Union and republic authority in this reshuffling were to be exercised concurrently, but in practice this meant centralization of authority. Nikolay Shchelokov, an old political ally of Brezhnev's, was made minister of the new central organization. With recentralization, the *militsiya* and criminal courts were once again given substantial responsibility for all law enforcement and adjudication; in fact, their powers were significantly increased.[6]

ADMINISTRATIVE DILEMMAS OF FRAGMENTATION

Several law enforcement problems within each country have fragmentation as a common theme—excessive concurrent authority exercised by agencies within the same or similar territory; unnecessary commingling of activities extraneous to the major police function, i.e., crime repression, with duties related to it; and even, in the USSR, the presence of a strong, quasi-police unit which interfered continuously with the regular police agency.

The United States

Local community responsibility, the traditional approach to law enforcement in the United States, is the genesis of many current problems in that country (President's Commission on Law Enforcement and Administration of Justice, 1967b: 68). For example, more than 39,000 of the approximately 40,000 police agencies in the United States employ fewer than 10 officers. There are only some 40 police agencies at any level which have more than 1,000 personnel. In all, there are approximately 355,000 state and local police officers in the country.

Aware of this fragmentation, many local government officials urged through their national associations the adoption of a federal grant-in-aid program for areawide planning and coordination. Collectively they argued that problems in providing police service cannot be artificially confined by political boundaries, but they did not advocate creating anything akin to a national police force (Norrgard, 1969; U.S. Congress, House Committee on Judiciary, 1967: 29, 322-325, 387). Suffice it to say that in the United States there was local support for altering the old basic policy of federal noninvolvement in local law enforcement problems to the extent of requesting financial assistance.

To encourage areawide coordination in local law enforcement planning, the original administration bill would have made grants-in-aid available only to those communities having a total population in excess of 50,000, or to two or more communities which jointly exceeded that number. Congressional opposition to this approach on the grounds that it did not properly recognize smaller, less metropolitan areas, in addition to other factors, forced a modification. Title I of Public Law 90-351 now stresses the need for a state master plan. Moreover, the guidelines prepared by the Law Enforcement Assistance Administration, U.S. Department of Justice (1968: 10) clearly state that "planning efforts on a regional, metropolitan area, or other 'combined interest' basis are encouraged and should receive priority." Each state has accordingly established a centralized state planning agency to prepare a statewide plan, incorporating plans developed by regionally based units within the state. This represents the initial phase of implementation, now completed, of the Safe Streets Act. The second phase is to begin expediting the various plans—both state and local—as they gain federal approval. This provision indicates that all such plans must be consistent with overall policy objectives of the federal government; otherwise federal financial aid is not made available.

Another dimension of the fragmentation problem in the United States is that police agencies often are called upon to perform duties not related to crime repression. A reference to this point can be found in the reports of the President's Commission on Law Enforcement and Administration of Justice (1967b: 88-90): police agencies were too often assigned responsibilities either not at all consistent with crime repression or at least tending to detract from their regular enforcement and peace-keeping duties. One typical recommendation of the commission was that the police be relieved of responsibility for operating correctional facilities.

Great Britain

The police of Great Britain, organized into 157 separate forces, include some 70,000 men under county and county-borough forces and about 18,000 men in the London Metropolitan Police. In times of crisis, as recently in Northern Ireland, military units are mobilized for police duty. The system has traditionally emphasized local control within the unitary system of state administration. This has meant that central coordination amounted to little more than infrequent inspection tours by Her Majesty's Inspectors of Constabulary. Scotland Yard, the headquarters of the Metropolitan Police, is consulted only when the crime eventually proves too much for local authorities.

This decentralization, within what is considered a classic unitary state, has been a boon to the highly mobile criminal for many years. The 1963 Great Train Robbery is but one example, admittedly a spectacular one, of modern urban-based criminals capitalizing on the lack of central coordination (Hewitt, 1965: 44-48; Nicholson, 1967: 197). The small police forces, concluded the Royal Commission, tend to be handicapped, lack flexibility, and cannot make full use of their manpower. Moreover, the efficient policing of large cities often is impaired by tradition-based police boundaries. The British Home Secretary in a 1963 statement to Parliament indicated that he had initiated on his own authority the implementation of some recommendations of the Royal Commission. Specifically, he created a research and planning unit (which would be utilized to develop closer coordination of the numerous police districts) and he increased the number of inspectors to coordinate regional police affairs more fully.[7]

The first significant effort to consolidate police forces in Britain took place in 1968 with final implementation occurring in the spring of 1969. As provided by the Police Act of 1964, the Home Secretary ordered the consolidation of 13 county-borough forces with the Lancashire county force creating a 7,000-man unit, the second largest in the country. Importantly, five boroughs objected to the enforced merger.[8] This action represents the only decisive step taken toward consolidation by the government since passage of the 1964 act.

British police, like their American counterparts, were saddled with numerous extraneous duties, spent too much of their time on traffic regulation and too little in dealing with crime, noted the Royal Commission on Police (1962: 96-97). Police officers were also required to serve as school-crossing guards, further limiting the time available for crime prevention work. The Commission felt that civilian workers could be employed in both situations to perform these tasks, freeing trained police officers for police duties.

The Soviet Union

Soviet law enforcement during most of the 1960s was fragmented in at least three ways. The first resulted from the 1960 devolution of authority to the republics, part of the slow decentralization programs in the post-Stalin era. At that time the Ministry of Internal Affairs (MVD) which includes the regular police (*militsiya*) was abolished. The militsiya was divided into fifteen separate forces (Republic Ministries for the Preservation of Public Order or MOOPs) without central bureaucratic coordination save for the Communist Party as the sole unifying element.[9] Although this hardly represents the kind of territorial fragmentation present in Great Britain, much less the United States, the post-Khrushchev leadership perceived that fragmentation was significantly retarding the Soviet effort to eradicate crime. Thus in 1966 (Postanovlenie, 1966), they created a central MOOP located in Moscow to direct and coordinate the efforts of the republic MOOPs. In 1968, recalling the pre-1960 centralized police, the MOOPs were renamed MVDs (Postanovlenie, 1968). The current system emphasizes the relative importance of authority at the national level consistent with Soviet federal practice.

To understand Soviet federal practice, it is useful to note the distinctions between the three types of "ministries" commonly utilized in the system. The first type is known as All-Union, and it characteristically deals with issues having scant relevance to the constituent republics (e.g., defense or foreign affairs), or are so important that tight central control is essential (e.g., defense industries, heavy industry). The second type, Union-Republic, is that in which some power is shared between a Moscow-based Union-Republic Ministry and ministries located in the republic capitals and belonging to the republic council of ministers. The degree of shared authority varies from ministry to ministry, and these ministries are reserved for matters of lesser, but national, importance such as agriculture, light industry, or the MOOP after 1966. The final type is the Republic Ministry which is created to deal with problems unique to a republic or which do not require national attention (e.g., local industry and public services, reclamation and water economy). Presumably the third type is also one means to denote a drastic change in importance. No doubt it was a combination of "unique" problems and drastic downplaying of the regular police function which led Khrushchev to regionalize the MOOPs.

The multifunctionality of the Soviet MOOP illustrates the second major problem of fragmentation. Between 1960 and 1968 the MOOPs were not merely responsible for the operations of the regular police. The various MOOPs, and after 1966 the Union Republic MOOP, also directed the internal passport system (which is, among other things, a method of controlling urban population size); all firefighting forces, civil defense units; the MOOP industrial police (factory guards–authority partly shared with the Soviet Army); the MOOP economic police (for prevention of internal economic sabotage); the administration of the penal colonies; the MOOP prisons; and, in formal conjunction with the Soviet Army, the MOOP railway police. Thus the Soviet police have been asked to perform a number of essentially nonpolice functions (e.g., firefighting) and a number of functions which either do not exist in the other two countries (e.g., internal passport system) or are undertaken by private police units (e.g., industrial guards). The resulting scale of operations has necessitated a bureaucratic complex which dwarfs police administration in the United States and the United Kingdom, if only in sheer number of personnel. The figure most often quoted for the size of the MOOP, before the 1969 renaming, is approximately 2,000,000 officers (Kozlov, 1968: 530-547; Conquest, 1968: 30-40). The present MVDs have continued to perform all of these functions.

Another aspect of this functional service problem in the USSR concerns the role of the Soviet Committee for State Security, or KGB. The internal operations of the KGB, usually described as those of counterintelligence (but which are actually more extensive), have tended to confuse Western analysts as well as Soviet practitioners. The organizational ancestor of both the MVD and the KGB is the NKVD, and this common heritage serves to augment some confusion in responsibilities. The present practice is that the MVD in its police functions will focus upon the "nonpolitical" aspects of crime while the KGB, primarily concerned with counterintelligence, will also resolve all cases of "political" crime. The Soviet definition of what constitutes political crime is, of course, quite broad; it includes such things as attempting to leave the Soviet Union, writing literature critical of the Soviet system, as well as the more familiar acts such as sabotage, assassination, or inciting to riot. The difficulties occur when responsibilities overlap (which the KGB sometimes promotes), and a clear line cannot be drawn between a criminal and a political act.

Although the 1966 and 1968 reforms were designed to make law enforcement agencies more efficient by centralizing and streamlining their operation, the problem of fragmentation due to police involvement in essentially nonpolice functions has not been dealt with, nor has it attracted anything more than cursory attention from the leadership, which is not the case in either the United States or Britain. Confusion between the roles of the MVD and that of the KGB will likely continue.

The third, and somewhat unique, fragmentation problem arises from the existence of Khrushchev-inspired popular organizations such as the volunteer police (*druzhiny*). Khrushchev's increased reliance on a nonprofessional organization for law enforcement was deeply resented by many professional law enforcement officers. The increasing power and size of the druzhiny organizations (over which the MOOPs had only a hazy jurisdiction and no real operational control) has been particularly abhorrent to the militsiya (Juviler, 1969: 14-15). Although the druzhiny, estimated by Raymond (1968: 265) to be about 5,500,000 strong, are charged with many of the nonpolice duties which have occupied trained police in the United Kingdom and the United States (e.g., parade duty, neighborhood patrols, certain kinds of traffic regulation), at the same time they have often been involved in more serious law enforcement, such as the prevention of hooliganism, theft, and, in some cases, aggravated assault and murder. Thus they assumed a kind of partnership with the militsiya (Vatsik, 1968).

The druzhiny were perceived by some police leaders as a significant threat, having performed their assigned duties badly, without either proper training or willingness to cooperate with the militsiya (Tikhunov, 1966). The militsiya strength and budget were cut as early as 1959 and kept at a correspondingly lower point through the mid-1960s as a result of reliance on the "popular" organizations. With the removal of Khrushchev, and the post-Khrushchev leadership's increased impatience with the continued existence of crime in the USSR, the role of the nonprofessional organization began to change. One of the principal points made by the 1966 police reforms was that the druzhiny must necessarily assume a secondary role to the regular militsiya.[10] After 1966 there was no longer any question, as some Communist Party theorists had suggested, of a "social" organization slowly supplanting the formal "organs of repression" such as the militsiya (Kuusinen, 1960: 788-878).

POLICE TACTICS AND COMMUNITY ATTITUDES

A second basic set of problems arises from tactics used by police agencies and individual police officers to repress crime. Each country has experienced difficulties with minority nationality or racial groups because of police tactics, or with the process of socialization and control of police personnel. One consequence has been a marked distrust of the police by minority groups. This, too, has evoked policy change at the national level.

In the United States, the President's Commission on Law Enforcement (1967b: 148) cited serious problems of minority hostility toward the police in virtually all medium-sized and large cities in the country. Eighty-five percent of the black population in the Watts area of Los Angeles believed that the police engaged in abusive tactics, nearly fifty percent saw such incidents, and somewhat less than twenty percent were victims of such tactics (Raine, 1966: 3). In Milwaukee, a moderately large city which has experienced rioting in ghetto areas, the official report of the incident noted that eighty-four percent of the blacks in the riot area listed police brutality as a cause of the riot. They also complained that the police frequently insulted blacks, unnecessarily frisked them, and beat them up.[11] These are but two examples of a larger number of similar incidents or expressions of feelings. The National Advisory Commission on Civil Disorders treated this subject extensively. There is substantial evidence that in the United States the ghetto resident, black or white, is convinced that the typical police officer regularly engages in abusive, oppressive tactics (President's Commission on Law Enforcement, 1967b: 148; Levy, 1968: 31).[12]

The President's Commission on Law Enforcement (1967b: 200-205) discussed at some length the experience of civilian review boards now operative in various cities in the U.S., but fell short of recommending that such units be established. Rather, the Commission suggested that citizen advisory committees be established in minority group neighborhoods to resolve conflicts between police and community (President's Commission on Law Enforcement, 1967a: 101).

The President's Commission on Law Enforcement (1967b: 126) also commented on police recruitment, selection, and training. It reported that "the quality of police service will not significantly improve until higher educational requirements are established for its personnel." A significant portion of the funds appropriated under the Safe Streets Act was intended to improve the general educational levels of the police through extensive loan programs to finance the return to school of officers employed full-time in law enforcement.[13] Moreover, the federal government has provided a number of ongoing national "information and training programs" including the FBI sessions at Quantico, Virginia, to which state and local law enforcement officers are invited for a series of classes and lectures concerning the "federal view" on minority problems, juvenile crime, and related concerns.[14]

Great Britain

Similar patterns can be detected in the United Kingdom. Of the total complaints against police reviewed by the Royal Commission on Police (1962: 123) the following breakdown was made: incivility, twenty-eight percent; excessive use of police powers, twenty-five percent; physical violence or assault, fifteen percent; corruption, five percent; and dereliction of duty, thirty-two percent. Niederhoffer (1969: 91-92) cites a number of such incidents and observes that the bobbies no longer enjoy the sacrosanct position they once did. It was observed by the Royal Commission, however, that the number of complaints against the police was small in relation to the number of policemen, and that there had been no significant increase in the number of complaints from year to year. This observation, though still essentially correct, would not hold if more recent figures from Northern Ireland or the university communities were included.

Detailed recommendations offered in Britain to improve the formal complaint procedure sought to guarantee that all complaints would be processed by the appropriate senior police official. In addition, a minority report to the official Royal Commission on Police report (1962: 193-194) called for the creation of a Commissioner of Rights to review all such matters, to ascertain that the police procedures were proper, and to exercise final review of all complaints upon appeal. No such position, however, has been created.

The Royal Commission on Police (1962: 90-95), like its American counterpart, found that the quality of personnel would have to be improved before the elimination of abusive police tactics could be achieved. Selection standards were poor, especially in the area of basic educational skills with insufficient in-service training provided to improve such skills. Additionally, the Commission stated that potential senior officers were lacking in advanced educational attainment, noting as an example that no university graduates had entered the police service. Steps have now been taken to attract such people. This, again, parallels U.S. trends.

The British have appeared less interested in the kinds of community relations programs U.S. law enforcement agencies have engaged in, preferring to rely on traditional socialization methods. While attempting to alter somewhat the image of the traditional foot patrol "bobby" to a more modern and mobile officer, the British still feel no pressing need for a major indoctrination program to "popularize" the police.

The Soviet Union

Soviet police problems with national minorities must of necessity be shaped by the nature of the population. There are nearly 200 officially recognized separate ethnic-language groups in the Soviet Union. Only a few of them have original native languages or customs even remotely related to those of the politically dominant Great Russia. Years of Russian and Soviet rule have made heavy inroads on this provincialism, but there are still areas in which Russian is rarely spoken.

Most of the national groups remain either in their traditional areas (e.g., Georgians still reside chiefly in the Georgian Republic) or in areas specifically set aside for them. The larger groups are represented politically through the federal system of the fifteen republics. For this and other reasons, there are no "ghetto" minority populations in Russian urban areas. Nonetheless, the republics and the numerous smaller political entities set aside for national minorities do form kinds of "ghettos" in which the population is controlled. The larger urban centers of these nationality areas may serve sometimes as battlegrounds for confrontations between police and minority groups. The police, whether locally recruited or not, are perceived as representatives of "Great Russian chauvinism," if not imperialism. If the difference in a given city is between a largely European militsiya force and an Asian population (as in Tashkent or Alma Ata, for example), the confrontation may sometimes take on a racial overtone (Zorinyan, 1968).

For police review, the Soviets have long maintained, in the office of the Procurator General of the USSR (public prosecutor), a unit specifically designed to investigate complaints against the police. Although the procuracy handles many such cases each year, the feeling is general among the Soviet population that the procuracy is not overenthusiastically fulfilling this function.[15]

Police recruitment and training programs are presently being extensively upgraded in the USSR. There has been a continuous push to recruit better qualified personnel, especially from the graduates of Soviet university law faculties.[16] Nevertheless, the educational level of the average militsiya officer is not significantly higher than his counterparts in Britain and the United States.

To complicate further the minority-police confrontation, there are indications of a recruitment pattern designed to prevent fraternization between police and certain minority populations. In Central Asia, militsiya senior officers appear still to be recruited almost exclusively from the European populations of the area (these officers rarely speak the native language but commonly insist that the natives speak Russian in any police transaction); this, despite the current formal program to recruit nationality cadres into the upper levels of administrative organizations. In other districts, such as the Georgian Republic, Georgian-speaking police are recruited mainly from the area of the Northern Caucasus in the Russian Republic. Despite their ethnic similarities and their ability to deal with the Georgian population in their own language, they are considered outsiders and representatives of foreign political and cultural standards.[17]

Soviet efforts to "popularize" the militsiya are certainly the most extensive and most amply funded of the three countries. Soviet newspapers constantly publish stories about individual police officers and the need for civilian-militsiya cooperation in various activities. The desire to "involve" the Soviet population seems to be the principal current theme (Krylov, 1969; Medynskiy, 1969). There is now even a day set aside (November 10) for honoring the militsiya; the newspapers run special promotional stories detailing the adventures of heroic policemen (Dyachkov, 1969; Korestkiy, 1968; Shchelokov, 1968). The campaign to encourage active public cooperation with the police has intensified (as in the United States through "Crime-Alert" programs) as the willingness of the general population to so respond has decreased. These advertising programs have improved in quality with the recentralization of police administration and the increased participation of Soviet Communist Party *aktivs* in the inner workings of the militsiya.

The vast discretionary authority vested in police departments and, particularly, in individual police officers is closely related to problems of community attitudes and especially of abusive police tactics. In all three countries this, too, has been of national concern.

Most police administrators in each of the countries would say that their departments adhere to a policy of "full enforcement" of all laws. In fact, however, few departments or individual officers could even begin fully to enforce all laws falling within their purview. At some point, discretion must be exercised as to which laws will be enforced, i.e., what the emphasis of the law enforcement program will be in a given location. In simple economic terms, no other course is prudent because a policy of full enforcement is beyond the financial capacity of virtually every local community or even nation.

Discretion is employed by a police agency in establishing priorities. The police might, for example, focus attention on crimes against property and choose to minimize enforcement provisions in other areas. Importantly, however, police discretion seems to lead to abusive practices as well. These abuses create the problems discussed earlier (e.g., rigid enforcement policy in black neighborhoods leading to extreme hostility toward police officers) and are difficult to control. As Goldstein (1967: 171) points out, "The nature of the police function is such that primary dependence for the control of police conduct must continue to be placed upon internal systems of control." By this is meant holding senior officers responsible for the actions of their subordinates and designing and implementing procedures to tighten internal discipline. Another control mechanism, suggests Goldstein, is the training program and other intradepartmental socialization processes which seek to influence the behavior of individual officers toward the use of nonabusive tractics. Niederhoffer (1969: 55-95) reinforces this point by demonstrating the debilitating effect peer group pressures have upon the behavior of a new police officer once his formal training program has been completed. Needed in addition to these internal controls, Goldstein also recommends, are certain external control devices such as a formalized and well-known complaint procedure, civilian review boards, and judicial review.

One reason for emphasizing internal controls as a means of regulating police behavior is that external control devices are subject to majority group domination. Majority groups in the population may be the very ones demanding the use of improper police pressure to manipulate minority groups or to preserve and maintain "law and order" in the streets. In the United States, for example, it is often under just such circumstances that most abusive police actions do, in fact, occur (President's Commission on Law Enforcement, 1967b: 32). This is why each nation seems to place so much importance on improving socialization processes within police agencies and strengthening police recruitment, selection, and training programs.

The Soviets, realizing the political liability of having operated an oppressive police system for so long, have publicly denounced police excesses (both secret and regular) committed during the Stalinist regime. The Soviet attempt to control police behavior, due to this legacy, has been more concerted than in the two Western nations which have chosen to rely upon traditional socialization processes. The "unleashing" of the militsiya in 1966 was thus greeted with a great deal more public opposition than might have been expected before Khrushchev's campaign against Stalin began. Police excesses were the subject of increasingly numerous complaints to the Procurator General's offices at all levels (see Malyarov, 1967). Instances of false arrest, mishandling of information, inefficiency and purposive red tape, physical "police brutality," and the like, increasingly confronted the units charged with investigation of such excesses (for examples, see Kochmarev, 1968; Shtanko, 1968).

These excesses, particularly against anything even remotely resembling hooliganism or juvenile crime, were given a degree of official sanction. By 1968 this policy had become a public liability while evidently not significantly decreasing street crime. Interurban organized crime and illegal drug traffic, apparently rising in the early 1960s, was virtually eliminated by 1968, in part because of the rigidly enforced population movement controls. The militsiya, given increased powers, assumed even more. They attempted to make the streets "safe" by methods scarcely less reprehensible than those of the criminal offenders pursued. These methods did not solve urban crime—they simply made it harder to find. As the intense campaign for law and order waned, those who had opposed granting the militsiya such sweeping powers began to point out the ineffectiveness of the new tactics. A period of reevaluation followed (Shchelokov, 1967; Gukovskaya and Yakovlev, 1968). The central leadership decided to "leash" once again the uniformed police and attempt greater internal supervision (Juviler, 1969). Recently, however, a number of legal changes have been made which lead again to an automatic increase in the militsiya's discretionary powers through such measures as preventive detention.[18] The United States is now considering similar legislation for the "federal" city of Washington, D.C., and there is increasing support for further augmenting police powers throughout the United States through devices such as "stop and frisk," "no-knock," and similar police state tools.

The druzhiny have caused similar problems. In some areas, these volunteer patrols exceeded their authority to the extent of using hooligan tactics on any passers-by. These excesses gave rise in 1968 to a number of stern national warnings and local measures to bring the druzhiny under proper control (Lyashenko, 1968).

Conflict within the economic system creates much of the problem the militsiya faces in determining which laws to enforce with full vigor. For instance, the sale of alcohol in the USSR today, under numerous complicated restrictions, is at the same time extremely profitable for state trade organizations. Alcohol may be sold and consumed only at specific and restrictive times and places; a complex set of regulations also governs its transport. While the laws restricting sale and consumption are complicated, those against various offenses committed under the influence of alcohol are nothing short of Draconian. The militsiya, however, seems to face an insurmountable problem in regulating the lucrative state alcohol monopoly. As a result, it has decided to let the liquor trade flourish while concentrating on manifestations of alcoholism. As alcohol sales, legal and illegal, now steadily increase, so do instances of violent crime committed under its influence (Juviler, 1969; Lukyanov, 1967).

In the United States and Great Britain, laws regulating vice (sex and gambling) are the ones most often subject to discretionary enforcement.

EMERGING NATIONAL PATTERNS

During the 1960s the Soviet Union, the United Kingdom, and the United States each became more actively involved in urban area law enforcement problems. At first this involvement was reflected by policy outputs developed to meet specific problems as they came to national attention. Ultimately, each nation devised a comprehensive program that resulted in a move toward centralization or recentralization of law enforcement powers at the national level.

It has been argued that crime has assumed a new physiognomy, at least prima facie evidence so suggests (Radzinowicz, 1966). Specifically apparent is a growth in motiveless destruction and hooliganism, an increase in new types of stealing (e.g., consumer durables), a shift to disintegrated behavior and drug crime, expanded juvenile crime, and a growth in relative rates of first offenders to recidivists. These trends occur in each of the countries under consideration.[19]

The leadership of each nation attends not only to the facts of crime but has begun to consider as well the question of what causes crime. There is no generally accepted theory on the cause of crime,[20] but one which has considerable support is that of differential association (Sutherland and Cressey, 1966: 77-100). The tenets of the differential association theory hold that criminal behavior is learned in intimate personal interaction with others, which involves learning (as in any other learning situation) techniques of committing crimes as well as motives, rationalizations, attitudes and drives, and results in a value structure predisposed to what has been defined through legal codes as deviant behavior. Importantly, the theory notes that the general needs of the criminal and the noncriminal are the same; the methods used to fulfill these needs are what distinguishes the one from the other.

The differential association theory focuses upon the gross facts of crime; it is not concerned as such with individual criminality. It is clear that in urban areas one is more likely than in rural areas to find social groups engaged in criminal behavior. As population density increases, so too does the propensity for criminality resulting from maximized opportunities for differential association with deviant social groups (Sutherland and Cressey, 1966: 95-96). This appears to be true of urban areas even in countries whose political systems differ radically.

Political leaders in the United States, while not specifically embracing the concept of differential association and its link with urbanization, have been influenced significantly by it, particularly in their perception of a relationship between urbanization and criminality. For example, a number of official commission reports have stressed the probability of a connection between the increase in crime and urban growth. In fact, one of these reports, that of the President's Crime Commission, was the principal input source for the first significant legislation pertaining to problems of urban crime.[21] A similar perception exists in the United Kingdom; the British rather consistently define the causes of crime in terms roughly corresponding to those of the differential association theory (British Information Services, 1960: 67-75).

A kind of Sutherland definition is also generally accepted in the Soviet Union. Survivals of bourgeois (i.e., negative antisocial) socialization and attitude formation among a small portion of the population are what cause crime (Karpets, 1966). There has been debate over both what constitute "survivals" and how they should be ranked in importance, but most Soviet specialists seem to agree that increased urbanization has resulted in shortcomings in contemporary Soviet society which, when combined with surviving negative factors, result in crime (Shlyapochnikov, 1964; Ostroumov and Chugunov, 1965; Pankratov, 1967).[22]

Urban crime, whether one is discussing the Soviet Union, the United Kingdom, or the United States, has a common facet today. Each national polity and its leadership have found it increasingly difficult to ignore hooliganism, burglary, assault, and theft. Even police problems associated with alcoholism and dangerous drug usage have cross-national similarities. "Law and order" has become (perhaps for different reasons in each country) an important political issue, a recurring theme in national political rhetoric, in the news media, in official reports of prestige groups, and among various interest groups. Urban crime has become truly a national concern in each of these countries.

The law enforcement policy of each country has begun to promote national involvement in matters previously or recently left to local jurisdiction. Each country's leaders have responded in some degree to demands for national restructuring and financing of law enforcement activities. Policy outputs in all three nations have been essentially the same. Specifically, the governments have sought to strengthen the national role in controlling local police affairs, have stressed the need for areawide planning and coordination (if not consolidation) of local police agencies to reduce fragmentation, have sought technological innovation and change, and have called for increased "professionalization" of police officers through improved recruitment, selection, and training standards, emphasizing the need for higher education. Nationality and minority group criticism of abusive police tactics has so far been dealt with only through superficial changes in the traditional police socialization processes.

Although the three countries evidence similar problems and responses, there are two important differences between the Soviet and Western crime profiles. The USSR today has virtually none of the organized interurban crime and little of the drug traffic that currently plague the two Western countries and troubled the Soviet Union as well in the early 1960s. Why this variation in profile?

First, a rigorous court-directed prosecution with poorly developed civil rights traditions characterizes the Soviet system of law enforcement and adjudication and leads, therefore, to less judicial restraint in the USSR than in the United States or Great Britain. Second, the Soviet Union has long practiced several forms of urban population control, closely restricting, among other things, the simple movement of people between urban areas. The barrier to any criminal's free movement that results from this control process is nonexistent in either the United States or Britain. Finally, the militsiya was recentralized in 1966 and given unlimited discretionary powers to reduce crime. No police agency in either Western state can begin to claim such freedom of action.

The Soviet Union has given its law enforcement agency an impressive array of "police state" tools for dealing with crime which have proved useful in curbing organized interurban crime and retarding illegal drug traffic. But, as Juviler (1969) and others have shown, these tools have been minimally effective in eliminating street crime. What, then, is the implication of Soviet experience for British and United States law enforcement?

The centralized police activity toward which each of the two Western nations is moving does seem to have played a significant role in the Soviet's successful eradication of organized interurban crime and dangerous drug traffic. Some sentiment appears to exist, especially in the United States, for providing police with the "police state" powers which the USSR has given its recentralized militsiya. The findings of this study suggest, however, that the kinds of crime a police state is able to handle are not those which create the great suburban and middle-class anxiety in the West. Street crime continues to exist in both the Soviet Union and the two Western states. Thus appears the paradox of a subpublic willing to alter fundamentally the existing political systems in the United States and Great Britain for a solution that is imperfect at best.

The solution to the "street crime"problem appears to lie not in the direction of a police state, but in widespread acceptance of some form of the differential association theory. Political leaders in each nation have indicated that more emphasis will be placed on the environmental setting as the breeding ground of crime. This may have some impact on street crime, although only a marginal effect on organized crime. Each of the three countries must decide which facet of urban crime demands the most attention, for the methods of eradicating organized crime are not the same as those of eliminating street crime, and the philosophical bases of the two approaches seem contradictory.

NOTES

1. By law enforcement is meant the prevention of nonpolitical crime and the apprehension of those who commit such crimes. Associated with this would be any supportive activity (e.g., training) necessary to fulfill this objective.

2. Most law enforcement activities are in fact carried out by local governments; the states, for the most part, provide only traffic law enforcement.

3. The Soviet concept of federalism stresses centralization, and most Western observers argue that it is federal in name only. Soviet writers, on the other hand, have consistently overstated the degree of responsible power and authority vested at the republic level. The answer likely lies between these extremes, as the Soviet system has vacillated between tight centralization and a degree of republic administrative autonomy on a number of questions, especially between 1955 and 1965.

4. Police Act of 1964, Part 1, Sections 1-9; Part 2, Sections 28-42.

5. New York Times, January 23, 1970, page 22.

6. Ukaz of the USSR Supreme Court, August 26, 1966, Byulleten Verkhovnogo Suda, Number 5, 1966, page 13. Also see the edicts of July 26, 1966, forming a Union Republic Ministry for the Protection of Public Order and three others, Vedemosti Verkhovnogo Soveta, Number 30, 1966, items 594-597.

7. London Times, May 10, 1963.

8. London Times, February 21, 1968, page 4.

9. Pravda, January 14, 1960.

10. Izvestia, February 23, 1969.

11. New York Times, November 10, 1968, page 75.

12. It is interesting to observe, however, that in both the U.S. and Britain, national opinion studies showed that more than seventy percent of the total population in both countries viewed the police as doing a good or better job in enforcing laws (President's Commission on Law Enforcement, 1967b: 145-146).

13. Public Law 90-351 provides for extensive financial support of in-service training programs and junior college, college, and graduate-level studies in fields related to criminal justice.

14. Public Law 90-351, Title I, Part D, Section 404(a).

15. Pravda, July 17, 1969.

16. Izvestia, August 16, 1969.

17. This material is based on information gathered by one of the authors during a period spent as an exchange scholar in the Soviet Union (spring 1966) and during a recent trip (winter 1969). Also see Zorinyan (1968).

18. Pravda, July 13, 1969.

19. For a summary of United States crime statistics see the FBI serial publication, *Uniform Crime Reports,* issued annually; for the United Kingdom, see the *Command Papers, Criminal Statistics, England and Wales.* Urban crime in Britain, while increasing somewhat more slowly than in the United States during the past few years, follows essentially the same profile—organized crime included (London Times, August 2, 1968, page 3).

The Soviet Union so closely guards crime statistics that these data are unavailable even to Soviet criminologists. Ostroumov (1968) cites this as a major obstacle to determining the nature and extent of crime in the USSR. Western experts are able to estimate, however, that the classes of urban crime rapidly increasing in their countries exhibit the same growth patterns in the USSR. These include all classes of juvenile crime (which has probably doubled in the 1960s), narcotics peddling, bribes, embezzlement, theft and burglary, hooliganism (especially while under the influence of alcohol), and even attacks on regular police (see Juviler, 1969 for a detailed review). During the period between 1966 and 1969 the Soviet press reported numerous attacks, many of them fatal, on individual militiamen acting in the line of duty (Izvesta, June 18, 1967; February 22, 1969; March 1, 1969; Pravda, April 13,

1969). A parallel can be seen in the United States where, for example, there were 33,604 assaults on police officers (FBI, Uniform Crime Reports, 1968: 152).

20. Radzinowicz (1966) discusses this subject at length and suggests that perhaps there is no single total theory. Rather, he postulates the presence of a number of theories, each of which has some empirical validity.

21. Public Law 90-351 is commonly known as the Omnibus Crime Control and Safe Streets Act of 1968. The Law Enforcement Act of 1965 (Public Law 89-197) was the forerunner of the 1968 act, but it was designed for "pilot" programs, not comprehensive ones.

22. A small but influential group of jurists and law enforcement officers in the Soviet Union seemed convinced that crime is caused by lack of individual moral fiber and encouraged by soft law enforcement and adjudiction, This belief, though not a total rejection of the environmental theory, marks a significant departure from accepted Marxist concepts (Smirnov, 1966; Tinkhunov, 1966; Juviler, 1969). The chromosomal theory recently propounded in the West has also been noted by the Soviets (Ledashchev, 1968).

REFERENCES

British Information Services (1960) Government and Administration of the United Kingdom. Harrow: H. M. Stationery Office.

CONQUEST, R. (1968) The Soviet Police System. New York: Frederick A. Praeger.

DYACHKOV, P. (1969) "Vsegda v stroyu, vsegda na strazhe." Pravda (April 6).

Executive Office of the President, Bureau of the Budget (1970a) The Budget in Brief, Fiscal Year 1971. Washington, D.C.: Government Printing Office.

——— (1970b) Special Analysis: Budget of the United States, Fiscal Year 1971. Washington, D.C.: Government Printing Office.

GOLDSTEIN, H. (1967) "Administrative problems in controlling the exercise of police authority." J. of Criminal Law, Criminology & Police Sci. 58: 160-172.

GUKOVSKAYA, N. and E. YAKOVLEV (1968) "Izuchenie prichin prestupnosti nesovershenstvoletnikh." Sotsialisticheskaya Zakonnost no. 12: 20-23.

HEWITT, W. E. (1965) British Police Administration. Springfield, Ill.: Charles C Thomas.

JUVILER, P. (1969) "The Soviet campaign for law and order." Presented at the Midwest Slavic Conference.

KARPETS, I. I. (1966) "O prirode i prichinakh prestupnosti v SSSR." Sovetskoe Gosudarstvo i Pravo no. 4: 82-91.

KOCHMAREV, N. (1968) "Krutitsya koleso." Pravda (March 14).

KORESTKIY, A. (1968) "Chtoby znali rebyata zakony." Pravda (September 16).

KOZLOV, Y. M. [ed.] (1968) Administrativnoe Pravo. Moskva: Yuridicheskaya Literatura.

KRYLOV, S. (1969) "Militsiya i vy." Izvestia (February 21).

KUUSINEN, O. V. (1960) Osnovy Marxizma Leninizma. Moskva: Izdatelstvo Politicheskoy Literatura.

LEDASHCHEV, V. (1968) "Protiv biologizatsii prichin prestupnosti." Sovetskaya Yustitsya no. 1: 13-14.

LEVY, B. (1968) "Cops in the ghetto: a problem of the police system." Amer. Behavioral Scientist 2: 31-34.

LUKYANOV, Y. (1967) "Nastupaet vecher. . . ." Izvestia (May 17).

LYASHENKO, V. (1968) "Klin Klinom?" Komsomolskaya Pravda (February 20).

MALYAROV, M. P. (1967) "Za dalneyshee ukreplenie zakonnosti v borbe c khuliganistom." Sovetskoe Gosudarstvo i Pravo no. 9: 50-58.

MEDYNSKIY, G. (1969) "I militsiya i my." Izvestia (May 30).

NICHOLSON, M. (1967) The System: The Misgovernment of Modern Britain. London: Hodder & Stoughten.

NIEDERHOFFER, A. (1969) Behind the Shield: The Police in Urban Society. New York: Doubleday Anchor.

NORRGARD, D. L. (1969) Regional Law Enforcement: A Study of Intergovernmental Cooperation and Coordination. Chicago: Public Administration Service.

OSTROUMOV, S. S. (1967) "Statisticheskie metody v kriminologii." Sovetskoe Gosudarstvo i Pravo no 7: 68-75.

— — and V. E. CHUGUNOV (1965) "Izuchenie lichnosti prestupniki po materialam kriminologicheskikh issledovaniy." Sovetskoe Gosudarstvo i Pravo no. 9: 93-102.

PANKRATOV, V. V. (1967) "Problema prichinnosti i printsip vzaimodeystviya v kriminologii." Sovetskoe Gosudarstvo i Pravo no. 6: 122-126.

Postanovlenie (1968) Summary: "v tsentralnom komitete KPSS i Sovet Ministrov SSSR." Pravda and Izvestia (November 29).

— — (1966) "Ob obrazovanii soyuzno-respublicanskogo ministerstva okhrany obshchestvennogo poryadka SSSR." Pravda (July 28).

President's Commission on Law Enforcement and Administration of Justice (1967a) The Challenge of Crime in a Free Society. Washington, D.C.: Government Printing Office.

— — (1967b) Task Force Report: The Police. Washington, D.C.: Government Printing Office.

RADZINOWICZ, L. (1966) Ideology and Crime. New York: Columbia University.

RAINE, W. J. (1966) Los Angeles Riot Study: The Perception of Police Brutality. Los Angeles: Institute of Government and Public Affairs, University of California.

RAYMOND, E. (1968) The Soviet State. New York: Macmillan.

Royal Commission on Police (1962) Final Report. London: H. M. Stationery Office.

SHCHELOKOV, N. A. (1968) "Shchit poryadka." Pravda (November 10).

— — (1967) "Pomogat cheloveky stat luchshe." Izvestia (July 31).

SHLYAPOCHNIKOV, A. S. (1964) "O klassifikatsii obstoyatelstv sposobsvuyushchikh soversheniyu prestupleniy." Sovetskoe Gosudarstvo i Pravo no. 10: 91-100.

SHTANKO, N. (1968) "Solo na buldozere." Izvestia (October 9).

SMIRNOV, L. (1966) "XXIII sezd KPSS i zadachi sudebnykh organov v borbe s prestupnostyu." Sovetskaya Yustitsya no. 14: 1-4.

SUTHERLAND, E. H. and D. R. CRESSEY (1966) Principles of Criminology. Philadelphia: J. B. Lippincott.

TIKHUNOV, V. (1966) "Snizheskhozhdeniya khuliganam ne budet." Izvestia (April 21).

U.S. Department of Justice, Law Enforcement Assistance Administration (1968) Guide for State Planning Agency Grants. Washington, D.C.: Government Printing Office.

U.S. Congress, House Committee on Judiciary (1967) Anti-Crime Program: Hearings on H. R. 5307, 90th Congress, 1st Session.

VATSIK, T. (1968) "Vernye pomoshchniki militsii." Izvestia (December 4).

WALSH, A. H. (1969) The Urban Challenge to Government: An International Comparison of Thirteen Cities. New York: Frederick A. Praeger.

WOLFGANG, M. E. (1967) "International criminal statistics: a proposal." J. of Criminal Law, Criminology & Police Sci. 58: 65-69.

YEGORICHEV, N. (1965) "Vospitanie molodezhi–delo partiynoe." Kommunist no. 3: 15-28.

ZORINYAN, E. (1968) "Ne proto ulichnoe proistesvie." Komsomolskaya Pravda (February 27).

PART TWO

Public Perceptions of Police Problems

Public Perceptions of Police Problems

In a democratic society, the ability of a government agency to resolve major social problems may be influenced both by the skill and efficiency of its personnel and by public evaluations concerning the actions of the agency. Political institutions are not only dependent upon public support for the appropriation of funds, but they may also require a broad sense of public confidence to sustain their operations. Perhaps in no area of government activity is this relationship more critical than in the conduct of law enforcement duties. Without the assistance of the community in reporting and providing information concerning crime, police departments could be immobilized. Moreover, in varied circumstances that range from the granting of increased legal powers to the control of major social disorders, public sentiments may have a crucial impact upon the performance of police functions. Police officers must achieve a high level of respect to secure popular cooperation and compliance with their authority. Public attitudes toward police behavior, therefore, can provide an important means of determining the effectiveness of law enforcement practices.

Perhaps one of the most essential tests of public trust in the police is reflected by attitudes concerning the legitimacy of law enforcement activities. The capacity of police departments to fulfill their responsibilities might be measured by the extent to which citizens are willing to rely upon policemen rather than upon forms of self-defense to protect their lives and property. Evidence compiled from a national survey of public opinion, however, suggests that large segments of the American people lack this fundamental confidence in the police. As Joe R. Feagin discovers, nearly two-thirds of black citizens and more than one-half of the white public are not prepared to depend upon policemen for protection from crime and violence. Furthermore, this lack of faith among whites appears to be associated with the development of mounting racial fears. The findings, therefore, seem to raise some vexing questions about whether or not the country actually satisfies the classic Weberian definition of a state as a community that maintains a monopoly over the legitimate use of physical force. In addition, they may indicate an emerging danger of armed attempts, especially among white sectors of the population, to usurp police prerogatives.

In addition to a general sense of public confidence, police officers also must receive extensive community support to achieve their goals. Increasingly, however, the issue of police conduct is becoming a major topic of social and political controversy. Police departments no longer can rely upon the tacit consent of the citizenry in establishing the limits of their authority; they must, like any government agency, subject their actions to public scrutiny and judgment. In an analysis of a pioneering survey of criminal victimization, Richard L. Block examines the attitudes of urban residents on measures extending the protection of civil liberties, such as civilian review boards and legal representation during police interrogation, and on plans for increasing police powers to stop and question suspects. Public sentiments regarding those issues often may appear to be complicated and confusing. Hence, law enforcement agencies that seek approval for expanding their authority may encounter divergent and often conflicting public demands. Yet, the finding that the fear of crime is directly related to support for civil liberties proposals among lower-class white as well as among black citizens seems to contain some important implications for police policies. The widely adopted and supposedly professional doctrine of "aggressive preventive patrolling," or stopping to question many suspects in areas with high crime rates, may provoke numerous abrasive encounters between policemen and local residents, while diverting police manpower from many other crimes that plague lower-class neighborhoods.

Growing public criticism of police practices, especially in urban ghettos, is not only a source of intense controversy, but it may also be an impetus for the occurrence of violent conflict. In the final article in this section, a survey conducted in the Twelfth Street area of Detroit shortly after the 1967 riots is employed to explore ghetto appraisals of police behavior before, during, and after violence. Although the results of the study revealed extensive local animosity toward law enforcement officers, they also seem to suggest that ghetto residents may be prepared to support strong measures for controlling a serious riot, provided that police impose strict restraints on the use of force and that their conduct is not perceived as deteriorating during the violence. As the initial article in the following section demonstrates, however, the attitudes of black citizens stand in marked contrast to the views of Detroit policemen concerning the riots. The development of extensive public respect for police authority in urban ghettos might not be an insurmountable problem, but it may be one of the most crucial and difficult challenges confronting law enforcement agencies.

Home-Defense and the Police

Black and White Perspectives

JOE R. FEAGIN
University of California at Riverside

Analysts of law enforcement systems have stressed that the police constitute a social control mechanism essential to the maintenance of order and legality in a modern society. Essential to the effectiveness of the police in this regard is the attitude of the private citizen. Emphasizing that the police provide one of the most basic social services, Reiss and Bordua (1967: 28) have suggested that citizen dependence on the police for protection against crime and violence, not on self-help, is critical to maintaining order and legality in a society: "One way the police serve the cause of legality, therefore, is to assure by their presence and performance that a set of rules prevails which make it unnecessary for the citizen to be continually prepared to defend himself or his property." Moreover, the extent to which people feel secure in their own homes and are willing to leave the protection of home and family to the government-established police forces may well be one important indicator of the extent to which a given human community can be viewed as an integrated "state."

STATE VERSUS PRIVATE PROTECTION

Max Weber (1958: 78) once defined a "state" as a "human community that (successfully) claims the *monopoly of the legitimate use of physical force* within a given territory." One interpretation of this view is that only the government-established police forces in a "state" exercise physical force legitimately; all other use by private organizations and individuals is illegitimate. Arthur Waskow (1966: 2-3) has averred that the United States has never been a full-fleged state by this definition, for this government has long tolerated the use of physical force by private individuals and organizations and has a lengthy ("frontier") tradition of quasi-legitimate private use of violence—lynching, riots, private business armies, violent labor disputes, and the like. However, writing in 1964-1965, Waskow apparently viewed American society as moving in the direction of a "state," increasingly concentrating the use of physical force in the hands of governmental agencies.

Yet the violent events of the mid- and late-1960s bring this argument into serious question, the current American situation being a problematical one in which the use of physical force by various private organizations and individuals—assassinations, ghetto revolts, raids by protective organizations, violent crimes, and similar occurrences—actually appears to be increasing. In recent years even groups of policemen have on occasion behaved as though they were vigilante organizations pursuing their own private ends. Moreover, in many of these cases the private use of force has been regarded as legitimate by certain segments of the American population.

These violent events on the local and national scene have had many effects on the operation of the police as a basic social control mechanism in this society. Doubtless one important effect has been on citizen attitudes toward the police. In the late 1950s and the early 1960s, on the basis of Waskow's analysis of trends, one would probably have expected citizen attitudes to reflect extensive reliance on the police for protection against crime and violence. Yet recent violent events might lead one to a contrary expectation for the late-1960s and the 1970s: substantial, perhaps majority, support for self-help measures among adult Americans.

ACQUISITION OF DATA

The purpose of this exploratory paper is to analyze this latter expectation in the light of some attitudinal data on adult Americans, available for both a white and a black sample, and to examine certain important demographic and attitudinal correlates of the protective orientations found.

THE SAMPLES

Data relevant to these issues were made available to the author for reanalysis by the Opinion Research Corporation (New Jersey). The data had originally been collected in May and June of 1968 for a CBS television program.[1] Two nationwide samples of respondents were interviewed, one black and one white. Both were "modified probability" samples, selected as representative of the adult populations of black and white Americans, and were by intention similar in size (551 whites and 468 blacks).[2] The questions asked dealt almost exclusively with race relations issues.

HOME-DEFENSE

Coming immediately after a series of questions about ghetto riots, crime, and civil rights demonstrations (including police responses to them), a key reality-oriented question in the ORC survey was the following: "Do you think that people like yourself have to be prepared to defend their homes against crime and violence, or can the police take care of that?" The responses to this question are tabulated, for black and white samples separately, in Table 1.[3] A majority of both samples said that people like themselves had to be prepared to defend their own homes against crime and violence, that such protection could not be left to the police. These data confirmed the general expectation that a substantial number of Americans living in the late 1960s would be oriented toward self-help measures. Only a minority of both groups, one in four among the blacks and four in ten among the whites, unequivocally responded that protection of their homes could be left in the hands of the police. The data in Table 1 also document a significant difference between the black and white samples; nearly two-thirds of the black respondents were "home-defense oriented," compared to just over half of the whites.[4]

TABLE 1

BLACK AND WHITE PERSPECTIVES ON HOME-DEFENSE
(ORC survey, 1968)

QUESTION: "Do you think that people like yourself have to be pre-pared to defend their homes against crime and violence, or can the police take care of that?"

	Defend Homes %	Leave to Police %	No Opinion/ Other[a] %	Total Percentage %	(Total n)
Black sample	65	24	11	100	(468)
White sample	52	41	7	100	(551)

$$x^2 = 36.303, p < .0001 \ (3 \ df)$$

a. About two-thirds of these answers were of the don't know/no opinion type.

SOCIAL AND ECONOMIC CORRELATES

Who were the Americans who felt they could not leave home protection up to the police? Table 2 presents cross-tabulations of responses to the home-defense item by certain key demographic variables, for both the black and white samples. Within the white sample there was no significant relationship relationship between sex and home-defense orientation, while in the black sample, male respondents were significantly more likely to be home-defense oriented than female respondents (seventy-three percent versus sixty percent).

Examination of the age variable revealed that the under-thirty black respondents were the most likely of all age groups, black or white, to feel that people like themselves had to be prepared to defend their homes; the proportion of those who were home-defense oriented decreased significantly with age. For the whites there was not much difference between the three age groups, although the percentage home-defense oriented also decreased somewhat with age. Were one to guess at the longitudinal trend on the basis of these age data, he might expect an increasingly large proportion of the population, black and white, to support self-help measures.

There was a significant variation by region in home-defense orientation for both the black and the white respondents, although the patterns were different. Among the blacks, those living in the northeastern and north central regions were the most likely to be home-defense oriented; the least likely to be home-defense oriented were the black southerners and the westerners. Yet among the whites those *most* likely to be home-defense oriented were the southerners. A majority of the whites in both the Northeast and the West were willing to leave the protection of their homes to the police, while a majority of the whites in the north central states were oriented to self-help measures. Moreover, comparing the two samples, one sees that only in the case of the southern respondents was the proportion of whites oriented to home-defense measures greater than that for Negroes.

As one moves up the ladder of urban size, the proportion of whites home-defense oriented goes down systematically. As one might expect, two-thirds of the whites in rural areas and small towns responded in terms of self-help measures, compared to about half of the whites in medium-sized cities and one-third of the whites in cities over one million in population. Within the black sample the pattern was quite different. Although majorities of the blacks in each urban category were home-defense oriented, those most likely to be home-defense oriented were the blacks living in the larger cities, with those living in rural areas and small

TABLE 2

HOME-DEFENSE ORIENTATION BY KEY DEMOGRAPHIC VARIABLES (ORC survey, 1968)

	Black Sample					White Sample				
	Defend Homes %	Leave to Police %	No Opinion/ Other %	Total Percentage	(n)	Defend Homes %	Leave to Police %	No Opinion/ Other %	Total Percentage	(n)
Sex[a]										
Male	73	18	9	100	(169)	51	43	6	100	(250)
Female	60	28	13	101	(299)	53	40	8	101	(301)
	$X^2 = 9.085$, p $<$ .02					$X^2 = 1.086$, n.s.[b]				
Age[a]										
18-29	73	20	7	100	(104)	54	38	9	101	(129)
30-49	70	20	11	101	(190)	54	41	4	99	(206)
50 +	53	33	14	100	(163)	48	43	9	100	(212)
	$X^2 = 14.880$, p $<$ .006					$X^2 = 4.621$, n.s.[b]				
Region[a]										
Northeast	63	24	13	100	(71)	38	56	5	99	(149)
North-central	74	20	6	100	(155)	54	39	8	101	(143)
South	59	27	15	101	(218)	75	21	5	101	(141)
West	58	29	13	100	(24)	40	50	10	100	(118)
	$X^2 = 11.921$, n.s.[b]					$X^2 = 51.205$, p $<$ .0001				
Urban[a]										
Under 2500 (rural)	64	15	21	100	(75)	67	27	6	100	(192)
2500-100,000	51	42	8	101	(65)	52	41	8	101	(106)
100,000-1 million	65	23	12	100	(128)	44	49	7	100	(167)
Over 1 million	69	23	9	101	(200)	33	61	7	101	(86)
	$X^2 = 22.535$, p $<$ .001					$X^2 = 36.804$, p $<$ .0001				

a. Percentages may not add to one hundred percent because of rounding-off procedures. Numerical totals vary a bit from table to table because respondents with "no answer/no data" on a given demographic variable have been deleted.

b. In this and subsequent tables the .05 probability level is used as the criterion of significance.

towns not far behind. In the under-one hundred thousand population categories the proportions of blacks and whites home-defense oriented were quite similar, while dramatic differentials appeared in the more metropolitan categories.

Discussions of the "frontier tradition" have sometimes suggested that the South and rural America remain the most important repositories of certain elements of that tradition (compare Cash, 1941). To the extent that the home-defense responses reflect the vestiges of the frontier spirit, the ORC data lend some support to this general argument, at least in the case of whites. Three-quarters of the southerners in the white sample—the largest proportion of any regional group—did not feel people like themselves could rely solely on the police to protect their homes. Moreover, those whites living in rural or small town areas were more likely to be home-defense oriented than other whites. However, among the blacks, the southerners were less likely than those in the North to be home-defense oriented. The blacks most likely to be home-defense oriented were to be found in the larger urban areas and in the north central region.

The data in Table 2 enable one to compare the percentages of blacks and whites who were home-defense oriented within each demographic subgroup. Out of thirteen possible comparisons, the proportion of whites home-defense oriented substantially exceeded that for the blacks in only one case—the southern respondents. In two other cases, the less-urban categories, the proportions for whites exceeded those for blacks, but only by a few percentage points.

But what about socioeconomic status? Table 3 presents the home-defense item cross-tabulated by two measures of socioeconomic status: education of respondent and occupation of chief wage earner in the household. For the white sample the proportion home-defense oriented generally goes down as one moves up the occupational and educational ladders. Sixty-five percent of the whites with a grade school education, and about six in ten of the whites in families headed by blue-collar wage earners, responded in home-defense terms, compared to about forty percent of the whites with a college education and of the whites in families headed by persons holding managerial or professional jobs. The one irregularity in the otherwise perfect stair-step patterns is to be found in the skilled blue-collar category. White respondents in skilled blue-collar families were a bit more likely to be home-defense oriented than those in lower-status, blue-collar families. The pattern for the black respondents was similar in the case of occupation, the percentage home-defense oriented being higher for blacks in families with an unskilled and semiskilled, blue-collar wage earner than for those with a chief wage earner

TABLE 3
HOME-DEFENSE ORIENTATION BY SOCIOECONOMIC VARIABLES (ORC survey, 1968)

	Black Sample					White Sample				
	Defend Homes %	Leave to Police %	No Opinion/ Other %	Total Percentage	(n)	Defend Homes %	Leave to Police %	No Opinion/ Other %	Total Percentage	(n)
Education										
8th grade or less	56	29	15	100	(167)	65	27	9	101	(102)
9-11	72	20	8	100	(136)	61	36	4	101	(104)
12	72	21	7	100	(87)	53	43	4	100	(162)
Some college or more	58	28	15	101	(69)	39	52	9	100	(174)
	$x^2 = 13.418$, p $<$ .04					$x^2 = 28.097$, p $<$ .0002				
Occupation[a] (chief wage earner)										
Unskilled, semi-skilled blue-collar	70	19	11	100	(247)	58	38	5	101	(109)
Skilled blue-collar	62	14	24	100	(29)	65	33	2	100	(103)
Clerical, sales	62	28	10	100	(29)	46	48	6	100	(112)
Managerial, professional[b]	55	36	10	101	(31)	41	51	8	100	(107)
	$x^2 = 10.208$, n.s.[c]					$x^2 = 16.544$, p $<$ .02				

a. Small n's are a result of the deletion of students, the unemployed, the retired, nonworking female heads of households, and "no answer" respondents from the tables.

b. Includes small business owners.

c. There were several small cells in this table.

in a managerial or professional position. For the black respondents, however, the association between education and home-defense orientation was curvilinear, with just over half of the blacks with grade school or college educations being home-defense oriented, compared to nearly three-quarters of those in the high school brackets. One important generalization was substantiated by these data: Among blacks and whites the highest-status respondents were the least likely to be home-defense oriented.

Moreover, in six of the eight educational and occupational categories the proportion of blacks home-defense oriented exceeded the comparable proportion of whites. The two exceptions were to be found in the grade-school and the skilled blue-collar categories. In both cases the proportions of whites home-defense oriented were somewhat higher than those for the blacks. Yet even in these two cases a majority of the black respondents took a position in favor of self-help measures.

GUN OWNERSHIP

To what extent did these home-defense attitudes reflect actual behavior? In what ways were people preparing to defend their homes? To what extent were they arming themselves with firearms? Although it is not possible to give comprehensive answers to these questions, given the limited character of the ORC data, partial answers (and a partial validation of the responses to the home-defense item) can be suggested on the basis of the gun ownership questions which were asked in the ORC survey.

The expectation that home-defense-oriented respondents would be more likely to be armed than those who were police oriented was confirmed by the data. No less than six in ten among the home-defense-oriented whites admitted that someone in the household owned a gun, compared to only thirty-five percent of those who felt that the police could take care of protecting their homes against crime and violence. In contrast, black respondents in both subsamples were less likely to report a gun in the house than either of the two white subgroups. One-third of the home-defense-oriented blacks had a gun in the household, compared to twenty-seven percent of those who were police oriented. The difference between the two black subgroups was not as striking as that for the whites, but it too was in the expected direction. These data jibe with the findings of a recent survey of gun owners, a survey which found that a majority of those with guns possess them, at least in part, for protective reasons.[5] Moreover, the actual differences between the two subgroups within the black and the white samples may be greater than those indicated in Table 4, since it may be that the figures on gun ownership, particularly for the home-defense-oriented respondents, are underestimates.

TABLE 4
GUN OWNERSHIP AND HOME-DEFENSE ORIENTATION
(ORC survey, 1968)

	Black Sample		White Sample	
	Defend Homes (n=302) %	Leave to Police (n=113) %	Defend Homes (n=286) %	Leave to Police (n=227) %
Gun in Household[a]				
Yes	33	27	60	35
No	56	66	34	58
No answer	11	8	6	7
Total	100	101	100	100
	x^2 = 2.890, n.s.		x^2 = 33.495, p $<$ .0001	

a. These response categories are actually composites of answers to two questions, one asking if the respondent owned a gun and a second asking if anyone in the household owned one. (Yes = yes, someone in the household owns a gun.)

In addition, in both samples those who were home-defense oriented were somewhat more likely than those who were police oriented to report knowing someone who had bought a gun within the last two years for protective purposes. Fifteen percent of the home-defense-oriented whites knew of someone who bought a gun for protection, compared to nine percent of the police-oriented respondents. The corresponding percentages for the black subsamples reflected a similar differential but were smaller: eight percent and three percent.

These survey data point to suggestive answers to the questions raised at the beginning of this section. Home-defense-oriented respondents, black and white, were more likely than the police-oriented respondents not only to travel in acquaintance circles some members of which have purchased guns for defensive purposes but also to have a gun in their own households. Extrapolating on the basis of these random samples, one can estimate that many white and black Americans have prepared to defend their own homes by arming themselves. However, these data also indicate that whites were more likely to be armed than blacks, whether they were home-defense or police oriented. Given these data, and the fact that white Americans constitute the bulk of the U.S. population, it would seem that a major potential threat to order and legality comes from white America.

One additional point is in order. Many respondents who were home-defense oriented, particularly the blacks, either would not admit to gun ownership or were thinking in terms of other weapons and/or preparatory procedures (such as knives, bats, karate, neighborhood protective organizations, and the like) which would enable them to defend their homes. And it may be that some respondents were talking in terms of what people like themselves ought to do, not so much in terms of what they had done up to that point in time.

THE POLICE

Why were majorities of the black and white samples home-defense oriented? One might suggest, following Waskow (1966) and other analysts of American society, that such home-defense orientations are vestiges of the frontier tradition surviving in a modern industrialized society, that is, an unwillingness to leave protection of home and family is not a new phenomenon in this country. Given an increasingly violent societal situation, together with a critical view of police protection, this traditional home-defense orientation might well be elicited or reinforced in the current situation. An added reason for this home-defense orientation among black Americans might be fear of "police brutality" within ghetto areas.

Explicit in the majority response to the home-defense item seemed to be fear of crime and violence, together with a critical view of the general protective capabilities of the police with regard to home and family. Although no additional questions in the ORC survey directly probed the reasons for the responses to this item, responses to three questions asking for assessments of police actions in regard to ghetto rioters and Negroes (presumably criminals) indicated that a critical view of specific police actions was associated with home-defense views, at least among the whites. Table 5 presents the distributions of responses to the questions for the black and white samples separately. Those whites who were home-defense oriented were significantly more likely than those who were not to criticize the police for being too soft in their general treatment of Negroes (thirty-eight percent versus sixteen percent), to think that the police should be tougher in handling riots (eighty-three percent versus sixty percent), and to believe that, after a warning, shooting one or two rioters as examples would be a good idea (forty-four percent versus twenty-six percent). Clearly, home-defense-oriented whites were more likely than police-oriented whites to be critical of police actions as not being tough enough with regard to Negro riots and crime. In contrast to the majority of blacks who complained about "police brutality," large proportions of white respondents—particularly those oriented to self-help measures—were disturbed about "police softness."

Looking at the data for the black sample, one finds a slightly larger percentage of "toughness" replies for the home-defense group than for the

TABLE 5

HOME-DEFENSE ORIENTATION AND ATTITUDES
TOWARD POLICE ACTIONS
(ORC survey, 1968)

	Black Sample[a]		White Sample[a]	
	Defend Homes (n=302) %	Leave to Police (n=113) %	Defend Homes (n=286) %	Leave to Police (n=227) %
Question No. 1[b]				
Too brutal	63	63	4	7
Too soft	3	3	38	16
Fair	24	26	51	69
No opinion	11	9	7	8
Total	101	101	100	100
	$x^2 = .3910$, n.s.		$x^2 = 30.487$, p $<$ .0001	
Question No. 2[c]				
Tougher	18	13	83	60
Easier	44	53	2	5
About right	23	20	11	23
No opinion	15	14	5	12
Total	100	100	101	100
	$x^2 = 2.966$, n.s.		$x^2 = 34.065$, p $<$ .0001	
Question No. 3[d]				
Good idea	7	4	44	26
Not good idea	89	89	50	68
No opinion	4	6	6	6
Total	100	99	100	100
	$x^2 = 1.726$, n.s.		$x^2 = 19.104$, p $<$ .0001	

a. "No opinion" responses to the home-defense question have been deleted from these tables.

b. "In general, what do you think of the treatment of Negroes by the police? Have the police been too brutal, or too soft, or have they generally been fair?"

c. "In handling riots, do you think the police should be tougher than they have been, or should they go easier than they have been, or what?"

d. "Is this a good idea or not a good idea: for police to warn the rioters and then shoot one or two as an example to the rest?"

police-oriented group in regard to two of the three questions (those dealing with riots), although the percentages for both subgroups are relatively small, and the nonsignificant chi-square statistics indicate that the small group differences are probably due to chance. However, it should be noted that these data did *not* support the expectation that home-defense-oriented blacks would be more critical of police practices (as too tough) than police-oriented blacks. Majorities, or near-majorities, of both subsamples were equally critical of police actions as too brutal or too tough.

Perhaps the most striking aspect of these data was the dramatic contrast between black and white perspectives on the police. A substantial majority of both black subsamples saw the police as too *brutal* in their general treatment of Negroes; nine out of ten spurned the riot remedy of shooting rioters as examples; and about half of both black subgroups said the police should go easier on black rioters. In striking contrast, the overwhelming majority of whites—in both subsamples, but particularly among the home-defense-oriented whites—felt the police were fair, or too *soft*, in their general treatment of Negroes and that police should be tougher on black rioters. And significant proportions of the whites subscribed to the extreme riot solution of shooting rioters as examples.

SOME ADDITIONAL RACIAL ISSUES

The police data just examined clearly have racial overtones. Several additional questions touching on racial fears also distinguished between the two white subsamples, but not between the black subgroups. A good example of this pattern can be seen in regard to the following critical item in a list of (possible) riot causes presented to both the black and white samples: "A way for black people to take over the cities." Respondents were asked to evaluate this as having "a lot," "something," or "nothing" to do with causing the recent ghetto riots. The distribution of responses to this item can be seen in Table 6. As can be seen, there is no significant relationship between the two variables for the black respondents. Those who were police oriented were no more likely than the others to see attempts at city take-over as having nothing to do with the riots. Yet among the whites, while a minority (thirty-six percent) of those who were police oriented saw attempts at city take-over as having "a lot" or "something" to do with the riots, a sizeable majority (sixty-one percent) of the home-defense whites felt that such an extreme goal lay behind the riots. White fears of ghetto riots as purposive were clearly related to feelings about home defense. And this was true in spite of the fact that many of the home-defense-oriented whites, particularly those in the smaller cities and towns, probably have not as yet been directly threatened by black uprisings.

A similar pattern appears when one examines questions on civil rights demonstrations. For example, the whites who were home-defense oriented

TABLE 6
HOME-DEFENSE ORIENTATION AND VIEWS OF RIOTS
(ORC survey, 1968)

"Black Takeover"[a]	Black Sample		White Sample	
	Defend Homes (n=302) %	Leave to Police (n=113) %	Defend Homes (n=286) %	Leave to Police (n=227) %
A lot, something	11	9	61	36
Nothing	77	76	32	55
No opinion	12	15	7	10
Total	100	100	100	101
	x^2 = .849, n.s. (3df)		x^2 = 41.701, p $<$ .0001 (3df)	

a. See text for wording of question.

were significantly more likely than police-oriented whites to regard peaceful demonstrations as an *illegitimate* way for Negroes and others to protest (seventy-four percent versus sixty percent), while the overwhelming majority of both black subgroups (seventy-two percent in each case) felt peaceful demonstrations were a *good* way for people to express their grievances.

In reply to a question which asked if "a high crime rate" was more true for Negroes than for whites (or vice versa), the home-defense-oriented whites were significantly more likely than the other whites to say that "a high crime rate" was more true of *Negroes* than of whites; in contrast, the black respondents who were home-defense oriented were significantly more likely than the police-oriented blacks to feel that "a high crime rate" was more true of *whites* than of Negroes. These data suggest that fear of crime on the part of the other racial group was yet another reason why many whites and blacks were unwilling to leave protection of home and family to the police.

The general pattern which emerges when one examines questions relevant to the issue of home defense and the police is that the whites who were home-defense oriented were more likely than police-oriented whites to see an attempted black take-over of cities lying behind riots, to see Negroes having a higher crime rate than whites, to take a negative view of civil rights demonstrations, and in general to hold negative attitudes in regard to Negroes.

For the black sample there was little difference between the two subsamples on these same indices; most blacks in both subsamples felt the riots were not attempts by blacks to take over the cities and that civil rights demonstrations were a legitimate means of protest. One significant difference did emerge, but the emphasis was rather different than that of the white respondents. Home-defense-oriented black respondents were more likely than police-oriented respondents to see "a high crime rate" as more true of whites than of Negroes.

SUMMARY AND DISCUSSION

In the late 1960s, extrapolating on the basis of these survey data, a majority of black and white Americans felt that people like themselves had to be prepared to defend their own homes against crime and violence, that such protection could not be left to the police. Do these majorities reflect a linear trend in the direction of growing support for self-help measures? An argument can certainly be made for such a trend based on impressionistic data, although a conclusive statement seems impossible given the unavailability of comparable data for the last few decades. Were one to speculate about the near future, on the basis of the age data alone, he might expect increasing support for private home-defense measures.

Analysts of police systems have argued that citizen dependence on the police, not on self-help, is critical to the maintenance of order and legality in a society. Yet police performance must be such that the rank-and-file citizen does not feel the need to be continually prepared to defend his home and himself. Reiss and Bordua (1967: 28) have argued that "we may, in fact, partly define the 'maintenance of law and order' as the maintenance of a set of social conditions such that over the society as a whole, the expectation of attack on person or property has a probability below the level at which the citizenry resorts to 'self-help'." This suggests that, when the people's fear of attack—whether reasonable or not—reaches a certain level, they will actually resort to self-help measures, and, when such is the case, stability and legality in a society are in jeopardy.

Although there are signs of growing citizen resort to private home-defense measures and protective organizations, there has not as yet been large-scale violence, or the wholesale breakdown of stability and legality, as a result of these measures. However, the self-help orientations and lack of confidence in the police reflected in the ORC survey suggest that there is a significant potential for an extensive breakdown of law and order. One prestigious federal commission on the police has argued (President's Commission on Law Enforcement, 1967: 144): "Hostility, or even lack of confidence of a significant portion of the public, has extremely serious implications for the police." And, one might add, for the society.

Why were so many black and white Americans supportive of self-help measures? We have previously suggested that such home-defense orientations have as their historical backdrop the American frontier tradition. Given a societal situation perceived as increasingly violent and threatening, this traditional home-defense orientation might well be elicited in the contemporary situation. Explicit in the majority response to the home-defense question itself seemed to be fear of attack, together with a lack of confidence in the ability of the police to protect home and family against crime and violence. Furthermore, examination of the relationships between home-defense orientations and attitudes toward police actions with regard to riots and crime indicated that—among the white respondents—those who were home-defense oriented were significantly more likely to be critical of police "softness" and more likely to recommend harsher measures to control riots than other whites. They were also more likely than other whites to be critical of civil rights demonstrations. This pattern of responses suggests that fear of attack or upheaval from these sources—riots, demonstrations, and the like—lay behind the home-defense orientations of many whites. At the very least, the two were closely related. Some data directly supporting this argument have been reported by Morris and Jeffries (1967: 7). Interviewing in white areas after the 1965 Watts riot, they found over half of their white respondents had feared for the safety of self or family during the riot, and, significantly, nearly one-third admitted that they had considered arming themselves. Morris and Jeffries note that in their data there was a "strong relationship between the consideration of the use of firearms and the amount of fear felt." Moreover, recent Harris polls (National Commission on Violence, 1969b: 226) have revealed that a sizeable segment of the white urban population is ready and willing to use their guns to shoot rioters in case of additional riots.

Also reflected in the responses of many whites, particularly the home-defense oriented, to questions about crime rates and riots as attempted city take-over seemed to be some aspects of traditional racist ideologies. Home-defense-oriented whites seemed more receptive to negative views of black America than were other whites. Nor is it likely that these were the only perspectives related to the home-defense views of the white respondents. The ORC survey was mainly limited to race relations issues and included no questions on recent student or anti-Vietnam demonstrations and disorders, or on specific types of violent crimes. Further research may well reveal that fear of attack or upheaval from these specific sources is also related to support for self-help measures.

However, with regard to riots and demonstrations the two subgroups within the black sample did not differ very much. Contrary to initial expectations, the home-defense-oriented black respondents were generally no more likely to be critical of police actions with regard to ghetto rioters in particular, and Negroes in general, than were the police-oriented respondents. Yet a majority, or near-majority of both subsamples viewed police practices as too brutal or too tough. And unlike the whites, majorities of both subsamples viewed civil rights demonstrations as legitimate. Responses to the one item that did distinguish between the two groups, that dealing with a "high crime rate," suggested that home-defense-oriented blacks might have been more fearful of white criminals than other blacks.

The lack of additional questions in the ORC survey dealing with the crime threat and ordinary police services *within* urban ghettos made it impossible to examine one possible explanation for the differential black views on home-defense measures. Previous surveys have revealed that a major worry of black urbanites has to do with ghetto crime and police services (Hahn and Feagin, 1970). On the basis of such data, one would expect the home-defense orientations of many black Americans to be closely linked to specific complaints about the amount and kind of ordinary police protection they receive both with regard to ghetto crime and, particularly in the South, with regard to attacks by white criminals.

Looking at the question of actual protective behavior, as contrasted with attitudes or perspectives, we presented data indicating that home-defense-oriented respondents were more likely than the others to have a gun in the household, most doubtless there for protective purposes. Other respondents may now be in the process of arming themselves. Moreover, various ORC, Gallup, and Harris Polls (compare National Commission on Violence, 1969a: 9) have shown that fifty to sixty percent of American households admit the possession of guns, and firearms statistics reflect a tremendous uptrend in the importation, production, and sale of guns in recent years. Particularly serious has been the growth in number of handguns, weapons mainly useful for protective purposes. An average of three million handguns was added to the civilian market in each decade between 1899 and 1948; no less than ten million handguns were added to that market in the decade ending in 1968 (National Commission on Violence, 1969a: 17). That such arming behavior has been related to recent societal upheavals is indicated by gun ownership data for cities, such as Detroit, which have seen riots or other violent outbursts, data indicating a doubling or tripling of guns owned within the narrow space of two or three years. Indeed, it is likely that the U.S. is now the best-armed major nation in the world, with twenty-five times as many handguns per

100,000 population as there are, for example, in Great Britain (National Commission on Violence, 1969a: 121).

Moreover, recent reports of the National Commission on Violence (1969a, 1969b) have noted the rapidly growing number of neighborhood protective organizations, both black and white; many of these organizations have armed themselves, or are in the process of doing so. The apparent motivation behind the arming varies greatly depending on the group, but such groups include certain black nationalist organizations, particularly those involved in policing the ghetto police, and neighborhood protective organizations in white residential areas. So far the significance of these groups for large-scale violence would seem to be more potential than actual; "to date, no extremist organization, white or black, has caused large scale violence" (National Commission on Violence, 1969a: 58). Yet incidents involving extremist groups seem to be increasing, doubtless contributing significantly both to the firearms buildup and the likelihood of violence in the name of self- and home-defense.

A CONCLUDING POLICY NOTE

While the implications of this situation are clear—a serious threat to order and legality in this society—the solutions to it are less so. The current emphasis on repressive measures, particularly on increased police force, to deal with protest and disorder, while it may well in the short run reduce the emphasis on self-help measures among many white Americans, is likely to alienate further America's protesting minorities. Given the fundamental social and economic causes lying behind much of the current upheaval and violence—causes now well documented by numerous distinguished presidential commissions—major structural reforms would seem to provide the only long-term solution ensuring the continued development of a democratic society:

> A democratic society cannot depend upon force as its recurrent answer to longstanding and legitimate grievances. This nation cannot have it both ways; either it will carry through a firm commitment to massive and widespread politic[al] and social reform, or it will develop into a society of garrison cities where order is enforced without due process of law and without the consent of the governed [National Commission on Violence, 1969b: 346].

NOTES

1. I am indebted to the Opinion Research Corporation (New Jersey) for making these data available for reanalysis and to the Columbia Broadcasting Company, Inc. and the McGraw-Hill Book Company for permission to publish them in this form.

2. These samples are slightly smaller than those discussed in ORC and CBS public statements on the same survey; the reason for this is that for this analysis I have excluded respondents on whom the racial information was ambiguous and have deleted "other nonwhite" respondents from the white sample.

3. The black and white samples are presented separately throughout the paper; they cannot be directly combined, because of their roughly equal size, into one sample for the purpose of calculating percentages.

4. The phrases "home-defense oriented" and "police oriented" will be used throughout this paper as shorthand for the more accurate but cumbersome terms which might be constructed to tag the two basic responses. It should be emphasized that those who were police oriented were thinking in terms of police defending their homes. The term self-defense oriented might have been used, but it does not seem to conjure up the image of a citizen preparing for the defense of his home as well as the phrase home-defense oriented. It is also likely that most of those who were home-defense oriented (particularly among the whites) felt the police had some part to play in home protection.

5. "Many Americans keep loaded firearms in homes, businesses, and on their persons for the purpose of protection. Evidence of this is found in a 1966 poll in which about 66 percent of householders with guns list 'protection' as one reason for having them" (National Commission on Violence, 1969a: 61).

REFERENCES

CASH, W. J. (1941) The Mind of the South. New York: Vintage Books.

HAHN, H. and J. R. FEAGIN (1970) "Riot-precipitating police practices: attitudes in urban ghettos." Phylon (forthcoming).

MORRIS, R. T. and V. JEFFRIES (1967) The White Reaction Study. Los Angeles: UCLA Institute of Government and Public Affairs.

National Commission on the Causes and Prevention of Violence (1969a) Firearms and Violence in American Life. Washington: U.S. Government Printing Office.

––– (1969b) The Politics of Protest. New York: Simon & Schuster.

President's Commission on Law Enforcement and Administration of Justice (1967) The Police. Washington: U.S. Government Printing Office.

REISS, A. J. and D. J. BORDUA (1967) "Environment and organization: a perspective on the police," pp. 25-55 in D. J. Bordua (ed.) The Police: Six Sociological Essays. New York: John Wiley.

WASKOW, A. I. (1966) From Race Riot to Sit-In, 1919 and the 1960's. Garden City, N.Y.: Doubleday.

WEBER, M. (1958) "Politics as a vocation," pp. 77-128 in H. H. Gerth and C. W. Mills (eds.) From Max Weber. New York: Oxford Univ. Press.

Support for Civil Liberties and Support for the Police

RICHARD L. BLOCK
Loyola University

In recent years, sociologists and jurists have become increasingly aware of the tension pursuant to achieving law and order. Laws which protect the citizen from the enforcers of law limit the efficiency of law enforcement agencies to maintain order (compare Skolnick, 1969: 1-22). To observers in the United States, the tension between law enforcement agencies and citizens has become increasingly apparent as the actions of the police have been increasingly circumscribed by decisions of the Supreme Court (Niederhoffer, 1967: 152-186; Sowle, 1962: 21-38).

This paper, however, is not an attempt to establish the existence of this tension between laws protecting the citizen from enforcers of the law and the ability of the police to maintain order; rather, it is an investigation of the relevance of this tension for the citizenry as a whole. The relationship between support for increases in the power of the police to enforce the law and support for increases in the protection of civil liberties will be considered.

It is assumed that all citizens recognize the existence of the tension. The question under investigation here is "How do citizens resolve the recognition of this tension in their support for increases in the protection of civil liberties and for increases in the power of the police?"

Four resolutions are possible. First, a respondent may support increases in neither the protection of civil liberties nor in the power of the police. He is satisfied with the status quo. Second, a respondent may support increases in the protection of civil liberties and in the power of the police—a resolution frequently found in surveys of residents of the black ghetto (National Advisory Commission on Civil Disorders, 1968: 299-310; Black and Reiss, 1967: 133-135). Third, a respondent may support increases in police power coupled with disapproval of increases in the protection of civil liberties, or, fourth, a respondent may support increases in the protection of civil liberties and oppose increases in police power. The last two resolutions will be defined as those which consistently resolve the tensions between civil liberties and civil order.

This research is based on a nationwide random sample survey conducted by the National Opinion Research Center (NORC) in the summer of 1966. This survey was commissioned by the President's Commission on Law Enforcement and the Administration of Justice and was designed to estimate the actual amount of crime occurring in the United States based on self reporting rather than on police reports (for methodological details, see Ennis, 1967).

A screening questionnaire was administered in 10,000 households. Each adult victim of crime or adult responding for a child victim was then administered a second questionnaire about the incident and a third questionnaire concerned with generalized attitudes toward crime and toward law enforcement agencies, the police, and the courts. The third questionnaire was also administered to a random sample of one in four nonvictims.

This paper is based primarily on the third questionnaire, of which 3,787 were administered. As discussed elsewhere, victimization seemed to have little effect on the respondent's attitude toward the police (Block, 1969: 124-130). Therefore, no attempt was made to weigh victims less heavily than nonvictims or to analyze the two categories of respondents separately.

This survey was administered from July to September 1966, "a long hot summer," and, therefore, is quite clearly bound in time. The climate of police-citizen relations may have been quite different during that summer than in either prior or subsequent years. Compared with other periods, the police may have had more support among whites and less support among blacks. Eventually the issues which compose the index of support for increased protection of civil liberties, namely support for civilian review boards of police activity and support for the suspect's right to a lawyer while under police interrogation, were less relevant than in 1966. Later, police-civilian review boards had been generally recognized as inefficient by both their early advocates and opponents, but in 1966 a major battle was fought between the mayor of New York and his police force over the continued maintenance of such a board.

The measure of support for increased police power is less bound in time. The question asks, "Do you favor giving the police more power to question people, do you think they have enough power already, or would you like to see some of their power to question people curtailed?"

If democracy presumes that some type of balance between the rights of the citizen and the protection of the state will exist at any point in time, then any citizen who supports increases in police power should also support increases in the protection of civil liberties to maintain this balance. However, if the citizen perceives an imbalance between the protection of civil liberties and protection of community, he will advocate measures to correct this imbalance. In the mid-1960s many people believed that there was an imbalance—a massive crime wave—and that court decisions protecting civil liberties had stripped the police of many of their powers to enforce the law (Wilson, 1963: 175-177).

However, surveys of the mid-1960s also found that blacks who frequently demanded increased police protection also demanded increased protection from the police. These seemingly inconsistent demands will be shown in this paper to be derived not from a deep sense of democracy, but from a fear of a community without order.

SUPPORT FOR THE POLICE AND SUPPORT FOR CIVIL LIBERTIES

Many respondents consistently resolved the tension between support for the police and support for civil liberties. Respondents who favored giving the police greater power to stop and question suspects were much more likely to oppose increases in the protection of civil liberties than those who rejected increases in the power of the police.

As seen in the last column of Table 1, of the total population sampled, seventy-one percent of those who supported neither measure to increase the protection of civil liberties supported an increase in the power of the police to stop and question suspects. Fifty-four percent of those who supported one measure and not the other, endorsed an increase in the power of the police. Of those who supported both measures to increase the protection of civil liberties, thirty-nine percent believed the police should have more power to stop and question suspects (gamma = -.37).

In Table 1, as in many others included in this paper, the percentage of respondents in each of three levels of support for increased protection of civil liberties who approved increases in police power to stop and question suspects is given. Gamma as a measure of relationship between support for the police and support for civil liberties is also presented. The larger the

TABLE 1

PERCENTAGE OF RESPONDENTS WHO SUPPORT INCREASED POLICE POWER
TO STOP AND QUESTION SUSPECTS BY RESPONDENT'S SUPPORT FOR
CIVIL LIBERTIES, RACE, REGION OF RESIDENCE, AND URBANIZATION

	White						Black			
	North			South					South	
Support Civil Liberties	Center City	Suburb	Other Urban/ Rural	Center City	Suburb	Other Urban/ Rural	North Center City	South Center City	Other Urban/ Rural	Total
Support Both (%)	34	39	46	41	37	58	26	30	34	39
Support One (%)	55	54	55	62	58	50	36	36	22	54
Support None (%)	73	76	69	63	72	64	33[a]	50[a]	–	71
Table n	575	883	637	207	189	304	179	88	46	3493
Gamma	-.47	-.44	-.26	-.27	-.42	.03	-.23	-.16	.31	-.37

a. Fewer than ten cases in a civil liberties support level.

magnitude of a negative gamma, the greater the probability that a member of a sample consistently resolved the tension.

Most respondents consistently resolved the tension between support for increased protection of civil liberties and support for increased police power. Returning to Table 1, however, approval of increased police power is less frequently linked with opposition to increased protection of civil liberties among southern respondents than among northern respondents and among blacks less frequently than among whites. Southern rural blacks were more likely to support increases in police power and in the protection of civil liberties than to support one and not the other.

The tension between support for civil liberties and support for increased police power is less often consistently resolved among northern urban black respondents than among northern urban whites. Seventy-three percent of those whites who favored neither measure to increase the protection of civil liberties supported increases in police power to stop and question suspects, while thirty-four percent of those who supported both measures to increase the protection of civil liberties also endorsed an increase in police power to stop and question suspects (gamma = -.47).

Only three of the one-hundred seventy-nine northern urban blacks opposed both measures to increase the protection of civil liberties. Of those who supported only one measure, thirty-six percent approved increases in police power to stop and question suspects. Of those northern urban blacks who supported both measures to increase the protection of civil liberties, twenty-six percent favored increasing the power of the police (gamma = -.23).

SOCIAL CLASS, CIVIL LIBERTIES
AND CIVIL ORDER

The remainder of this paper will consider only residents of the urban North. As shown elsewhere, the responses of suburban or rural residents are somewhat different than those of urban respondents, and those of southern respondents are different from those of northerners (Block, 1969). Unfortunately, there was not a sufficient number of black respondents from any area except the urban North for further analysis.

Overall, northern urban blacks were much less aware of the antithesis of support for civil liberties and support for police power than comparable whites, but among those of the lowest stratum of either race, among those who were either poor or poorly educated, the tension between support for the police and support for civil liberties was consistently resolved least often.

As we see in Table 2, among northern urban blacks with less than a high school education, support for measures to increase police power and support for measures to increase the protection of civil liberties were unrelated (gamma = -.01). Among similar northern urban whites, the relationship was fairly strong (gamma = -.37), but was weaker than among whites with more education. Blacks with more than a high school education were more likely to link support for increased protection of civil liberties with opposition to increased police power than their white counterparts ($\text{gamma}_{\text{black}}$ = -.84, $\text{gamma}_{\text{white}}$ = -.55).

TABLE 2

PERCENTAGE OF RESPONDENTS WHO SUPPORT INCREASED POLICE POWER TO STOP AND QUESTION SUSPECTS BY RESPONDENT'S SUPPORT FOR CIVIL LIBERTIES, EDUCATION, AND RACE (northern urban respondents only)

	Education					
	White			Black		
	-HS	=HS	HS+	-HS	=HS	HS+
Support None (%)	67	81	71	33[a]	—	—
Support One (%)	55	56	66	35	28	57
Support Both (%)	35	38	28	35	21	10
Table n	234	203	179	98	52	29
Gamma	-.37	-.50	-.55	-.01	-.19	-.84
Net Partial		-.46			-.09	

a. Fewer than ten cases in civil liberties support level.

Among whites, education was not found to be strongly related to the respondent's consistent resolution of the tension between support for the police and for civil liberties, although the tension was less consistently resolved among the uneducated. Among blacks, the poorly educated were not likely to consistently resolve this tension, and a majority of the black respondents had less than a high school education. Therefore, gamma as a measure of consistent resolution of the tension is reduced from .23 to -.09 by controlling for education among blacks.[1]

One might be led to conclude that those respondents who were poorly educated were generally so little aware of the world around them that they could not discern the tension between support for the police and support for civil liberties, but this would be an incomplete conclusion.

As seen in Table 3, poor northern urban respondents who supported increases in the protection of civil liberties were less likely to oppose increases in police power than respondents from other income groups who gave equivalent support to the protection of civil liberties. Poor blacks were more likely to support both increases in police protection and in the protection of civil liberties than to support one and not the other (gamma = .53).

TABLE 3

PERCENTAGE OF RESPONDENTS WHO SUPPORT INCREASED POLICE POWER TO STOP AND QUESTION SUSPECTS BY RESPONDENT'S SUPPORT FOR CIVIL LIBERTIES, FAMILY INCOME, AND RACE (northern urban respondents only)

| | Income | | | | | | | |
| | White | | | | Black | | | |
	-3000	3000-5999	6000-9999	10000+	-3000	3000-5999	6000-9999	10000+
Support None (%)	44[a]	86	70	75	00	—	100[a]	—
Support One (%)	44	56	61	66	13	46	38	40[a]
Support Both (%)	32	16	41	41	30	19	29	18
Table n	86	129	230	134	47	58	45	16[b]
Gamma	-.20	-.78	-.36	-.42	.53	-.58	-.32	-.50
Net Partial		-.44				-.26		

a. Fewer than ten cases in civil liberties support level.
b. Gamma calculated on fewer than twenty cases.

Thirteen percent of those low-income, northern, urban blacks who supported only one measure to increase the protection of civil liberties favored increased police power to stop and question suspects, but thirty percent of those who supported both measures for expanding safeguards of civil liberties also favored increased police power. Although many poor, northern, urban whites did not relate support for the police and support for the protection of civil liberties, the two measures were inversely related (gamma = -.20).

Both the respondent's income and education were, therefore, related to the probability that he would couple support for increased police power with opposition to increased protection of civil liberties. But education and income are, of course, strongly related; therefore, to clarify the importance of each of these social class factors in affecting the probability of a consistent resolution to the tension of support for civil liberties and police power, it is necessary to simultaneously hold income and education constant.

As we see in Table 4, among white respondents who were both poor and poorly educated there was no relationship between support for increases in police power and increases in the protection of civil liberties (gamma = -.05). Among those blacks who were both poor and poorly educated those who supported both increases in the protection of civil liberties were much more likely to endorse increases in the power of the police than those who supported only one increase (gamma = .75). There appears to be no relationship between education and the ability to

TABLE 4

GAMMA, SUPPORT FOR INCREASED PROTECTION OF CIVIL LIBERTIES AND SUPPORT FOR INCREASED POLICE POWER TO STOP AND QUESTION SUSPECTS, CONTROLLING FOR RESPONDENT'S EDUCATION, FAMILY INCOME, AND RACE
(northern urban respondents only)

Respondent's Education	Family Income							
	White				Black			
	-3000	3000-5999	6000-9999	10000+	-3000	3000-5999	6000-9999	10000+
Less than High School	-.05	-.63	-.42	-.49	.75	-.33	-.11[a]	1.00[a]
High School Graduate	-.17[a]	-.83	-.26	-.70	1.00[a]	-1.00[a]	-.33[a]	-1.00[a]
More than High School	-.63[a]	-.88	-.40	-.27	-1.00[a]	-1.00[a]	-.63[a]	.00[a]
Net Partial			-.42				-.04	

a. Fewer than twenty cases used to calculate gamma.

consistently resolve the tension of support for police power and civil liberties once income is held constant, and no relationship between income and this ability once education is controlled. Overall, holding constant both income and education had almost no affect on white respondents' consistent resolution of the tension between civil liberty and civil order. By holding income and education constant a total gamma of -.47 was reduced to a net partial of -.42. But among urban black respondents there was no relationship between support for the police and support for civil liberties once income and education were held constant (gamma$_{net partial}$ = -.04). This lack of relationship, however, is based on the large proportion of blacks who are both poor and poorly educated.

CIVIL ORDER, CIVIL LIBERTY, FEAR OF CRIME, AND FEAR OF THE POLICE

Very poor northern, urban blacks supported increases both in police protection and in protection from the police. Perhaps among the very poor, both black and white, a consistent resolution of the tension between support for civil liberties and support for civil order includes support for both. Police violations of civil liberties may be so common that civil order is imperiled. A citizen living in such a situation may not believe it is possible to maintain civil order without increasing the protection of civil liberties. Thus far, however, it has *not* been shown that fear of crime or fear of the police do in fact affect the respondent's support for increases in police power or in the protection of civil liberties. A relationship between fear and support for actions affecting the police may assume a rationality which is not present in the real world.

Unfortunately, the NORC survey did not include a direct measure of fear of the police; however, respondents were asked to evaluate the respectfulness of the police in their community and this question will be used as an indicator of fear of the police. It is assumed that the more respectful an individual evaluates police treatment, the less will be his fear of the police. Whites were found to evaluate police respect much more favorably than blacks (gamma = .58). Poor whites evaluated police respect less positively than whites of higher income (gamma = .27), but there was no relationship between income or education and evaluation of police respect among blacks or between education and evaluation of police respect among whites.

For this analysis, fear of crime is measured by the respondent's rating of the probability of attack while walking in his neighborhood. Whites generally believed the probability of attack in their neighborhood was less than did blacks (gamma = -.42). Among both blacks and whites, respondents of higher income (gamma$_{black}$ = -.16, gamma$_{white}$ = -.10) and of higher education (gamma$_{black}$ = -.26, gamma$_{white}$ = -.13) rated the probability of attack as somewhat less than those respondents of less income or education. There was a slight tendency for respondents to link fear of crime and fear of the police (gamma$_{black}$ = .15, gamma$_{white}$ = .11), but among most respondents the two variables seemed to be independent.

As we see in Table 5, controlling for fear of crime *did* affect the probability that an individual would consistently resolve the tension between civil order and civil liberties. However, the effect of fear of crime on whites was different from that on blacks. Those whites who believed the probability of attack in their neighborhood was very high were much more likely to couple support for enhanced police power to stop and question suspects with opposition to increases in the protection of civil liberties than other whites. Of those whites believing that attack was very likely, ninety-three percent of those who opposed both measures to increase the protection of civil liberties wanted to strengthen the power of the police to stop and question suspects. Of those whites who rated the probability of attack as somewhat likely, seventy-three percent of those opposing both measures to increase the protection of civil liberties supported greater police power.

TABLE 5

PERCENTAGE OF RESPONDENTS WHO SUPPORT INCREASED POLICE POWER TO STOP AND QUESTION SUSPECTS BY RESPONDENT'S SUPPORT FOR CIVIL LIBERTIES, FEAR OF ATTACK, AND RACE (northern urban respondents only)

Support for Civil Liberties	White				Black			
	Very Likely	Somewhat Likely	Somewhat Unlikely	Very Unlikely	Very Likely	Somewhat Likely	Somewhat Unlikely	Very Unlikely
Support None (%)	93	73	69	70	50[a]	—	—	00
Support One (%)	72	61	55	56	35	25	53	38
Support Both (%)	31	39	32	32	45	19	15	13
Table n	63	175	227	154	52	56	50	17[b]
Gamma	-.76	-.41	-.44	-.45	.15	-.18	-.73	-.40
Net Partial			-.45				-.25	

a. Fewer than ten cases in civil liberties support level.

b. Gamma calculated on fewer than twenty cases.

Whites who feared crime most were especially apt to be consistent about the tension between support for increased police power and increases in the protection of civil liberties. Of all whites, they were most likely to support increases in police power and oppose increases in the protection of civil liberties. However, blacks who feared crime most were least likely to see a relationship between support for heightened police power and opposition to the growing protection of civil liberties. Fear of crime did result in support for increased police power to stop and question suspects, but among blacks, support for increased police protection was linked to support for increased protection from the police.

Thirty-five percent of those blacks who believed attack was very likely in their neighborhood and who supported only one measure to increase the protection of civil liberties favored increases in police power, while of those who supported both measures, forty-five percent endorsed strengthening police power (gamma = .15). Of those blacks who believed attack to be somewhat unlikely in their neighborhood, fifty-three percent of those granting moderate approval to measures for the protection of civil liberties favored increases in police power, while fifteen percent of those who supported both measures approved expanding police power to stop and question suspects (gamma = -.73).

As we see in Table 6, fear of the police, as measured by evaluation of the respectfulness of police treatment had almost no effect on the relationship between support for the police and support for civil liberties

TABLE 6

PERCENTAGE OF RESPONDENTS WHO SUPPORT INCREASED POLICE POWER TO STOP AND QUESTION SUSPECTS BY RESPONDENT'S SUPPORT FOR CIVIL LIBERTIES, EVALUATION OF POLICE RESPECT, AND RACE (northern urban respondents only)

| | Evaluation of Police Respect | | | | | |
| | White | | | Black | | |
	Very Good	Pretty Good	Not So Good	Very Good	Pretty Good	Not So Good
Support None (%)	77	58	100[a]	—	—	100[a]
Support One (%)	63	53	31	56	31	13[a]
Support Both (%)	41	28	31	40	13	12
Table n	382	165	31	54	74	34
Gamma	-.44	-.42	-.32	-.21	-.51	-.42
Net Partial		-.43			-.39	

a. Fewer than ten cases in civil liberties support level.

as it was observed by whites, although fear of the police was related to both support for increased police power (gamma = .37) and increased protection of civil liberties (gamma = -.34).

Black respondents who did not fear the police related support for expanded protection of civil liberties with opposition to increases in the power of the police to stop and question suspects less frequently than blacks with more fear of the police or than whites who did not fear the police. Fifty-six percent of those blacks who did not fear the police (rated police respect very good) and who supported only one measure to increase the protection of civil liberties favored increased police power (gamma = -.21). Of those with some fear of the police (evaluated police respect as pretty good) who also gave low approval to measures extending guarantees of civil liberties, thirty-one percent wanted more police power, while thirteen percent of those who supported both measures to increase the protection of civil liberties also endorsed increases in police power (gamma = -.51).

As seen in Table 6, with fear of the police controlled, there was little difference between blacks and whites in the probability that the tension between support for the police and support for increases in the protection of civil liberties would be consistently resolved. Holding constant fear of the police, the relationship had a gamma of -.43 among whites and -.39 among blacks. Only among those blacks who greatly feared the police was the relationship between support for civil liberties and support for the police weaker than among whites.

The reason for the strong inverse relationship between support for increased police power and for increased protection of civil liberties among blacks who greatly feared the police is clear. The greater a black respondent's fear of the police, the more likely that he sanctioned both measures to protect civil liberties and also opposed increased police power to stop and question suspects. Of those blacks who did not fear the police (those who rated police respect as very good), thirty-nine percent approved both civil liberties proposals and opposed increases in police power. Of those blacks who were somewhat afraid of the police, forty-six percent responded in that manner. Of those who greatly feared the police, sixty-five percent supported both increases in the protection of civil liberties and opposed extensions of police power to stop and question suspects.

As seen in Table 7, among whites, fear of the police only affected the probability that an individual would consistently resolve the tension between support for the police and support for increased protection of civil liberties if fear of crime was low. Under this condition, those who had little fear of the police were quite likely to have consistently resolved the

TABLE 7

PERCENTAGE OF RESPONDENTS WHO SUPPORT INCREASED POLICE POWER TO STOP AND QUESTION SUSPECTS BY RESPONDENT'S SUPPORT FOR CIVIL LIBERTIES, EVALUATION OF POLICE RESPECT, FEAR OF ATTACK, AND RACE

(northern urban respondents only)

	WHITE ATTACK					
	Likely			Unlikely		
	Evaluation of Police Respect					
	Very Good	Pretty Good	Not So Good	Very Good	Pretty Good	Not So Good
Support None (%)	80	66[a]	100[a]	75	53	—
Support One (%)	68	63	57	61	48	10
Support Both (%)	45	36	33	39	50	30
Table n	150	61	12	230	104	20
Gamma	-.43	-.43	-.74	-.43	-.03	.59
Net Partial			-.39			

	BLACK ATTACK					
Support None (%)	—	—	100[a]	00[a]	—	—
Support One (%)	50	29	00[a]	63[a]	40	33[a]
Support Both (%)	47	17	13	33	00	10
Table n	29	48	21	24	23	13
Gamma	-.05	-.34	-.29	-.33	-1.00	-.50
Net Partial			-.36			

a. Fewer than ten cases in a civil liberties support level.

tension (gamma = -.43). Among those who had some fear of the police, those opposing both measures to extend the protection of civil liberties were no more likely to approve increases in police power than those who supported both measures (gamma = -.03). Of those few whites who greatly feared the police, those who supported only one measure to increase the protection of civil liberties were less likely to approve expansions of police power than those who supported both measures (gamma = .59). Those who gave low approval to measures extending the protection of civil liberties became less willing to support increases in police power as fear of the police mounted. Those who supported both proposals to bolster the protection of civil liberties, perhaps feeling insulated from the police, were apparently less affected in their support of the police by alleged fear of the police.

As we also see in Table 7, the effect of fear of crime and the police on the probability that a black consistently resolves the tension between support for civil liberties and support for the police was more nearly additive than among whites. There was no relationship between support for the police and support for civil liberties among those who had little fear of the police but great fear of crime (gamma = -.05). Although blacks were increasingly more likely to support the expansion of safeguards on civil liberties with increases in fear of the police and black attitudes on police power and fear of crime also were related, the probability of consistent resolution of the tension between support for the police and support for civil liberties is approximately of the same magnitude for all other combinations of fear of the police and fear of crime.

Holding fear of the police and fear of crime constant, there is little difference between blacks and whites in consistent resolution of the tension between support for the police and support for civil liberties. With these controls, the net partial gamma, as a measure of the consistent resolution of the tension is -.39 for whites and -.36 for blacks.

Fear of crime and of the police affect the probability that an individual will support increases in the protection of civil liberties and in the power of the police. Social class as measured by either income or education also affects the ability of an individual to consistently resolve the tension between support for the police and support for civil liberties. Those who are poor or poorly educated frequently perceive no tension. Perhaps, the reason for their inconsistent resolution can now be understood. The relationships between fear of crime, fear of the police, support for the police, and support for civil liberties are different among the poor than among members of other social classes.

As we see in Table 8, holding education constant, fear of crime had relatively little effect on either support for increases in police power or support for increased protection of civil liberties among most whites, while fear of the police was strongly related to both support for the police and support for civil liberties. In general the relationship was as predicted. Among white respondents of all education groups, fear of crime was directly related to support for the police, and fear of the police was inversely related to favoring the police but directly related to approval of the protection of civil liberties.

Among low education respondents, however, as fear of crime increased, support for civil liberties also increased. As we see in Table 8, of those whites with less than a high school education who believed attack was likely in their neighborhood, twenty-five percent supported both increases in the protection of civil liberties. Of similar whites who believed the probability of attack was low, seventeen percent supported both methods

TABLE 8

PERCENTAGE SUPPORTING INCREASES IN POLICE POWER AND IN THE PROTECTION OF CIVIL LIBERTIES BY EDUCATION, FEAR OF CRIME, FEAR OF THE POLICE, AND RACE

	WHITE					
	Fear of the Police					
	% More Police Power			% Support Both Civil Liberties		
	-HS	=HS	+HS	-HS	=HS	+HS
Not Good	35	37[a]	63[a]	44	37[a]	30[a]
Pretty Good	49	46	35	36	35	48
Very Good	58	63	66	19	25	22
Gamma	-.23	-.35	-.44	.44	.25	.33
n	215	189	167	234	195	170
	Fear of Crime					
Likely	59	61	62	25	30	30
Unlikely	47	56	51	17	27	29
Gamma	.24	.10	.22	.15	-.09	-.05
n	230	199	179	239	206	195
	BLACK					
	Fear of the Police					
Not Good	20	17	00[a]	56	75	100[a]
Pretty Good	23	6	31	48	63	54
Very Good	55	37	00[a]	59	55	100[a]
Gamma	-.51	-.47	-.16	-.09	.27	.07
n	87	46	25	96	48	26
	Fear of Crime					
Likely	35	25	23	57	56	67
Unlikely	37	19	21	42	70	87
Gamma	-.04	.16	.05	.27	-.30	-.52
n	96	50	27	108	52	30

a. Percentage based on fewer than ten cases.

of protecting civil liberties (gamma = .15). Among whites with little education, fear of crime and support for civil liberties were directly related. Among blacks with little education, fear of crime was also directly related to support for civil liberties (gamma = .27). Of those blacks with less than a high school education who believed attack was likely, fifty-seven percent supported both increases in the protection of civil liberties. Of those who believed attack was unlikely, forty-two percent supported both increases (gamma = .27). Of those blacks with a high school education who believed attack to be likely, fifty-six percent supported both increases in the protection of civil liberties, while of those who believed attack to be unlikely, seventy percent supported both increases (gamma = -.30).

Among all blacks, fear for the police was inversely related to support for the police, but had little relationship to support for civil liberties. The greater a black man's fear of the police, the less likely he supported increases in police power to stop and question suspects. The direct relationship between support for civil liberties and fear of crime among the poorly educated, a relationship not found in other respondents, may account for their frequent inconsistent resolution of the tension between support for the police and support for civil liberties.

IMPLICATIONS

Why is it that ghetto blacks support both increases in police power and increases in the protection of civil liberties? This paper clearly indicates that those who are poor and/or poorly educated are less likely to consistently resolve the tension between civil order and civil rights in their support for the police than other respondents, and that fear of crime and fear of the police also affect the ability of an individual to consistently resolve this tension.

It is shown, however, that simultaneous support for both increases in police power and in the protection of civil liberties among poor blacks may result in the inverse relationship between fear of the police and support for the police and the direct relationship between fear of crime and support for civil liberties among this group. That support for the police decreases as fear of the police increases is not surprising. That support for civil liberties increases as fear of crime increases is an unexpected finding.

Perhaps, aggressive police patrols in the ghetto have an unexpected effect on ghetto blacks. If aggressive patrols are most frequent in areas with the greatest probability of crime, and if many innocent people have their rights violated by aggressive patrols, then residents of those neighborhoods where fear of crime is strongest may be most likely to support increases in the protection of civil liberties even though they realize that it may cut down on the efficiency of the police. Therefore, fear of crime resulting from police action without regard for the rights of citizens leads to demands for more protection of citizen rights.

Among most blacks, fear of crime has little effect on support for the police, but fear of the police strongly affects support for the police.

Among most whites, fear of the police does not affect either support for the police or support for the protection of civil liberties. Thus, the most effective method for the police to gain support in the community is not through efficient maintenance of order only but through respectful treatment of citizens.

NOTE

1. This research makes use of the net partial gamma developed by James A. Davis. Following Goodman, Davis interpreted the net partial gamma to be how much more probable it is to get like than unlike orders in measures A and B when pairs of individuals differing on A and B and tied on C but unselected on any other measure are chosen at random from the population. See Davis (1967).

REFERENCES

BLACK, D. J. and A. REISS (1967) "Patterns of behavior in police and citizen transactions," pp. 133-135 in A. Reiss (ed.) Studies in Crime and Law Enforcement in Major Metropolitan Areas, Vol. II. Washington, D.C.: U.S. Government Printing Office.

BLOCK, R. L. (1969) "Foundations of citizen support for the police." Ph.D. dissertation. Chicago: University of Chicago (August).

DAVIS, J. A. (1967) "A partial coefficient for Goodman and Kruskal's gamma." J. of the Amer. Statistical Assn. 62: 189-193.

ENNIS, P. (1967) Criminal Victimization in the United States. Washington, D.C.: U.S. Government Printing Office.

NIEDERHOFFER, A. (1967) Behind the Shield: The Police in Urban Society. Garden City, N.Y.: Doubleday.

REISS, A. [ed.] (1967) Studies in Crime and Law Enforcement in Major Metropolitan Areas. Washington, D.C.: U.S. Government Printing Office.

SKOLNICK, J. H. (1969) The Politics of Protest. New York: Ballantine Books.

SOWLE, C. R. [ed.] (1962) Police Power and Individual Freedom: The Quest for Balance. Chicago: Aldine.

National Advisory Commission on Civil Disorders (1968) Washington, D.C.: U.S. Government Printing Office.

WILSON, O. W. (1963) "Police authority in a free society." J. of Criminal Law, Criminology & Police Sci. 54: 175-177.

Cops and Rioters

Ghetto Perceptions of Social Conflict and Control

HARLAN HAHN
University of California at Riverside

Among the seemingly new and insurmountable problems that confront law enforcement officers, perhaps few are more demanding than the outbreak of civil disorders. As the governmental agency vested with primary authority to maintain public order, local police departments must assume the major responsibility for curbing urban violence. Yet, as the experience of many American cities indicates, policemen often are exposed to severe criticism for their role in provoking as well as in controlling major riots. Police officers may encounter strong public antagonism before riots, during the disorders, and after the rioting has subsided. Hence, the duty of curtailing civil disturbances may be one of the most crucial and difficult obligations imposed upon law enforcement agencies.

PUBLIC HOSTILITY TOWARD POLICE

Perhaps the primary obstacle to the task of police officers in civil disorders has been intense public hostility toward police activities in urban ghettos. Numerous studies of areas that exploded in violence (Kraft, 1966; Raine, 1967; McCord and Howard, 1968; Feagin and Sheatsley, 1968) as well as of communities that were relatively calm (Marx, 1967: 36-37; Campbell and Schuman, 1968; Bayley and Mendelsohn, 1969) have found that resentment of police practices has been a common and persistent grievance in predominantly black neighborhoods. In addition, many of the nation's most serious and destructive riots apparently have been triggered by police behavior. As the Kerner Commission (1968: 206) noted,

"Almost invariably the incident that ignites disorder arises from police action." The conduct of law enforcement officers in riot-precipitating incidents frequently seemed to spark a smoldering sense of mutual suspicion and animosity between policemen and ghetto residents that flared into violence.

As a result, assessments of police behavior, and especially the charge of "police brutality," have been accorded the status of what Lupsha (1969: 282-283) termed "folk theories" of riots (see also Levy, 1968). Both the prevalence of strong public disapproval of police conduct in areas that experienced riots and the presence of police officers at precipitating events appeared to be more than coincidental. In a fundamental sense, moreover, rioting has represented a deliberate repudiation of external social controls and a continuing defiance of police efforts to reimpose social controls upon the community. The course of many civil disorders, therefore, has indicated that ghetto perceptions of police actions may have been an important source of the unrest that exploded in major riots.

Perhaps even more important than the role of policemen in sparking ghetto riots, however, is their activity in attempting to halt the disturbances. Ironically, civil disorders might be characterized as a social phenomenon in which the major responsibility for terminating the disruptions is delegated to the same political agency that may have been instrumental in provoking them. Although definitive evidence of police misconduct has been difficult to amass or to evaluate, some accounts of civil disturbances (see, for example, Walker, 1968; Hersey, 1968) indicate that police actions may tend to exacerbate conflict and to undermine public confidence in law enforcement authority. The methods that policemen employ in an effort to control rioting, thus, may be one of the most critical features of their involvement in civil disorders.

In general, studies of riot control measures have focused upon two opposing strategies that reflect what Conant (1968: 427) has termed the problem of "under-control and over-control." Although no extensive plans were developed for restraining civil disorders prior to the riots of the 1960s, many observers have accepted the belief that "exhibitions of force, in overwhelming strength, have prevented outbreaks on numerous occasions" (Grimshaw, 1969: 283). On the other hand, the use of harsh or repressive force to quell ghetto disturbances also has been cited as a measure that could both intensify existing antagonisms toward policemen and escalate the violence (see Skolnick, 1969: 345). As a result, some commentators have advocated the removal of police officers from potential riot areas. Hundley (1968: 637) noted that "in some cases, the total withdrawal of police simply enhances riot activity." Yet, no general consensus apparently has been reached concerning the efficacy of either an impressive display of force or the withdrawal of large police contingents as a means of curbing ghetto disorders. As the Kerner Commission (1968: 332) commented:

> The larger question, however—whether police should withdraw from the disorder area and let the community leaders or forces seek to cool the rioting raises a number of critical issues. . . . The Commission believes that only the mayor—who has the ultimate responsibility for the welfare and safety of the community—can, with the advice of the police administrator, make the critical judgment.

While the most appropriate strategy for ending civil disorders—like many other problems relating to urban violence and police activities—eventually must be resolved by political decisions, perhaps studies of major riots also have yielded information concerning some issues, such as ghetto assessments of riot control measures, that might assist civic and police officials in making this determination.

Discussions of riot control, however, usually have considered this problem as an essentially technical issue. Although police planning and preparations for civil disorders frequently have emphasized the mobilization and deployment of manpower, the development of rapid communication systems, and the acquisition of riot control weapons, relatively little attention has been focused upon public reactions to the role of law enforcement officers in urban riots (Applegate, 1969: Momboisse, 1967). In part, perhaps this neglect has been justified by the intensely critical attitudes of ghetto residents toward riot control policies. Police efforts to restrain urban violence not only have been condemned as harsh and vindictive, but they also have been attacked as weak and ineffectual. While many persons who live in riot areas have been inclined to interpret active police intervention in a riot as a sign of hostility and oppression, others have censured the alleged failure of policemen to provide adequate protection for their lives and property. As a result, ghetto sentiments seldom have appeared to provide a firm basis of support for riot control activities.

The effectiveness of riot control measures, however, eventually may be determined by ghetto attitudes toward police actions. Unlike military operations, civil disorders cannot be stopped by a decisive, armed victory over the opposition. Attempts by policemen to curtail urban violence usually require at least a minimal amount of cooperation and support from the residents of a riot area. Public appraisals of the conduct of law enforcement officers in civil disorders, therefore, could be as important as actual police behavior in affecting the success of riot control policies. Since the growth of public animosity toward police officers often has seemed to be associated with the outbreak of rioting, changing perspectives that reflect either increasingly favorable or increasingly hostile images of policemen during the disorders also may have a major impact upon the willingness of local residents to comply with police efforts to control the rioting. In addition, perceptions of police activities during civil disturbances could influence the ability of law enforcement officers to reimpose legal constraints upon public behavior in the aftermath of violence. The purpose of this research, therefore, is to explore the attitudes of ghetto residents who have experienced civil disorders concerning both riot control issues and police conduct before the riots, during the disturbances, and after the violence had ended.

PERCEPTIONS OF POLICE CONDUCT
AND THE DETROIT RIOTS

An unusual opportunity to investigate ghetto perceptions of police conduct as a source of discontent and as a factor in the control of civil disorders was provided by a modified quota sample survey of 270 black adults in the Twelfth Street area of Detroit, where the riots of 1967 originated. This survey was conducted shortly after the disorders. In addition, however, those data have been supplemented in this study by responses collected in another citywide panel survey, based upon an area probability sample of both white and black adults in Detroit conducted after the 1965 and 1966 elections, respectively.[1]

Information from the latter surveys permitted an examination of trends in public sentiments concerning police activities prior to the outbreak of violence. In both the 1965 and 1966 surveys, respondents throughout the city were asked if they tended to "approve or disapprove of the way the Detroit police are doing their jobs." Table 1 reports the changes in public attitudes toward policemen that emerged among white and black residents of Detroit before the riots of 1967.

Apparently, during the years preceding the riots, criticism of Detroit policemen was increasingly centered in black segments of the community. As the total percentages by' year indicate, from four-fifths to approximately three-fourths of the white respondents expressed a favorable view of police conduct in 1965 and 1966, respectively, but approval of police activities by black adults dropped from three-fifths to slightly more than one-half between the two years. In addition, two-thirds of the black residents who disapproved of local law enforcement officers in 1965 remained critical of their performance one year later. By contrast, a thin majority of whites who criticized police actions in 1965 had been

TABLE 1

CHANGES IN WHITE AND BLACK PERCEPTIONS OF
POLICE PRACTICES IN DETROIT, 1965-1966
(in percentages)

Perceptions of Police Conduct—1965	Perceptions of Police Conduct—1966					
	Whites			Blacks		
	Approve	Disap-prove	Total 1965	Approve	Disap-prove	Total 1965
Approve	79	21	81	66	34	61
Disapprove	51	49	19	33	67	39
Total—1966	74	26	—	53	47	—
n	174	61	235	59	52	111

converted to a position of approval in the following year. Although this period was not marked by any unusual visible evidence of deteriorating relations between police officers and minority groups in Detroit, the surveys did indicate that the police force was gradually gaining the support of formerly hostile white sectors of the population while black resistance was stiffening slightly during the years prior to the civil disorders. The findings suggested, therefore, that a growing division between white and black perceptions of police behavior in Detroit may have promoted the development of community tensions that eventually exploded in violence.

POLICE CONDUCT AS A SOURCE OF GHETTO DISCONTENT

The survey conducted after the riots of 1967 also revealed that antipathy toward police behavior, as well as other grievances (Hahn, 1969b, 1969d), may have been especially prevalent in the Twelfth Street ghetto of Detroit, which was the principal scene of the disorders. More than eighty percent of the black respondents in this neighborhood, for example, did not feel that police officers treated people equally; slightly more than half evaluated police treatment of local residents before the riots as "not good" or "poor." This criticism of police conduct, moreover, seemed to reflect a basic distrust of the entire legal system (see Hahn, 1969a). Eighty-seven percent of the ghetto residents did not believe that most laws "are fair to all people," and ninety-two percent denied that "laws are enforced equally."[2] In general, residents of the Detroit ghetto that had exploded in serious riots seemed to lack even a minimal faith in the impartiality of police officers and of the legal regulations that they administered.

The overwhelming resentment of both the law and law enforcement that was uncovered by the surveys, as well as the police raid that had precipitated the disorders, therefore, suggested that perceptions of police conduct may have played a major role in igniting the Detroit riots. A survey of ghetto areas conducted by the Detroit Urban League after the 1967 disorders also revealed that black residents ranked "police brutality" at the top of a list of twenty-three possible causes that may have had a great deal to do with the rioting (Meyer, 1967). In the study of the Twelfth Street area, however, when respondents were asked about the "two or three main reasons" for the violence, only twenty-four percent mentioned police practices, an equivalent proportion cited the general issue of discrimination or the denial of civil rights, and thirty percent referred to the specific problem of a lack of job opportunities. Another question disclosed that more than two-thirds of the residents in the Twelfth Street neighborhood believed that high unemployment rather than inferior housing or poor police practices was "most likely" to produce civil disorders. Thus, a pervasive and deepening distrust of police officers may have contributed to the tensions that were developing in the neighborhood prior to the outbreak of rioting, but many ghetto residents tended to identify more general—and perhaps more pressing—problems such as discrimination and unemployment as the principal sources of the violence.

To probe the association between perceptions of police behavior and rioting, however, residents of the Twelfth Street area were questioned about the manner in which police officers normally treated five major groups in the ghetto: young blacks who are out of work, whites who live in the neighborhood, black homeowners, persons who speak out for black power, and black teenagers. At a later point, respondents also were asked to evaluate the participation of each of the groups in the rioting. The mean scores and the simple coefficients of correlation between those measures of police mistreatment and riot involvement for the five groups are presented in Table 2.[3]

As the mean scores for different groups indicate, unemployed black youths, black power advocates, and black teenagers were more likely to be perceived both as the victims of police abuse and as active in the rioting than black homeowners or whites. Yet, the coefficients of correlation also suggested that perceptions of increasing riot participation were not closely related to comparable appraisals of police misconduct toward critical segments of the ghetto population, except for young unemployed blacks, who were also regarded on the average as most heavily involved in the rioting. In fact, the associations between the extent of perceived police mistreatment and riot participation were inverse for all of the remaining

TABLE 2

PERCEPTIONS OF POLICE MISTREATMENT AND RIOT INVOLVEMENT FOR SELECTED GROUPS IN THE TWELFTH STREET GHETTO OF DETROIT

Groups	Mean Riot Involvement Score	Mean Police Mistreatment Score	Coefficients of Correlation	n
Young unemployed blacks	3.61	2.91	$+.16^a$	198
Black power advocates	3.42	3.01	$-.10^b$	154
Black teenagers	3.44	2.89	$-.10^b$	227
Black homeowners	1.92	1.85	$-.01^c$	214
White residents of the neighborhood	2.13	1.37	$-.15^b$	142

a. Significant at the .001 level.
b. Significant at the .01 level.
c. Not significant.

groups. A separate examination of respondents who were operationally identified as members of three groups of black adults also disclosed that assessments of the intensity of police mistreatment and riot involvement were inversely related among both members and nonmembers of the groups, again with the exception of unemployed youths.[4] The findings, therefore, indicated that, for most sectors of the community, measures of riot activity and police mistreatment were not closely associated either among ghetto residents generally or among persons who were themselves defined as members of specific groups.

The direct association between perceived police mistreatment and riot involvement in the case of unemployed black young people, however, suggested that those persons may have been commonly regarded—by themselves and by other residents of the neighborhood—as especially susceptible to both police abuse and riot participation. Hence, the evidence seemed to support the speculation that ghetto unrest inspired by unemployment and other grievances has been exacerbated by frequent conflict between police officers and segments of the population that have encountered severe economic obstacles. This problem also may have been intensified by so-called professional law enforcement procedures such as "aggressive preventive patrolling" and "stopping and frisking" suspicious persons in high crime rate areas (Fogelson, 1968). Perhaps those policies have produced numerous hostile encounters between ghetto residents and policemen searching for suspects in serious crimes, while diverting police manpower from the investigation of the many supposedly minor offenses that plague lower-class neighborhoods (see Hahn and Feagin, 1970). As a group that might have been particularly vulnerable to the appeal of participation both in the riots and in the many illegal activities that flourished in this locality during normal periods, unemployed black young people may have become a special target of police suspicion and harassment. Perhaps the simple charge of "police brutality" has failed to reflect the complex set of variables that could spark civil disorders, but specific police practices such as "preventive patrolling" may have fostered increasing friction between policemen and residents of the community who were widely regarded as most active in the rioting.[5]

The results of this investigation, therefore, seemed to support an interpretation of urban riots that focused primarily upon general problems of discrimination and economic inequality rather than police conduct as a major impetus for the disorders. Police behavior might not have been the single most important source of ghetto unrest, but it may have promoted the growth of community tensions that eventually exploded in violence.

POLICE CONDUCT AND RIOT CONTROL STRATEGIES

Even though police practices may have been a contributory rather than an instrumental source of ghetto discontent, the overwhelming distrust of law enforcement officers that permeated the neighborhood where the disorders erupted seemed to impose severe burdens upon police actions to control the rioting. Attempts to gain public respect for police authority during civil disorders probably have been impeded by a deep legacy of mutual antagonism and resentment. In addition, the duty of restoring order often has appeared to require the use of police tactics that might intensify local criticism of their behavior. Yet, ghetto animosity toward police activities allegedly has been focused not only upon harsh or repressive riot control measures but it also has been directed at the failure of policemen to contain serious outbreaks of violence. As a result, law enforcement agencies frequently have been damned both for their action and for their inaction during civil disturbances.

In the Detroit riots of 1967, the role of the police department seemed to reflect an ambivalent strategy that, at least during the initial stages of the disorders, appeared to rely more heavily upon the withdrawal of police personnel than upon a massive display of strength as a means of curtailing the violence. According to the city police commissioner, the principal riot control measure adopted by law enforcement officers was "a loose policy in the early phase of the Detroit rioting, assuming that local civilian Negro leadership would contain the disorder" (Janowitz, 1968: 14). Ghetto residents who were affected by the disorders, however, seemed to be highly critical of this strategy. The results of the Twelfth Street area survey revealed that seventy-seven percent of the black respondents felt that policemen had "waited too long" in moving into the riot area, fifteen percent believed they went in "at about the right time," and only eight percent thought that they "should have waited longer and let people in the area try to handle it." In a serious riot such as the civil disorders in Detroit, the total withdrawal of police officers appeared to arouse the strong opposition of most persons who lived in the neighborhood which had been the principal scene of violence.

On the other hand, the residents of the Twelfth Street ghetto also were evenly divided on the issue of employing a display of strength as a riot control technique. Approximately one-half of the respondents felt that "if the police had gotten tough right away . . . they could have stopped the trouble then," but another half believed that this strategy simply "would have made matters worse." The replies to both questions, therefore, appeared to reflect highly critical perspectives on riot control policies. While nearly three-fourths of the residents seemed to castigate Detroit policemen for their failure to intervene promptly in the disturbances, at least one-half also apparently thought that a strong display of police strength might have intensified the violence.

Since ghetto assessments of police efforts to contain the violence may have been shaped by previous animosity, however, persons who harbored disparaging perceptions of police conduct before the riots might have been expected to manifest the principal opposition to the display of force as a riot control strategy. Yet, the survey data provided only slight support for this proposition. While forty-nine percent of the respondents with favorable attitudes toward police behavior before the riots were willing to endorse a "get tough" policy at the start of the disorders, forty-one percent of those with previously unfavorable views of police conduct also expressed support for this technique. Appraisals of police activities during the violence, however, seemed to be somewhat more closely associated with opinions concerning riot control measures. Seventy-four percent of the respondents who said that police actions had improved also felt policemen "should have gotten tough right away," but seventy-eight percent of those who perceived police behavior as deteriorating during the riots thought that this policy "would have made matters worse." A display of police strength also was favored by fifty-four percent of the respondents whose attitudes about police conduct remained unchanged during the disorders. An examination of the earlier perceptions of residents who maintained consistent perspectives on police activities, however, disclosed another pattern. Persons who held favorable images of police conduct before the disorders and who had not altered their opinions during the riots were somewhat less likely to sanction a strategy involving the display of force than those who had not changed their previously unfavorable assessments of police behavior. Whereas only forty-nine percent of the former respondents favored a "get tough" policy, fifty-six percent of the latter group approved of this technique. Changing perceptions of police actions during the riots—in either a positive or a negative direction—apparently were related to opinions concerning riot control measures, but, among respondents whose attitudes remained relatively stable, persons who had approved of police conduct before the riots appeared to be somewhat more cautious about endorsing the display of force than those who disapproved of police behavior prior to the disorders.

Ghetto sentiments concerning riot control measures, however, may have been shaped both by perceptions of general police conduct and by other attitudes and experiences that emerged during the disorders. An effort, therefore, was made to examine the perceived reasons for the failure of police officers to utilize a display of force at the inception of the Detroit riots. When the residents of the Twelfth Street ghetto were asked why policemen had been unable to control the rioting during its initial phases, sixty-six percent stated that "they were not allowed to use enough force" and thirty-four percent simply said that "they were outnumbered by the crowds." Most ghetto residents appeared to attribute the principle blame for the growth of violence in Detroit to police inaction rather than to aggressive police behavior during the early stages of the riots.

Nonetheless, many respondents also seemed to chastise law enforcement agencies for the alleged use of of excessive force in ending the disorders. More than half, for example, asserted that the actions of policemen in stopping the riots were "too strong." The residents of the Twelfth Street neighborhood, therefore, seemed to demonstrate strong disapproval of the riot control techniques adopted by Detroit policemen both at the initial and at subsequent stages of the riots. Although nearly two-thirds of the residents apparently believed that police restraint in the use of force was a primary reason for their original failure to control the disorders, at least one-half also seemed to feel that police efforts to stop the rioting were overly repressive.

The responses, therefore, seemed to suggest that ghetto sentiments concerning both general riot control issues and the actual means employed by policemen to stop the Detroit riots may have been based upon hostile views of police inaction during the early phases of the disorders. Since most ghetto residents believed that policemen were under formal orders to exercise initial restraint, many persons who continued to hold favorable images of police conduct, as well as other respondents, may have felt that the display of force in a neighborhood that was basically hostile to police interference might simply have exacerbated the conflict or "made matters worse." On the other hand, residents who perceived that police officers were outnumbered at the beginning of the riots might have thought that increased police strength could have stopped the disturbances. Similarly, at subsequent stages of the violence, as the conflict escalated and as accounts of police misconduct began to spread throughout the neighborhood, persons who believed that policemen were previously restrained by departmental orders may have condemned law enforcement personnel for ultimately resorting to the use of unnecessary force in an effort to end the disorders, but those who felt that police officers were formerly outnumbered may have regarded their later actions as either inadequate or appropriate. This interpretation, therefore, seemed to suggest that antagonistic perceptions of early police restraint, as well as changing appraisals of police conduct during the disorders, may have been closely related to attitudes toward riot control measures both at the initial and at subsequent stages of the violence. Table 3 presents the associations between assessments of police restraint and opinions concerning riot control techniques among respondents with both stable and changing evaluations of police conduct before and during the riots.[6]

The analysis, however, did not appear to confirm this speculation regarding public criticism of the riot control techniques adopted by Detroit policemen. The apparent condemnation of police restraint in the use of force during the early stages of the riots actually may have been the basis for public approval of strong riot control measures. Although considerable care must be exercised in interpreting these data due to the small number of cases in many of the cells, the findings indicated that, among all respondents except those who felt that police behavior had deteriorated during the riots, ghetto residents who believed that police officers had been prevented from using sufficient force to quell the disturbances were more likely to endorse a "get tough" policy and to approve of the actions taken by Detroit policemen in stopping the riots than people who thought that police officers had been outnumbered by the crowds. With this one exception, therefore, residents of the Twelfth Street neighborhood who perceived police officers as adopting initial restraint were inclined to support active police intervention in the riots, regardless of their earlier assessments of police conduct. Even among respondents who had been highly critical of police actions before the riots and who had not changed their minds during the violence, for example, persons who felt that policemen had respected strict limits on the use of force were willing to approve relatively firm methods of controlling the

TABLE 3
PERCEIVED REASONS FOR POLICE RESTRAINT AND RIOT CONTROL ATTITUDES BY CHANGING PERCEPTIONS OF POLICE CONDUCT DURING THE DETROIT RIOTS

Changing Perceptions of Police Conduct During the Riots	Perceived Reasons for Police Restraint	Riot Control Attitudes					
		Use of Force During Detroit Riot:			Appraisals of the Display of Strength as a Riot Control Measure:		
		About Right or Not Strong Enough %	Too Strong %	n	Police Should Have Gotten Tough Right Away %	This Policy Would Have Made Matters Worse %	n
Improved	Police were outnumbered	0	100	5	20	80	5
	Police were not allowed to use sufficient force	71	29	12	94	6	16
Remained Good	Police were outnumbered	27	73	11	33	67	12
	Police were not allowed to use sufficient force	78	22	54	56	44	52
Remained Poor	Police were outnumbered	10	90	10	10	90	10
	Police were not allowed to use sufficient force	66	34	41	71	29	41
Deteriorated	Police were outnumbered	10	90	40	21	79	38
	Police were not allowed to use sufficient force	10	90	10	36	64	14

disorders. The issue of police restraint appeared to have little impact upon the attitudes of people who thought that police mistreatment had increased during the riots. Among the remaining respondents, however, the perception that policemen had used self-restraint in the early phases of the rioting seemed to be closely related to the acceptance of both an impressive display of force and strong measures to control the disorders.

Apparently, ghetto residents who had experienced a major riot were not unalterably opposed to police efforts to control the disorders. The principal opposition to firm riot control measures seemed to be centered among persons who felt that policemen had been initially outnumbered and those who believed that police conduct had deteriorated during the riots. The belief that the police department had imposed sharp limitations upon the use of force at the beginning of the Detroit riots, therefore, did not seem to represent a sweeping condemnation of police inaction. In fact, the appearance of police caution and restraint may have been an essential means of securing public respect for riot control activities.

The results of this investigation also appeared to suggest that, in carefully controlled circumstances, an impressive display of police strength could be an appropriate—and perhaps even an acceptable—riot control strategy. In general, respondents who did not perceive police behavior as deteriorating and who felt that policemen had obeyed preliminary orders to avoid the excessive use of force were prepared to endorse relatively strong riot control measures both initially and at later stages of the rioting. The exercise of restraint in the use of physical force and the avoidance of actions that could signify increasing police misconduct, therefore, may have been two basic prerequisites for a riot control policy that would gain the cooperation and support of ghetto residents.

CIVIL DISORDERS AND FUTURE POLICE AUTHORITY

The control of violence perhaps has been the major immediate task of law enforcement agencies in civil disorders, but the outbreak of ghetto disturbances has also imposed a heavy responsibility upon police officers after the rioting subsides. While existing animosities may have hampered attempts to control a serious riot, police actions during urban disorders also have seemed to increase the difficulty of restoring police authority in the ghetto afterwards. Thus police behavior in seeking to control riots may have had an important impact upon their subsequent ability to reimpose social control and to maintain order in a riot-torn ghetto neighborhood.

The results of the Twelfth Street area survey yielded little evidence that police conduct during the Detroit riots had enhanced local respect for law enforcement duties. Perhaps the most striking finding of the survey, for example, was that eighty-three percent of the black residents of the neighborhood reported hearing stories that some policemen during the riots "were involved in taking things or in burning stores." In addition, increasing hostility toward police officers seemed to be most prevalent among respondents who were sympathetic to the riots and who regarded violence as the most effective means of securing racial progress (see Hahn, 1969c). The outbreak of ghetto riots, therefore, may have tended to erode the legitimacy of police authority among those segments of the community that had been especially critical of police conduct before the riots started.

The growth of local resentment toward police officers during the riots seemed to pose a serious problem for police departments both in avoiding future disorders and in regaining the faith and confidence of ghetto residents. Since assessments of departmental limits on the use of force were closely related to positions on riot control issues, an effort was made to examine the impact of perceptions of police restraint upon expectations concerning police behavior in the future. As a measure of increasing optimism or pessimism about police conduct, respondents were classified by their evaluations of police activities before and after the riots in a manner similar to the categories that were used to code the differences in their attitudes prior to and during the disorders. Table 4 presents the association between appraisals of police restraint and changing perceptions of police behavior in the aftermath of the riots.

Apparently increasing pessimism about police conduct after the disorders was associated with the belief that police officers had not exercised restraint in the use of force during the early stages of the rioting.

TABLE 4

PERCEIVED REASONS FOR POLICE RESTRAINT AND CHANGING PERCEPTIONS OF POLICE CONDUCT AFTER THE DETROIT RIOTS
(in percentages)

Perceived reasons for police restraint	Changing Perceptions of Police Conduct After the Detroit Riots			
	Will Improve	Will Remain Good	Will Remain Poor	Will Deteriorate
Police were out-numbered	20	26	44	83
Police were not allowed to use sufficient force	80	74	56	17
n	69	61	55	18

Respondents who predicted that police actions would deteriorate or remain poor in the future tended to attribute the failure of the police to stop the riots initially to the fact that they were outnumbered, but those who foresaw improvements or continually favorable police conduct generally believed that law enforcement personnel had observed departmental limitations upon the use of force. The application of police restraint, therefore, may have been an important requirement not only for securing public acceptance of riot control measures but also for restoring social controls in the ghetto after the violence had ended.

SUMMARY

The outbreak of civil disorders in many of the nation's major cities has confronted police departments with serious problems and major obligations. Surveys of ghetto areas that exploded in major riots have disclosed overwhelming and intense animosity toward the policemen that patrol those neighborhoods. Moreover, during urban disorders, police officers usually have become primary targets of local hostility both in the precipitating incidents that sparked the disturbances and at later stages of the rioting. Nonetheless, police officers have been compelled to assume the tasks not only of controlling the disorders but also of maintaining order in those communities after the rioting has subsided. The duties assigned to law enforcement agencies in civil disorders perhaps have been among the most difficult responsibilities that have been bestowed upon any branch of local government.

The results of the survey conducted in the Twelfth Street neighborhood of Detroit, however, indicated that, while the problems facing police officers in the ghetto may have been immense, they might not have been totally insoluble. Although an overwhelming proportion of the black respondents expressed a deep distrust of law enforcement activities, for example, some evidence suggested that police behavior was widely regarded as a contributing rather than a primary source of ghetto discontent. The data did reveal that segments of the community confronting major economic adversity, such as unemployed black youths, were generally viewed as the principal objects of police mistreatment. But this finding also seemed to suggest that the modification of some police practices such as the policy of "preventive patrolling" might have reduced mutual tensions and antagonisms between policemen and members of the community who were regarded as active in civil disorders.

Police action or inaction during the riots also seemed to promote the growth of public resistance to the efforts of law enforcement officers to contain disturbances. However, only a small fraction of the respondents felt that, in moving into the principal scene of the rioting, police officers "should have waited longer and let people in the area try to handle it." On the other hand, the residents of the Twelfth Street area were evenly divided by the issue of employing a prompt mobilization of police strength as a method of riot control.

Although the attitudes of ghetto residents toward riot control measures have appeared to be intensely critical, this investigation indicated that, at least in a major riot such as the civil disorders in Detroit, a sizeable proportion of the community was willing to accept both an impressive display of strength and relatively strong measures to control the disorders, provided that police imposed strict restraints upon the use of force and that police conduct was not perceived as deteriorating during the riots. From the perspective of many ghetto residents, those two imperatives seemed to be basic and essential conditions for the success of riot control measures. In other situations, perhaps the total withdrawal of police personnel from a riot area might have been an effective method of containing civil disturbances. When circumstances seem to require the mobilization of police manpower, however, the results of the Detroit survey appeared to suggest that this strategy might gain public approval or cooperation only if police officers are restrained from using excessive force and from engaging in behavior that could be perceived as denoting increased police mistreatment of local residents.

The exercise of self-restraint in controlling civil disorders seemed to offer another major advantage for law enforcement agencies. Ghetto residents who appeared optimistic about police activities in the future generally had regarded policemen as obeying limits on the use of force during the initial stages of the rioting, but those who were pessimistic tended to attribute police inaction to other causes. The belief that policemen had adopted restraint in the use of force during a major riot, therefore, may have provided an important means of overcoming local hostility and of regaining public confidence in police authority after the rioting had ended.

Although this study has focused upon perceptions of the role of policemen in civil disorders, it also appeared to contain implications concerning police practices at other times. Despite the overwhelming distrust that has developed between the police officers and urban minorities, public approval of law enforcement activities in ghetto neighborhoods has not been entirely absent. Even in a major upheaval such as the Detroit riots, many black citizens seemed willing to accept relatively firm police action to restore order. By exercising restraint in the use of force, policemen may have been able to secure the respect of local residents that was necessary to control the disorders. Similarly, during periods that are not marked by serious violence, attempts to develop a basis of support for law enforcement duties may require major changes or modifications in police procedures. The effort to gain public support for police work in urban ghettos, however, might not be a hopeless task. In fact, it may be one of the most important goals that law enforcement agencies can adopt.

NOTES

1. The panel surveys of 1965 and 1966 were supported by general research support grants from the University of Michigan School of Public Health, and the 1967 survey was supported by a special grant from the University of Michigan. Field work and interviewing for the 1965 and 1966 surveys were performed by National Analysts, Inc. and the National Opinion Research Center of the University of Chicago, respectively. Interviews for the 1967 survey were collected by the Market Opinion Research Corporation of Detroit, which also conducted the Detroit *News* Poll.

2. Residents of the Twelfth Street ghetto also did not regard police officers as incorruptible. In response to another question, approximately ninety percent asserted that "most Detroit policemen break the rules for their personal gain."

3. The measures of police mistreatment and riot involvement were obtained from two questions which asked respondents to evaluate the manner in which each of the five groups was treated by Detroit policemen before the disorders and the extent to which each group was involved in the riots. Responses to the questions were assigned unweighted scores ranging from zero to four denoting the severity of police mistreatment (very bad, poor, not good, good) and the scope of riot involvement (a great deal, somewhat, very little, not at all) for each of the groups. Kendall's r was used in calculating the coefficients of correlation between the two measures. Missing data were omitted from this analysis.

4. The three groups, of course, were young blacks who are out of work, persons who speak out for black power, and black homeowners. Whites who live in the neighborhood and black teenagers were omitted from this analysis. The identification of black homeowners, of course, did not present a serious problem. For the purposes of this study, however, unemployed black youths were arbitrarily identified as persons under thirty-five years of age with irregular employment records; black power advocates were roughly defined as persons who supported violence as a means of securing racial progress and who endorsed black separatism. Although the simple coefficient of correlation between perceived police mistreatment and riot participation for unemployed black youths was considerably stronger among persons who were identified with this group (+.39) than among nonmembers (+.08), none of the remaining coefficients of correlations reflected similar differences between the perceptions of members and nonmembers, and all of them were inverse.

5. Some support for this perception was provided by research (Fogelson and Hill, 1968: 236) which indicated that a relatively high proportion of persons arrested in the disorders of 1967 were unemployed.

6. As a general measure of changing assessments of police behavior, respondents in the Twelfth Street area initially were classified into four major groups: persons who believed that police conduct had improved during the riots, ghetto residents whose perceptions of police actions remained generally favorable, those who continued to hold unfavorable images of police behavior, and people who thought that police activities deteriorated or grew worse during the violence. Table 3 examines the intervening effect of perceptions of police restraint upon attitudes toward riot control measures among each of these groups.

REFERENCES

APPLEGATE, R. (1969) Riot Control: Material and Techniques. Harrisburg, Pa.: Stackpole Books.

BAYLEY, D. H. and H. MENDELSOHN (1969) Minorities and the Police. New York: Free Press.

CAMPBELL, A. and H. SCHUMAN (1968) "Racial attitudes in fifteen American cities," pp. 1-69 in Supplemental Studies for the National Advisory Commission on Civil Disorders. Washington, D. C.: U.S. Government Printing Office.

CONANT, R.W. (1968) "Rioting, insurrection and civil disobedience." Amer. Scholar 37 (Summer): 420-433.

FEAGIN, J. R. and P. B. SHEATSLEY (1968) "Ghetto resident appraisals of a riot." Public Opinion Q. 32 (Fall): 352-362.

FOGELSON, R. M. (1968) "From resentment to confrontation: the police, the Negroes, and the outbreak of the nineteen-sixties riots." Pol. Sci. Q. 83 (June): 217-247.

--- and R. B. HILL (1968) "Who riots? a study of participation in the 1967 riots," pp. 217-248 in Supplemental Studies for the National Advisory Commission on Civil Disorders. Washington, D. C.: U.S. Government Printing Office.

GRIMSHAW, A. D. (1969) "Actions of police and military in American race riots," pp. 269-287 in A. D. Grimshaw (ed.) Racial Violence in the United States. Chicago: Aldine.

HAHN, H. (1969a) "Philosophy of law and urban violence." Soundings 52 (Spring): 110-117.

--- (1969b) "Ghetto sentiments on violence." Sci. & Society 33 (Spring): 197-208.

--- (1969c) "The political objectives of ghetto riots." Presented at the annual meeting of the American Political Science Association, New York.

--- (1969d) "Violence: the view from the ghetto." Mental Hygiene 53 (October): 509-512.

--- and J. R. FEAGIN (1970) "Riot-precipitating police practices: attitudes in urban ghettos." Phylon (forthcoming).

HERSEY, J. (1968) The Algiers Motel Incident. New York: Alfred A. Knopf.

HUNDLEY, J. R., Jr., (1968) "The dynamics of recent ghetto riots." J. of Urban Law 45 (Spring-Summer): 627-639.

JANOWITZ, M. (1968) Social Control of Escalated Riots. Chicago: University of Chicago Center for Policy Study.

Kerner Commission (1968) Report of the National Advisory Commission on Civil Disorders. New York: Bantam Books.

KRAFT, J. F. (1966) "The attitudes of Negroes in various cities," pp. 1383-1423 in Vol. 6 of Federal Role in Urban Affairs, Hearings before the Subcomittee on Executive Reorganization, Committee on Government Operations, U.S. Senate, Washington, D. C.: U.S. Government Printing Office.

LEVY, B. (1968) "Cops in the ghetto: a problem of the police system." Amer. Behavioral Scientist 11 (March-April): 31-34.

LUPSHA, P. A. (1969) "On theories of urban violence." Urban Affairs Q. 4 (March): 273-296.

McCORD, W. and J. HOWARD (1968) "Negro opinions in three riot cities." Amer. Behavioral Scientist 11 (March-April): 24-27.

MARX, G. T. (1967) Protest and Prejudice. New York: Harper & Row.

MEYER, P. (1967) "The people beyond Twelfth Street." Detroit Free Press (August 20).

MOMBOISSE, R. M. (1967) Riots, Revolts and Insurrections. Springfield, Ill.: Charles C Thomas.

RAINE, W. J. (1967) The Perception of Police Brutality in South Central Los Angeles. Los Angeles: UCLA Institute of Government and Public Affairs.

SKOLNICK, J. H. (1969) The Politics of Protest. New York: Ballantine Books.

WALKER, D. (1968) Rights in Conflict. A Report Submitted to the National Commission on the Causes and Prevention of Violence. New York: Bantam Books.

PART THREE

Police Perceptions of Public Issues

Police Perceptions of Public Issues

Perhaps the most critical test of the effectiveness of police work is reflected in the relationship between law enforcement officers and members of the public. In fact, the performance of many police functions, including the control of crime and other duties, could be determined by the nature of interactions between policemen and private citizens. Yet, the outcome of those encounters may be shaped both by public assessments of police practices and by police sentiments on public conduct. Contacts between law enforcement officers and civilians can represent either mutual animosity and suspicion or mutual cooperation and respect. As a result, the study of police perceptions of the public, as well as public appraisals of the police, seems to constitute a necessary approach to the examination of law enforcement problems.

The growth of extensive public hostility toward police behavior and the outbreak of major violence in many American cities have appeared to provide clear and dramatic evidence of the necessity for increased communication and understanding between policemen and urban residents. But the survey conducted by Robert A. Mendelsohn of police responses to the Detroit riots disclosed relatively little awareness of this issue. Many law enforcement officers below the highest ranks in police departments apparently have failed to recognize the need for improving police-community relations. In expressing their views about both the causes and the cures for urban riots, most policemen emphasized the adoption of strong measures of social control rather than the amelioration of ghetto conditions. Although the attitudes of higher-echelon officers could form the basis of increased police-community relations programs, the results of the study seemed to imply that those efforts might be seriously impeded by the sentiments of policemen who patrol urban neighborhoods.

The judgments formed by police officers in ghetto areas, as well as elsewhere, may be affected both by their prior predispositions and by the circumstances that they confront in the community. Since opinions founded upon personal attributes might be more resistant to change than viewpoints based upon social conditions or events, the relative influence of those factors could have a critical effect upon the reciprocal perceptions of policemen and the people. In a study of 522 policemen assigned to ghetto areas in 13 American cities, W. Eugene Groves and Peter H. Rossi investigate characteristics such as race, age, rank, feelings of racial prejudice, acquaintance with local residents, and city differences that may mold police appraisals of ghetto hostility. By finding that personal traits exert a greater impact upon police perceptions than features of the community, the implications of this research also seem to underscore the potential difficulty of improving police-community relations.

In addition to forming individual opinions about public conduct, however, law enforcement officers may comprise a critical linkage between the population and the civil authorities. The function of policemen as boundary personnel is examined by Howard Aldrich and Albert J. Reiss, Jr., in a survey of police officers and small businessmen in Boston, Chicago, and Washington, D.C. The conclusions of this investigation of similarities in the sentiments of both groups regarding the controversy over "law and order" also appear to contain important omens for the resolution of law enforcement issues. Policemen not only develop images of city residents that affect the performance of their duties, but they also might play a major role in the transmission of attitudes toward the public and toward political leaders. The sentiments of police officers, therefore, may exert a crucial impact upon the eventual outcome of the pressing problems that confront both the community and law enforcement agencies.

Police-Community Relations

A Need in Search of Police Support

ROBERT A. MENDELSOHN
Department of Mental Health, State of Michigan

As the society responds to changes in technology, increased educational levels, redistribution of population centers, admission to civil society of previously excluded groups, and a host of other structural phenomena, so does the role and method of operation of the police. One major consequence of these trends for the police has been to place them under considerably more restraint than was true even a short time ago (Bordua, 1968; President's Commission on Law Enforcement and Administration of Justice, 1967b). Thus, it would be reasonable to assume that instances of "police brutality" are less frequent than in the past, and that police officers are less able to administer "street justice." Though officers may complain about the role of Supreme Court decisions and the activities of civil liberties groups in these changes, their real source lies in the far-ranging developments listed above. A second major result of these broad social changes has been an increasing demand, among the black

Author's Note: *The research on the Detroit Police Department reported herein was supported by a grant from the National Institute of Mental Health. The author wishes to acknowledge the contribution to the police study of numerous colleagues, most notably Elliot Luby, M.D.; James Hedegard, Ph.D.; and Sue Smock, M.S. Appreciation is expressed to former Police Commissioner Ray Girardin and officers of the Detroit Police Department without whose cooperation the study would not have been possible.*

citizenry, for improved police services combined with an increasing impatience and anger at police for real and imagined mistreatment of citizens. A third major consequence has been the impetus for increasing police professionalization. This in effect is an attempt to transfer the motivating forces on officers from control by a given subcommunity to internalized standards of conduct. These standards are presumably derived from the canons of effective and responsible police work.

POLICE-COMMUNITY NEGATIVISM

All these changes increase the stress on the police by disrupting traditional methods of operation or by requiring an increased degree of contact with, and understanding of, negatively viewed groups.

Yet it is reasonably clear that, unless a disastrous and panicky repression sets in, these are the trends of the future, if for no other reason than they are consistent with trends in the larger society.[1] In fact, moreover, the potential for improving police work that resides in these trends is quite substantial. It is a truism that effective police work requires the support of the community. As the President's Commission (1967b: 144) puts it:

> Even if fairer treatment of minority groups were the sole consideration, police departments would have an obligation to attempt to achieve and maintain good police-community relations. In fact, however, much more is at stake. Police-community relationships have a direct bearing on the character of life in our cities, and on the community's ability to maintain stability and to solve its problems. At the same time, the police department's capacity to deal with crime depends to a large extent upon its relationship with the citizenry. Indeed, no lasting improvement in law enforcement is likely in this country unless police-community relations are substantially improved. . . . A dissatisfied public will not support the police enthusiastically . . . when the police and public are at odds, the police tend to become isolated from the public and become less capable of understanding and adapting to the community and its changing needs. . . . Poor police-community relations adversely affect the ability of the police to prevent crime and apprehend criminals.

While no one would be naive enough to believe that improved police-community relations will in themselves, given the multiple causes of crime and riots, eliminate these disruptive events, it is difficult to see how much can be done without a change in police attitudes toward the black community.

The truism, unfortunately, may be a truism for only a minority of officers. Within the department in Detroit, there was, following the riot, a most striking absence of concern with the importance of police-community relations as a riot deterrent.[2] There was also a lack of appreciation of the role police play in contributing to riot etiology. Strikingly illustrative of this disinterest are the responses to the question, "What needs to be done to prevent future riots?"[3] although responses to other questions would perhaps do as well. As can be seen, until the inspector and above rank (labelled "inspectors")[4] is attained, there is no support whatever among white officers for improved police-community relations; indeed, far and away the most popular response calls for a better trained, better equipped, and larger force, and "stricter" law enforcement.[5] Certainly, there is little in this to suggest that there is any comprehension of, much less support for, the idea, which I will advocate, that the role of the police should include close ties with persons in the community, considerable openness to public scrutiny, increased community service, and a major advocacy role for the disadvantaged and oppressed.

The irony of this reaction is that the police, despite a self-conception that their role is one of apprehending law-breakers and keeping blacks in

TABLE 1

WHAT NEEDS TO BE DONE TO PREVENT FUTURE RIOTS?

(in percentages)

Race[a]	White					Black
Rank[b]	Insp. (n=93)	Lt. (n=41)	Sgt. (n=52)	Det. (n=60)	Ptr. (n=113)	All Ranks (n=54)
Program						
Law and/or more efficient police	21.5	43.9	55.8	66.7	65.5	18.5
Social action (e.g., education, better race relations)	37.7	31.7	25.0	20.0	25.6	46.3
Improve police-community relations	19.4	4.9	3.8	3.3	0.0	13.0
Other	21.5	19.5	15.4	10.0	8.8	22.2
TOTAL	100.1	100.0	100.0	100.0	99.9	100.0

a. Although the views of black officers are not the main focus of this paper, it is instructive to examine the difference in views of white and black officers. Accordingly, the views of black officers are included in this and the other tables.

b. The data in the table record the first two reasons mentioned by the respondents. Accordingly it is a table of responses rather than subjects. Those officers who responded with "don't know" or not applicable answers are not included. This was the case for four inspectors, five lieutenants, six sergeants, seven detectives, nineteen patrolmen, and two black officers.

their place (Edwards, 1968), in fact, probably provide more essential services to lower-class residents than most other governmental service organizations. Intervention in family quarrels, running an "ambulance service" working with troubled youth, and a large variety of other responsibilities consume more police time than the apprehension of criminals. As can be seen even by this superficial recitation, many of these are among the most difficult or most undesirable to be found in large cities. Yet it is the police who perform these services, not the professionals who flee the city after daylight hours. Furthermore, even though many police officers think of themselves as functioning to control the black population, it is probably easier, as Bordua (1968) has pointed out, for a ghetto resident to obtain a needed service from the police than from a teacher, a social worker, a housing inspector, a psychiatrist, or a sanitation man. More specifically, then, the irony is that the police are already providing many of the services that potentially form the basis for an effective police-community interaction but cannot grasp its implications for improving their effectiveness in the area of crime control—the very area in which their conception of police work requires them to be effective.

The failure to make the connection between police-community relations and the perceived role of the police in crime prevention and control may be attributed to two main factors. First, the average officer is undereducated and the ability to perceive what is, after all, a complex connection requires analytical abilities that are distinctively functions of education. As Skolnick (1969) has pointed out, the average officer joining the force is less educated than his civilian peers, and the educational level of officers has actually been declining since the Depression.[6] It is this, rather than the assumed authoritarian character structure of the officer, that matters. In fact, while studies of police officers' personalities are rare, the available evidence (Niederhoffer, 1967)[7] would indicate that officers, on joining the force, are not particularly authoritarian. They are, however, certainly conventional and become authoritarian and cynical as they continue with the force.

The second main factor blocking improved police-community relations is the police attitude toward the people with whom they would have to frankly and intimately interact if they are to develop an effective program. Numerous studies presented or reviewed in Skolnick (1966, 1969) have clearly shown that many, indeed most, police officers manifest considerable anti-black feeling and find it difficult to avoid viewing themselves, literally, as front line troops against the rebellious and uncivilized blacks. To be sure, white police officers are not particularly different from working-class whites in general in this anti-black feeling; rather perhaps, the average officer is more direct in his verbal utterances than the equivocating, but just as hostile, civilian.

The study in Detroit provides some of the dimensions of this dislike. The typical white officer, lieutenant and below, interprets the motives for the riot in predominantly negative terms. He clearly does not see it as a meaningless event but, rather, as a reflection of the undisciplined, hostile or morally corrupt nature of the black community. This is shown in Table 2. This interpretation is consistent with his general view of the black community. As Table 3 shows, he sees the black community as a privileged minority which, rather than rebelling against white authority, obviously ought to be grateful to that authority. Furthermore, he sees the lower-class black community as manifesting relatively little respect for law and order. This comparison takes on more significance when it is compared to his view of the white community. These data are presented in Table 4.[8]

TABLE 2

**WHAT DO YOU THINK WAS THE LONG TERM
CAUSE OF THE RIOT?**

(in percentages)

Race	White					Black
Rank[a]	Insp. (n=94)	Lt. (n=40)	Sgt. (n=43)	Det. (n=49)	Ptr. (n=104)	All Ranks (n=53)
Cause						
Persons (e.g., agitators, militants)	18.1	22.5	14.0	14.3	26.9	9.4
Undisciplined self-interest (e.g., something for nothing)	6.4	10.0	32.6	26.5	17.3	11.3
Protest (e.g., frustration, jobs, mistreatment)	43.6	17.5	20.9	20.4	22.1	54.7
Temper of the times (e.g., violence elsewhere, no respect for authority)	27.6	50.0	27.9	34.7	31.7	24.5
Other	4.2	0.0	4.6	4.1	1.9	0.0
TOTAL	99.9	100.0	100.0	100.0	99.9	99.9

a. The data in the table record the first two reasons mentioned by the respondents. Accordingly, it is a table of responses rather than subjects. Those officers who responded with "don't know" or not applicable answers are not included. This was the case for five inspectors, nine sergeants, three detectives, fifteen patrolmen, and five black officers.

TABLE 3

HERE IS A LIST OF AREAS IN WHICH SOME PEOPLE SAY
NEGROES ARE NOT TREATED FAIRLY. DO YOU THINK
THEY ARE TREATED VERY UNFAIRLY, SLIGHTLY UNFAIRLY,
THE SAME AS WHITES, OR THAT THINGS ARE ACTUALLY
IN THEIR FAVOR?

(in percentages)

Race	White					Black
Rank	Insp. (n=59)	Lt. (n=33)	Sgt. (n=36)	Det. (n=36)	Ptr. (n=86)	All Ranks (n=36)
Area						
Housing						
VU	24	12	22	6	12	67
U	34	39	39	28	29	25
S	30	33	25	56	37	3
F	10	12	14	11	19	3
DK, NA	2	3	0	0	3	3
Schools						
VU	3	0	0	0	0	47
U	7	6	3	3	0	33
S	44	45	31	33	40	14
F	41	48	67	64	59	3
DK, NA	5	0	0	0	1	3
Jobs						
VU	15	3	11	6	5	56
U	25	18	14	22	17	33
S	30	36	44	56	43	8
F	29	42	31	17	31	0
DK, NA	0	0	0	0	3	3
Welfare Agencies						
VU	0	0	0	0	0	8
U	2	0	0	0	0	19
S	25	15	14	11	10	39
F	64	79	83	86	86	28
DK, NA	8	6	3	3	3	6
Stores						
VU	12	3	8	0	1	22
U	5	9	8	8	13	33
S	71	76	72	86	70	36
F	5	9	8	6	13	3
DK, NA	7	3	3	0	3	6
Law Enforcement Agencies						
VU	2	0	6	0	0	56
U	14	15	14	3	7	31
S	68	55	53	72	57	6
F	14	30	28	25	34	3
DK, NA	3	0	0	0	2	6

TABLE 4

MEAN PERCEIVED SCORES ON RESPECT FOR LAW AND ORDER
(at the present time) IN MIDDLE-CLASS AND
SLUM COMMUNITIES BY RACE

Race			White			Black
Rank	Insp.	Lt.	Sgt.	Det.	Ptr.	All Ranks
Group						
Black middle class	6.8	6.5	6.3	6.4	6.0	7.0
White middle class	8.0	7.6	7.6	7.8	7.6	7.4
Black slum	4.1	2.6	2.4	2.6	2.0	3.0
White slum	4.7	3.7	3.6	4.3	3.3	4.1

Finally, the officer's view of citizen hostility toward him as an officer shows a clear differentiation between white and black. He is not unsympathetic toward white hostility, as Table 5 shows, but he interprets black hostility (Table 6) in highly negative terms with relatively little insight into its likely causes or the police contribution. This interpretation is, of course, consistent with a warfare view of his relations with the black community and with his other views which have been presented above.

TABLE 5

MANY PEOPLE HAVE NOTED THAT THE AVERAGE WHITE
CITIZEN OFTEN HAS NEGATIVE FEELINGS TOWARD THE
POLICE. WHY DO YOU THINK THEY FEEL THAT WAY?
(in percentages)

Race	White				Black
Rank[a]	Lt. (n=33)	Sgt. (n=36)	Det. (n=36)	Ptr. (n=86)	All Ranks (n=36)
Reason					
Antisocial nature of white community	12.1	2.8	5.6	8.1	11.1
Unpleasant experiences; everyone hates authority a little bit	57.6	69.4	52.8	48.8	41.7
Statement not true	15.2	8.3	11.1	18.6	11.1
Other	15.2	11.1	16.7	18.6	22.2
DK, NA	0.0	8.3	13.9	5.8	13.9
TOTAL	100.1	99.9	100.1	99.9	100.0

a. Unfortunately, inspectors and above ranks were not asked this question.

TABLE 6

A RECENT SURVEY IN THE *FREE PRESS* FOUND THAT
A MAJORITY OF NEGROES IN THE RIOT AREAS
FELT THAT POLICE BEHAVIOR TOWARD NEGROES
WAS A MAJOR CAUSE OF THE RIOT.
WHY DO YOU THINK THEY FEEL THAT WAY?
(in percentages)

Race	White					Black
Rank	Insp. (n=59)	Lt. (n=33)	Sgt. (n=36)	Det. (n=36)	Ptr. (n=86)	All Ranks (n=36)
Reason						
Police behavior or perception of police behavior by Negroes[a] (e.g., Negroes treated unfairly)	54.2[b]	27.3	19.4	19.4	19.8	69.4
Antisocial nature of black community (e.g., no respect for law and order; more Negroes are criminals)	0.0	33.3	55.6	50.0	39.5	5.6
Statement is not true	15.2	6.1	11.1	11.1	11.6	5.6
Other	23.7	18.2	8.3	8.3	19.8	19.4
DK, NA	6.8	15.2	5.6	11.1	9.3	0.0
TOTAL	99.9	100.1	100.0	99.9	100.0	100.0

a. Very few white officers believe that police *in fact* discriminate against blacks with the exception of inspectors (see note b). Most of the officers responding within this category are saying that Negroes *feel* police discriminate. Black officers reverse the explanation. The majority responding in this category believe police *in fact* do discriminate.

b. Half the inspectors responding in this category state blacks feel the way they do because the police represent the power structure. Only inspectors give this reason.

Summing up, the typical white officer (below the rank of inspector[9]) views the black community as a privileged minority, unsatisfied with its already privileged position and prepared to use violence[10] to attain still further advantage over the white community. The community is perceived, further, as susceptible to the influence of agitators capable of galvanizing into action a people without real grievances. Finally, the black community is viewed as deficient in respect for law and order. Implicit in this view is a conception of the black community as primitive, emotional, and easily aroused to antisocial action, and with an ultimate goal of domination over whites rather than a goal of equality.[11]

This is, of course, not to say that he acts on this conception in all his interactions while on duty. Quite the contrary—most of the time, as Skolnick (1966) has pointed out in his discussion of the warrant policeman, practical considerations play a major role. Further, the professional standards to which most officers strive to adhere are of great influence. But obviously an officer carrying around such a view of the black community is going to act on it at some points. For example, a view of blacks as hostile toward him predisposes an officer to use unnecessary force when he interprets the situation as threatening. In turn, what he decides to be threatening is a function, in part, of his generalized belief system about the black community. If he is wrong, or at times even when he is right, the resulting police-community tensions can have far-reaching and explosive consequences. In terms of the concern of this paper, however, even if he is able to behave judiciously despite these views, they hardly would incline him toward concern with improving police-community relations, and that is, as I have been arguing, a critical need.

These beliefs, then, make such far-reaching programs for police-community relations, as proposed by the President's Commission (1967b) and Bordua (1968), most difficult, perhaps impossible, to attain. The following considerations complicate adequate solution still further: (1) the increasing crime rate[12] with its demands for more vigorous police control despite the likely failure of such tactics to affect the crime rate in the long run (Menninger, 1968); (2) the pervasive feeling among officers that theirs is a disrespected profession[13] (Wilson, 1963; President's Commission, 1967b) with its concomitant and resulting reinforcement of in-group loyalties and alienation from the larger society; and (3) the reluctance of the police to add still another "disrespected" group to the list of police responsibilities. It thus becomes apparent that implementation of an effective and revolutionary program in police-community relations is highly problematical. Still, given the strategic importance of the police, an effort must be made.

Such an effort must begin where there are positive potentials at work. These may be identified as follows. First, from the black side, there is an increasing demand for better police services. Studies reported by the President's Commission (1967b) clearly indicate that a majority of blacks would support, indeed desperately want, a fair and effective police presence. This is hardly surprising since it is predominantly blacks who are the victims of crime.

Second, there is, among many—particularly higher echelon—officers, some recognition of the need for effective police-community relations and a corresponding realization that the police contribute, at least in some measure, to the problems in the community. For example, sixty-six percent of officers of the rank of inspector agree with the statement that "the behavior of the police in the past has contributed to the tense situation that exists in the Negro areas of the city." Sixty-nine percent of inspectors favor increased police involvement with the community. Furthermore, these officers have a positive view of the purpose of police-community relations work. Twenty-nine percent of inspectors hope such programs will produce closer contact between police and community or open lines of communication, seventeen percent feel it would let people present their problems and complaints to the police, forty-nine percent believe it would promote better understanding of *each other's problems* and improve police relations with the black community, and seventeen percent think it would help in the pursuit of solutions to police and community problems that are mutually acceptable. By contrast, very few inspectors cite using such contacts as an intelligence source, to promote a positive police "image," or to get citizens to respect law and order. Finally, fully eighty-one percent of these executive officers thought the police should do more in the way of police-community relations.[14] Fifty-four percent of those who believed more should be done felt it should take the form of increased involvement in community affairs, many advocating more meetings with citizens' groups.[15]

Among lower-echelon officers, there is considerably less support but, even here, a majority of officers state that they favor a human relations approach toward the black community. It is doubtful that this support goes very deep but it may be something on which to build. In addition, there is some evidence from Niederhoffer that many officers begin their police careers with some idealism and desire to help others. While his data clearly show that most of this idealism is lost, it may be possible to recapture it. Suggestions for how this might be done are presented below.

RECAPTURING THE IDEALISM

Considering the balance of positive and negative forces, presented here, affecting the development of an effective police-community relations program, the conclusion must be that to date the negative forces predominate. If this situation is to change, a number of steps are required.

First, there must be an explicit redefinition of the police role, reinforced by strongly supported professional norms. This redefinition would conform with what police in fact do in providing public service. Explicit recognition must be given to the police responsibility for assisting citizens who lack resources or sufficient power to obtain such resources. Equally important, the redefinition of the police role must provide a rationale for the importance of this work from both a general humanitarian and a practical point of view. This is to say, the officer needs to learn the connection between good community relations and greater effectiveness in crime control. Given the attitudes of most officers, it is difficult to see how this redefinition can be accomplished without strong professional norms supporting such activity. Professional norms would also shield the police, to some extent, from those groups in the community that reflect antipathy toward black Americans. Another way to put this last point is that so long as the police permit themselves to be used to carry out the mandate of large segments of the white population, they will always be cast in the role of victimizers and victimized. They will carry out the mandate of the white citizenry but unlike the citizenry cannot avoid that policy's implications. They thus become the visible representatives of the white power structure, a point not lost on a number of police administrators.[16]

There is good reason to believe that those professional norms which implicitly require officers to disengage themselves from a firmly held set of attitudes before they take action will not be easily inculcated. As Wilson has pointed out, police officers' conception of their roles is often at variance with idealized professional norms. For example, many officers regard violence as a way of instilling "respect" for police, a belief that most professionally oriented officers would reject. In addition, there are some professional norms that fly in the face of the hostility many officers feel toward blacks. Both impediments to the adoption of professional norms do not seem to be functions of specific police experience with black citizens.[17] Rather they come from attitudes learned from their primary reference groups in the process of growing up in a society that discriminates against black Americans and from generalized police tradition and attitudes. Since police agencies have no control over the early socialization experiences of the men who become officers, it is they who must take primary responsibility for the education of their officers.

This discussion leads to the second and third recommendations. There must be increased university training for police officers and more effective in-service training programs. Such programs will provide the intellectual background for understanding the centrality of police-community relations. As indicated earlier, the need for increased education has been recognized by the Detroit Police Department. Third, it is absolutely essential that command and executive officers reward, through promotion and other positive reinforcements, officers who exemplify good relations with the community and who innovate new techniques for improved relations. Of all the steps that can be taken, none may be more potent than reward by superiors of officers who exemplify commitment to positive community attitudes.

A fourth recommendation is that a program of research must be vigorously undertaken to evaluate the effect of new (and old) programs pertaining to police-community relations. Nothing succeeds like demonstrated success. Research may provide that evidence of success. This means that close ties between the police and the academic community must be vigorously established.

Finally, innovation and willingness to try new ideas in the area of police-community relations must be strongly rewarded. Included must be a recognition that old solutions are not adequate. The following are several programs suggested by Bordua and briefly noted here. They really deserve complete discussion but are presented mainly to provide an idea as to what innovation might involve. Police must be willing to talk with all groups in the community, including militants. As the most visible representatives of law and order, they must make that role more than a euphemism for repression by adopting an advocacy role in regard to the poor and disadvantaged. Police must expand and professionalize their Youth Bureaus. To earn the confidence of the community, they must develop a citizen observer program (with observers recruited from all political groups). They must know community mores and through careful program and operations analysis determine which police practices offend such mores without commensurate pay-off in crime reduction or decrease in police-community tensions.

The police are inevitably and inextricably involved in the black community. The sole question is how they will relate to that community. While obviously substantially improved police-community relations will be just one factor in reducing both urban crime and the likelihood of further riots, it is a certainty that the way the police handle their relations with the black community will play a major role in the direction that American cities take.

NOTES

1. Bordua argues that there has been a relative shift from coercion as a method of social control. He cites human relations approaches to industrial management, child rearing techniques, and other evidence. He goes on to argue that social control is becoming more and more "distributive" in nature. Included in this latter category are economic sanctions, persuasion, and a vast array of welfare state programs.

2. Although it may be argued that these responses occurred two years ago and in response to a cataclysmic event, it is the author's belief that the beliefs expressed in these responses are stable and have not changed markedly in two years. Probably

some shifts in belief have occurred in this time span but whatever shifts have occurred are hardly commensurate with the need.

3. This question and all other data from Detroit referred to in this paper come from a survey on police attitudes, particularly about the riot of 1967, carried out from November 1967 through March 1968. A random sample, stratified by rank and race, were exhaustively questioned on riot interpretation, police response to the riot, police work in general, attitudes toward both blacks and whites, morale, and police-community relations. In addition, the usual demographic material was obtained along with a variety of responses to the officers' status and hopes. The white officers interviewed were fifty-seven inspectors and executives, thirty-three lieutenants, thirty-six sergeants, thirty-six detectives, and eighty-six patrolmen. The black officers interviewed included thirty-eight officers. In the tables, the thirty-six black officers of rank of lieutenant and below are not differentiated by rank. The number of black officers in each rank is too small for such a breakdown. The two black inspectors are included with the inspectors. For further details, see Mendelsohn (1969).

4. Inspectors include officers from the highest professional rank, the superintendant, to various executives and to those with the rank of "inspector." This group as a whole generally exercises command and executive functions. For example, an inspector will ordinarily be in command of a precinct. Lieutenants are superior to sergeants who, in turn, are superior to patrolmen, the lowest rank. If assigned to a precinct, a lieutenant may command a platoon. Detectives may be of various ranks but in the sample of this study, they do not carry additional rank such as detective sergeant. Those with ranks of detective sergeant or detective lieutenant were coded as sergeant and lieutenant respectively. This is the correct procedure for two reasons: (1) they are superior in rank to that of detective; (2) they were obtained, respectively, from the sergeant and lieutenant rosters provided by the Police Department. With a few exceptions, these ranks constitute all the ranks within the department.

5. Obviously, there is not that much support at the inspector level either. Evidence to be presented later, however, indicates that a need for improved police-community relations is recognized by a substantially larger group than shown in response to this question. How deep and insightful this support is will be discussed later.

6. This deficiency has been recognized by the Police Department in Detroit and is also a central point in the reforms suggested by Locke (1969), a former administrative assistant to the commissioner, in his recent book on the Detroit riot. Officers are encouraged to pursue college studies and are rewarded for this by reducing the time spans required to take promotional exams and by other rewards as well.

7. Niederhoffer (1967) notes that recruits to the New York Police Department score about average on the California F Scale. They seem reasonably idealistic about police work but rapidly change in the direction of the substantial cynicism that characterizes the veteran officer. Interestingly, this increase in cynicism occurs while they are still in the Academy and before they have any real street experience. Later in this paper, I will discuss the effects of street experience on police attitudes.

8. Most striking, of course, is the fact that the officers' chief differentiation is along class lines, even though all officers (including black ones) always rate whites as higher in respect for law and order than blacks. This class differentiation made by white officers is potentially of great value to an effective police-community relations

program. It hardly needs to be said, however, that to most officers, a black is lower class unless the citizen proves otherwise. Then there may be a change in attitude toward him. By then, however, it is often too late. The seriousness of the officers' dislike of the lower-class black is compounded by the fact that, despite the increased entry of blacks into the middle class, proportionally larger numbers of blacks are lower class than are whites.

It should also be pointed out that black officers make the same differentiations as do white officers. They rate the middle class as higher than the slum group and, within class, evaluate white citizens as having more respect for law and order than black citizens. Black officers, however, assign higher respect for law and order, among blacks, than all white officers (except inspectors). Most significantly, they do not assume that anger at the police by black citizens is a function of the antisocial nature of the black community but is rather due to real or perceived police mistreatment of black citizens.

9. Of all white officers, the inspectors present the most understanding and sympathetic view of the black community as can be seen from the tables. This likely comes about from their increased sophistication, their contact with leaders and concerned citizens of the black community, and their removal from the confrontations of the street. It may also be a function of the kind of persons who become inspectors. The issue is discussed in Mendelsohn (1969).

10. The majority of white officers below the rank of inspector responded "yes" to the question "Do you believe the more that Negroes get the more they want and the more they will rely on force to get it?"

11. Except for the emphasis on law and order and a disinclination among officers of ranks of detective and above to see the riot as planned, there is nothing especially distinctive about white officers' interpretation of the riot or their views of the black community. The same may be said for black officers. White officers mirror the views of the white citizenry, particularly the working-class citizenry, and black officers mirror the views of the black community. Further, although persons in the community sample of the Detroit study were not asked about whether blacks suffer from discrimination, past and recent polls (Pettigrew, 1964; Newsweek, 1969b) show that police attitudes in this matter are quite similar to those of whites in general. It is clear that most of the variance in riot interpretation and view of the black community is a function of race and class. This suggests that there is little variance remaining to be influenced by the effects of experience as a police officer qua officer in these matters. This indeed turns out to be the state of affairs. Patrolmen who have served only in all white precincts are not differentiable in attitudes from those whose sole experience has been in all black precincts. Nor are officers (of ranks from lieutenant to patrolmen) whose major experience has been in white areas differentiable from officers whose major experience has been in black areas. Certainly the claim that officers' attitudes are understandable in the face of the dangers they face and the experiences they have with blacks is challenged by such data.

Since, as innumerable surveys (Herbers, 1968; Hedegard, 1969; Newsweek, 1969a) have shown, the goal of the overwhelming majority of black citizens is equality rather than domination, integration rather than separation, the potential for misunderstanding and conflict between white officers and black citizens is ominous.

12. The best evidence would suggest that, even accounting for more efficient methods of reporting crime, the rate has been rising (President's Commission, 1967a). Whether, however, it is in fact higher than in previous eras of our nation's history is open to question.

13. This is an incorrect belief particularly as it applies to the white community. The President's Commission (1967b) reviews the evidence of public reaction to the police, and, by and large, the police are positively viewed by whites.

14. Response to this question may be an over-estimate of the commitment of the inspectors to police-community relations. The question specified should police do more *if time and money were available*. Thus the question avoids the issue of priorities on police time and money.

15. Though these responses are correctly cited as positive potentials, it must be pointed out that there remains a large group of police executives who are not convinced of the importance of even these minimal programs. Perhaps more significant is the fact that only a handful of officers see improved police-community relations as functionally related to reducing crime. Finally, police executives more strongly support programs for crime reduction and riot avoidance which place the responsibility on other social forces or agencies. For example, the two most popular responses given by these officers on ways to prevent future riots is improvement in the socioeconomic and educational status of blacks and the imposition of stiffer penalties by the courts. Both kinds of social change are well beyond the power of the police to effect. It is undoubtedly true that improvement in the status and skills of the black community is a critical step to make in eliminating riots and reducing crime. It is also true that this police response attests to some sophistication and sympathy and is a realistic one. The danger, however, is that, given this view, the police will be inclined to do less than they could. Of course, quite aside from the inspectors' views, there remains the problem of getting the cooperation and support of lower-echelon officers.

16. As Table 5 shows, twenty-seven percent of inspectors believe the reason blacks blame police for the riot is that police represent the white power structure. With second mentions included, this rises to thirty percent. This explanation is totally absent among officers below this echelon.

17. As indicated earlier, the specific assignment of officers (with the exception of those at the inspector level) does not seem related to attitudes. This suggests that police attitudes toward blacks (and indeed work norms) is a function of police tradition and attitudes, and primary reference group attitudes. These provide the "filtering system" through which experience is channeled. Thus, it is the filtering system that matters and which must be changed if officers are going to accept the changes being advocated.

REFERENCES

BORDUA, D. J. (1968) "Comments on police-community relations." Unpublished paper.
EDWARDS, G. (1968) The Police on the Urban Frontier: A Guide to Community Understanding. New York: Institute of Human Relations Press.
HEDEGARD, J. M. (1969) "Detroit community attitudes on race and urban rioting." Detroit Riot Study, unpublished paper.
HERBERS, J. (1968) "Study says Negro justifies rioting as social protest." New York Times 118 (July 28): 1 ff.
LOCKE, H. G. (1969) The Detroit Riot of 1967. Detroit: Wayne State Univ. Press.

MENDELSOHN, R.A. (1969) "The police interpretation of the Detroit riot of 1967: an examination of the dimensions and determinants of the interpretation." Detroit Riot Study, unpublished paper.

MENNINGER, K. (1968) The Crime of Punishment. New York: Viking Press.

Newsweek Editors (1969a) "Report from black America." Newsweek 73 (June 30): 17-35.

––– (1969b) "The troubled American: a special report on the white majority." Newsweek 74 (October 6): 28-68.

NIEDERHOFFER, A. (1967) Behind the Shield. New York: Doubleday.

PETTIGREW, T. F. (1964) A Profile of the Negro American. Princeton: D. Von Nostrand.

President's Commission on Law Enforcement and Administration of Justice (1967a) The Challenge of Crime in a Free Society. Washington, D.C.: U.S. Government Printing Office.

––– (1967b) Task Force Report: The Police. Washington, D.C.: U.S. Government Printing Office.

SKOLNICK, J. H. (1969) The Politics of Protest. New York: Ballantine Books.

––– (1966) Justice Without Trial. New York: John Wiley.

WILSON, J. Q. (1963) "The police and their problems: a theory." Public Policy 12: 189-216.

Police Perceptions
of a Hostile Ghetto

Realism or Projection

W. EUGENE GROVES
Johns Hopkins University

PETER H. ROSSI
Johns Hopkins University

Self-fulfilling prophecies create a larger share of the results of social interaction than we sometimes care to admit. So it may be with the police and some of the local communities in which they are charged with maintaining "law and order." In the last few years, there have been a number of instances where police departments, anticipating disorders either from black populations or white protestors, have acted in such a manner as to ensure that the anticipated disorders actually occurred. The Walker Report (1968) to the National Commission on the Causes and Prevention of Violence assails the Chicago police for acting with such unrestrained violence and vindictiveness toward the protestors during the Democratic National Convention in 1968 that formerly peaceful demonstrators were led to more militant actions.

Perhaps the clearest case of police expectations leading to the outbreak of a civil disorder was described by an unpublished staff report of the National Advisory Commission on Civil Disorders (The Kerner Commission)[1] on the 1967 civil disorders in Cambridge, Maryland. The scheduling of a speech in that city by H. Rap Brown led the police to anticipate that civil disorders would break out, to mobilize their reserves, and to place the Maryland National Guard on an alert status. The speech itself appeared to have added to the police perception of immediate threat to the point that when Brown was walking with the remnants of his audience down the street in the general direction of the downtown area of Cambridge, the local police began firing on the group. Soon after that, several carloads of local whites drove through the black residential section firing guns out of the windows. Blacks and whites quickly hardened into positions of hostility and the result was a minor civil disorder in which a local school and a local motel (both used by blacks) were burnt down. The conflict was brought under control after the State Police and National Guard with cooler heads intervened to de-escalate the conflict.

In other disorders, particularly Newark; Detroit; and Plainfield, New Jersey, there is considerable evidence that violent police overreaction to relatively slight hostile acts led what might have been minor incidents into major disorders with heavy tolls of life and property.

Although not as well documented because the actors in collective disorders rarely leave behind records, it is probably the case that black populations have also overreacted to specific actions of police. Thus in the 1967 Detroit riot, the raiding of a "blind pig" by a very large task force of Detroit policemen dressed in a new type of uniform led the local populace to believe that the raid in question was an unusual and especially harsh intervention into local privileges. During the riots which ensued photographs were circulated in the black ghetto of a badly mutilated black man allegedly tortured to death by the police.[2] Many blacks had come to expect through past experience that they would not be treated fairly and humanely by the police, so that any rumor, especially one originating in a situation where police were essentially unrestrained, seemed credible.

The dramatic instances of overreaction on the part of police or their clients occur in connection with major civil disturbances. But what is the day-to-day manifestation of these attitudes? On the beat, policemen and blacks meet, interpret each other's behavior in terms of the meanings each imputed to the actions of the other, and act on those bases. In situation after situation, an officer has to make a judgement whether or not a particular person is hostile, friendly, or indifferent—and act accordingly. Conversely, the civilian black encountering an officer has to judge how the latter is going to behave in the encounter and judge how to act accordingly. These are the judgements and actions which are more difficult to study and assess, yet are the stuff out of which police-community relations are formed.

The relationships between police departments and the black populations of our cities are made up cumulatively out of the day-to-day actions and reactions of the two groups. In this paper, we wish to examine some of the conditions under which police view the residents of the black ghetto as hostile, whether police perceptions are primarily a response to the actual expressed antagonism of blacks, or whether they arise more from causes independent of the black community. It is a critical issue, if we assume, as has been shown in so many cases, that perceptions of others tend to strongly influence one's own actions toward others. And it is particularly important, since police are the primary representative of white power with which blacks continuously come into potentially threatening personal contact.

Of course, to look at police perceptions of blacks is to look at only one of the two major self-fulfilling prophecy mechanisms that may be at work in police-black relationships. There is also the question of how blacks view the police, an issue into which we will not go in this paper. But, in a real sense, the attitudes of the police are more critical. In theory, at least, police are supposed to serve the communities where they patrol, and be accountable to political authority. And from a practical policy viewpoint, one can do more to affect the views of policemen than to affect the views of ghetto blacks. Police are organized into a para-military organization, making them more accessible (at least from within the police organization) and more likely to respond to organizational efforts to change their practices and behavior.

CONTACT, PREJUDICE AND THE PERCEPTION OF HOSTILITY

Unlike some other public services which are delivered to local neighborhoods in an impersonal way, the services of a police department are essentially activities conducted in face-to-face encounters between local neighborhood residents and police personnel. One might, therefore, expect that the officers on daily patrol in a neighborhood would have ample opportunity to build an empirical base underneath their perceptions of how their services are viewed by local residents, assuming, of course, that they make an effort to understand and be informed about the community. In particular, we would expect that officers on daily patrol in black neighborhoods would have a very good chance to form assessments of the general tone of the community that might easily reflect the level of hostility that black citizens generally direct towards police officers. In addition, the interchange among police colleagues concerning their individual experiences should provide policemen in any particular city with some common assessment of the support and approval they can expect, and the dangers they face, in their patrol neighborhoods.

On the other hand, most of what we know from studies in the psychology of perception would lead us to expect that prior definitions of the situation, generalized expectations, and pressure from peers often will override the content of specific experiences, so that generalized social assessments will not reflect simply the content of a myriad of specific encounters. Furthermore, such prior definitions may affect the extent to which a policeman will penetrate a neighborhood—in the sense of developing a wide network of acquaintances and reliable sources of information. In short, a policeman may be in a neighborhood but penetrate it only superficially. He may be out of touch with the residents either because he does not make efforts to become acquainted or because his personal antagonism toward the residents prevents such acquaintances from developing.

Under such conditions, minor incidents, or even harmless street corner gatherings, may be blown out of proportion, and interpreted as exceptionally hostile in confirmation of the policeman's preexisting mental set. The policeman may then assault a person who used incautious phrases, or may summarily order a group to disperse, thus engendering the actual hostility he initially imagined. This self-fulfilling prophecy may be at work early enough in the cycle of police-community interaction to prevent the development of (or perhaps to partially create) a realistic basis for local neighborhood assessments.

Thus we pose two models to characterize an aspect of police-community relations in the black community. One model suggests that a policeman's assessment of the hostility of local black neighborhoods is based largely on the actual level of friendliness or hostility toward the police. The other model suggests that these assessments are generated by processes that have little to do with the black community, but may arise from prior attitudes, from definitions of the situation shared by certain police subcultures, or from unique experiences the policeman himself generates by his own friendly or hostile actions toward residents. Of course, models set up in opposition to each other have a distressing tendency not to be clearly separable when applied to empirical data. Hence, we have to consider that both sets of processes may be going on at the same time: the actual level of community hostility toward the police, and the perceptual screens of the individual may both bear a significant relationship to the policeman's final assessments.

THE SAMPLE

To examine which of these models is more plausible, we have drawn upon the results of interviews with five hundred and twenty-two policemen drawn from thirteen major central cities. These interviews were part of a study conducted for the Kerner Commission[3] concerned with the attitudes toward blacks displayed by persons who occupy positions on the interfaces between local institutions and residents of the ghettos. The interviews were conducted in the Spring of 1968; most were completed before the round of civil disorders broke out following the assassination of Martin Luther King. The study design was based upon drawing a sample of fifteen cities, five of which had major riots or widespread civil disorders in 1967 (Detroit, Newark, Milwaukee, Boston, and Cincinnati), five of which had riots in previous years or only a low level of disorder in 1967 (Brooklyn, Cleveland, Chicago, Philadelphia, and San Francisco), and five which had had no major disorders in 1967 or earlier (Washington, D.C. , Pittsburgh, Gary, Baltimore, and St. Louis).[4]

About forty policemen were quota sampled in each city, quotas being set to obtain twenty-four white patrolmen, six white supervisors, eight black patrolmen and two black supervisors. To qualify for interviews, the policemen had to be working in police districts which were predominantly black and hence, hopefully representative of the policemen black ghetto residents encounter.

Respondents were in most cases chosen by local police officials and hence, can be expected to be biased toward the kinds of policemen officials felt might present their cities in the best light. The interview contained questions about local community problems, items concerning their perceptions of civil disorders, about their patrol practices, about their own attitudes toward blacks, and about their backgrounds.

Samples were obtained from only thirteen of the fifteen cities in the sample. The police departments of Milwaukee and Boston not only refused official participation but also forbade their policemen from granting interviews on their own. The analysis which follows is based on the five hundred fifteen usable interviews obtained in the thirteen cooperating cities.

If police assessments of black hostility are sensitive to actual experiences in patrolling the ghetto, then we would expect that there would be significant variation from city to city. After all, at the time of our interviews some of the cities (notably Detroit and Newark) had recently experienced widespread civil disorders, and other cities (notably Baltimore, Gary, and St. Louis) had not even experienced minor disorders. The salience of police behavior as an issue in the civil rights agitation also varied considerably. In New York and Baltimore, for example, local public officials had instituted policies stressing police restraint in the ghettos of those cities, while in other cities, like Chicago, Milwaukee, and Newark, police departments had notorious reputations among blacks for mistreatment and brutality. Qualitative interviews with public officials in each of these cities demonstrated considerable variation in the control which mayors exercised over their police departments, and similar interviews with black leaders showed differences from place to place in the extent to which police behavior was a local issue in the struggle for black parity.

RESULTS

Overall, the police perceived a large proportion of the residents as hostile. Thirty-one percent felt that "most Negroes regard police as enemies," another 31% felt that "most Negroes regard police as on their side," and 36% felt that "most Negroes are indifferent toward the police." When asked about young adults, 42% felt that young blacks considered police as enemies, while only 16% thought they considered police as friends. From these two questions and three others ("How much respect does the average resident of this precinct have for the police?" and "How do people *in general* in this precinct regard the police?" and "How satisfied are you with the respect you get from citizens?"), all of which were related to all others with gamma (γ) greater than .47, we constructed an index of perceived hostility. (Responses to each question were given a -1, 0, or +1 for perception of friendliness, neutrality, and hostility, respectively, and the responses to the five questions added together.)

The resulting index gave scores from -5 to +5, with a mean of -0.28 (as shown in Table 1) and a population standard error of 2.91, indicating that, on the average, police perceived the residents of these largely black precincts as indifferent toward the police. As we would expect, black police perceive the population as less hostile than do white police. (The difference is significant at $p \leqslant .001$, two-tailed test.)

When we examine the average (of all black and white policemen) perceived hostility in each of the thirteen cities, differences do emerge. Baltimore is the lowest with an average index score of -1.83, while Detroit is the highest with a score of +0.92. An analysis of variance of city differences shows that 8.7% of the total variance among policemen is accounted for by differences in city means[5] (see Table 2). We can, therefore, reject the hypothesis that cities do not differ at a level of significance beyond $p = .001$. Separate analyses for white and black policemen lead to interesting findings: among blacks, the intercity differences account for 19.3% of the total variance among individuals, while among whites only 7.4% of the variance can be "explained" (see Table 5).

TABLE 1

SCORES ON PERCEIVED HOSTILITY INDEX

	Mean	Standard Error of Mean
All respondents (n=515)	-.28	.13
White respondents (n=391)	-.04	.15
Black respondents (n=124)	-1.09	.24

TABLE 2
CONTRIBUTION TO VARIANCE OF INDEPENDENT VARIABLES
IN LINEAR MODEL (n=515)
(perceived hostility is dependent variable)

	R^2	Unique[a] Contribution to R^2	F Ratio for Unique Contribution	Significance Level[b]
City Differences (12 variables)	.087[c]	.078[c]	4.26	.001
Individual Attributes (5 variables)	.158[c]	.150[c]	19.10	.001
Race	.024	.0002	0.15	n.s.
Rank	.027	.0011	0.72	n.s.
Age	.071	.0352	22.95	.001
Prejudice	.092	.0521	34.00	.001
Acquaintance	.031	.0075	4.91	.05
City + Individual Attributes (17 variables)	.236[c]	—	9.05	.001

a. "Unique contribution" indicates the amount that is subtracted from multiple R^2 when the variable (or set of variables) is removed from the model. Thus the unique contribution may be less than the R^2 from that variable by itself, since that variable may be correlated with other independent variables in the model.

b. Significance with which we can reject the hypothesis that the attribute(s) has no effect independent of the other variables in the model.

c. Multiple R^2.

In terms of the two basic models posed earlier, this result suggests that black policemen have an assessment of residents' hostility that may be more closely related to the actual differences in city characteristics. We should normally expect black policemen to be more closely in touch than white policemen with residents of the black community, and therefore, that their perceptions of residents would more accurately reflect the actual attitudes they confront in daily encounters—as suggested in our first model.

In order to more adequately determine whether intercity differences in perceived hostility do, in fact, reflect real differences in the level of hostility, we would need to develop some measure that accurately characterized the antipolice hostility among blacks in each city. In this paper we will not attempt to employ such a measure. Therefore we can only observe that the differences between cities in the way police perceive black residents may be due not only to differences in actual hostility, but also to such factors as police hiring and assignment practices, variations in city sampling biases, or aggregation or compositional effects in different police departments. It will not be possible, therefore, to examine the exact extent to which our first model describes the source of police perceptions about residents.

However, it is clear that once we control for city differences, 91.3% of the variance among police (black and white combined) remains to be explained. Obviously there are individual characteristics of each policeman that make—in total—ten times as much difference in his perception of hostility as do city characteristics. Put another way, the variation within city among individuals is ten times as great as the variation across cities. The important determinants of police perceptions, therefore, do not depend upon the characteristics (including the black communities) of the cities themselves. The most interesting problem to explore, then, is whether we can find measurable characteristics of individuals that are at least as important as city differences and which can clarify exactly how our second model operates.

To carry out this analysis we examined the residuals after removing city means from a number of variables, in order to find relationships between perceived hostility and other attributes that would be unconfounded with intercity variation. We conjectured that a number of attributes might be related to individual variation in perceived hostility: education, human relations training, prejudice against blacks,[6] acquaintance with residents of the community,[7] age, rank, participation in community affairs, assignment to interracial patrol, and race. Since we were not certain of the accuracy of representation of a quota sample, especially in establishing generalizable zero-order relationships, we selected for further analysis only those variables which showed a zero-order correlation to perceived hostility at a level of significance greater than $p = .001$ (two-tailed test). A correlation coefficient of at least .15 met this criterion.

Five variables achieved at least this level of significance in their relationship to perceived hostility. They are listed in Table 2, along with the variance they "explain" alone, and the unique addition to variance "explained" which they account for in a liner model of individual attributes and city effects. The five individual attributes together account for almost twice as much variance as do city differences. At least fifteen percent of the variation among individuals (both before and after city effects are controlled) can be "explained" by race, rank, age, prejudice, and acquaintance. To illustrate the magnitude of the effects of individual attributes, we have dichotomized individuals into these who scored higher and lower than the median in each city on appropriate variables. The zero-order effects are illustrated in Table 3.

TABLE 3

EFFECTS OF INDIVIDUAL ATTRIBUTES
ON PERCEIVED HOSTILITY

Variable	Value	% who are above city median in perceived hostility
Race	white	.53
	black	.34
Prejudice[a]	low	.37
	high	.61
Acquaintance[a]	low	.53
	high	.43
Age[b]	young	.59
	old	.37
Rank	patrolman	.52
	supervisor	.31

a. "High," "low" mean above or below city median, respectively.

b. "Young," "old" mean above or below city median, respectively.

Two of these five individual attributes, race and rank, do not have a significant relationship to perceived hostility, when we control for the other variables. To clarify why race and rank have no independent direct effect, we can first examine the correlation matrix of these five variables and perceived hostility (Table 4).

There are two pairs of fairly highly related variables: age and rank, and race and prejudice. The nature of the causal relationships in these two sets can be seen more clearly by setting out reasonable causal hypotheses and examining partial correlation coefficients. With race and prejudice, for example, the reasonable alternative hypotheses are (1) race affects both

TABLE 4

INTERCORRELATIONS OF VARIABLES DETERMINING
PERCEIVED HOSTILITY
(based on variables as deviations from city means)

	Rank	Age	Prejudice	Acquaintance	Perceived Hostility
Race	-.027	+.000	-.560	.161	-.157
Rank		.434	-.056	.098	-.161
Age			.017	.198	-.262
Prejudice				-.129	.297
Acquaintance					-.176

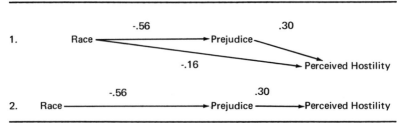

Figure 1: ALTERNATIVE HYPOTHETICAL CAUSAL MODELS RELATING RACE, PREJUDICE, AND PERCEIVED HOSTILITY
(zero order correlations are listed for each relationship)

prejudice and perceived hostility, or (2) only prejudice affects perceived hostility directly, while race acts entirely through its effect upon prejudice (see Figure 1).

Which hypothesis is more supported by the data can best be seen by comparing the partial correlation coefficient of race and perceived hostility with prejudice controlled. In hypothesis one we would expect some, but not substantial reduction in the partial compared to the zero order correlation coefficient. In hypothesis two we would expect the partial correlation to approach zero. The partial is .018, compared to a zero order correlation of -.157, indicating that hypothesis two is the better representation of the data, i.e. race has little effect upon perception once we have accounted for the effect of the policeman's prejudice, but it does explain a sizeable fraction of the variation in prejudice.

This suggests that black and white policemen with similar levels of prejudice react similarly to actions by people in their precincts. Furthermore, since for obvious reasons the average level of "prejudice" among black police (if the index can even be appropriately interpreted for blacks) is much lower than the average level for whites (mean of 2.07, compared to 5.84 for whites, in a 12-point index), and the population variance on the prejudice index is about one-third as high for blacks as for whites (2.53 compared to 7.18 for whites), it is clear that most of the variation in hostility that is related to prejudice comes from the variation in white prejudice. To further substantiate this claim, we have separated black from white policemen, and analyzed separately the variance explained for each by the remaining 4 independent variables, viz. rank, age, prejudice, and acquaintance. The results are shown in Table 5.

The hypothesis that the effects of these four variables is nil for blacks cannot be rejected even at a level of $p = .10$. The hypothesis of no effect is clearly rejected for whites (at a level of $p \leqslant .001$). This result rather

TABLE 5

IMPORTANCE OF TWO SETS OF VARIABLES IN "EXPLAINING" WHITE AND BLACK PERCEIVED HOSTILITY

		Multiple R^2 for Set	F Ratio	Unique Contribution to R^2	F Ratio	Level of Significance of Unique Contribution
	City differences	.074	2.54	.074	3.07	p = .005
White (n=391)	Four individual variables	.167	19.40	.167	28.22	p = .001
	City + individual	.242	7.47	—	—	p = .001[a]
	City differences	.193	2.21	.169	1.92	p = .05
Black (n=124)	Four individual variables	.043	1.33	.019	0.95	n.s.
	City + individual	.212	1.80	—	—	p = .05[a]

a. Refers to multiple R^2 for full model.

strongly indicates that the background variables we earlier suggested might be related to the ascription of hostility are *only* important for white policemen. The significance of the individual attributes of whites, versus presumably more objective city attributes affecting blacks, is more clearly exemplified when we recall the much greater importance that city differences played in determining black perceptions of hostility. We can see in Table 5 that for whites the individual attributes are more than twice as important as intercity differences, while for blacks, the individual differences are quite small compared to intercity differences.

We can dispense with another attribute in the analysis. Rank does not contribute a significant unique amount to the variance "explained." The only reasonable causal chain connecting age, rank, and perceived hostility is shown in Figure 2. The two partial correlation coefficients (age by perceived hostility controlling for rank, and rank by perceived hostility controlling for age) can clarify what the predominant relationship is. If $r_{13.2} = 0$, then age acts entirely through its effect on a person's rank. But if $r_{23.1} = 0$, then the correlation between rank and perceived hostility is spurious, arising from the effect that age has upon both. We find that

$$r_{13.2} = .22 \qquad r_{23.1} = .055$$

indicating that the age is the important determinant, with rank largely related spuriously to perceived hostility due to older people occupying higher ranks.

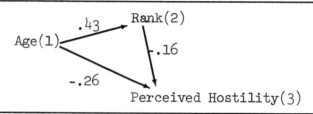

Figure 2: HYPOTHETICAL RELATIONSHIP AMONG AGE, RANK, AND PERCEIVED HOSTILITY
(zero order correlations are listed for each relationship)

HOW INDIVIDUAL ATTRIBUTES WORK

We have concluded that for *white* police, three individual attributes have a significant independent relationship to perceived hostility: age, prejudice, and acquaintance. Of these the unique contribution to variance "explained" by prejudice is most significant, that by acquaintance least significant (see Table 2). Table 6 shows the relationships between these three variables and perceived hostility, with individuals dichotomized at the city medians on all variables (thus the effects are not confounded with the actual level of hostility in each city, unless, of course, there is an interaction between level of hostility and the operation of these variables—which we have not yet examined). The fraction of police who are above city medians in perceived hostility ranges from twenty-three percent of the old, low prejudice, low acquaintance group, to seventy-five percent of the young, high prejudice, low acquaintance group. Both higher prejudice and younger age increase the perceived hostility under all combinations of the other attributes (though the magnitude of the effects is not uniform). Acquaintance, however, does not change perceptions in the same direction in all cases. The apparent interactions bear closer examination.

A higher level of acquaintance may conceivably either raise or lower the perception of others as hostile, depending upon what other factors are at work. Initial strong antagonism toward blacks could be an important enough screen through which a policeman would view his interaction with the residents that increased contact might add to his perceptions of hostility, as each encounter reinforces his own preconceptions. Or, on the other hand, the necessity that a good policeman make peace with the residents and have a friendly working relationship in order to more adequately perform his duties might constitute enough of an overriding imperative that a latently hostile policeman would be forced to look more fairly upon the black residents he is supposed to serve. The latter suggestion seems more plausible from our data. Table 6 indicates that for

TABLE 6
PERCEPTION OF HOSTILITY BY WHITE POLICEMEN
(proportion higher than city median in perceived hostility)

	Young	Old	All Ages
Low Prejudice			
Low acquaintance	.51	.23	.39
	(49)	(39)	(88)
High acquaintance	.60	.29	.41
	(25)	(41)	(66)
High Prejudice			
Low acquaintance	.75	.63	.71
	(88)	(52)	(140)
High acquaintance	.63	.37	.49
	(51)	(46)	(97)

the high prejudice policemen, a higher level of acquaintance implies a lower level of perceived hostility (chi square is significant at $p \leqslant .001$). On the other hand, for those with low prejudice, acquaintance makes little difference in perceived hostility—if anything, the trend suggests that the more acquainted, but less prejudiced individuals, might perceive more hostility, perhaps from a realization that some of the residents are, in fact, hostile, even though the policeman may be sympathetic with their complaints.

It is clearly the highly prejudiced, out of touch, white policeman—regardless of his age—who believes the residents to be antagonistic. Or put another way, most white policemen, like most other white Americans, tend to project their own prejudices and fears upon blacks, ascribing to them a level of hostility that more adequately reflects the hostility of the perceiver. Fortunately, however, it appears that a great deal of "reality testing" can somewhat temper these projections.

The significant difference between age groups is a little more difficult to interpret. A number of observers have suggested that older policemen are typically more prejudiced and also more accustomed to the "old days" before civil rights protests had gained significant strength—when police were much freer to act the way they wanted toward black citizens. One of the problems police departments often claim they face is that human relations training may have little impact on a recruit after he has spent some time on the beat being socialized by older policemen into the way "it is really done." But to counter this influence, most police departments have taken steps in the last decade to recruit more highly educated, less prejudiced, and more psychologically stable cadets.

If these measures have been at all successful in fulfilling their claims, we should expect to find the younger policemen less prejudiced, and would hope to discover that they had developed a more realistic perception of the residents. There was no significant relationship between age and prejudice in our sample. But we did discover a significant difference in the perception of hostility depending upon age—the younger police viewed the residents as *more* hostile. From Table 6 it is clear that age makes a striking difference in perception for all except those who are highly prejudiced and not well acquainted with the community.

The greater amount of hostility perceived by the younger policemen may have to remain an interesting but unexplained finding. Given the trends in the general society and the trends in recruitment, training, and the like, in police departments over the past decade one would expect to find the younger policemen more receptive to an unstereotyped approach to the black ghetto. One may speculate that these younger policemen are given different—perhaps more difficult and dangerous—tasks in patrolling the ghetto, that they may be self-selected from among the more apprehensive young whites and so on. It also may be the case that young white policemen are more the target of black hostility than their older colleagues. Whatever the ultimate explanations, these differences do not bode well for the future of relationships between police departments and the black communities they serve.

CONCLUSIONS

A large proportion of the police who serve in the black communities of our major cities see themselves as pursuing their tasks in, at worst, a hostile, and, at best, an indifferent environment. Less than one in three sees his clients as friendly. Urban police find themselves to a large extent in the position of troops who are sent to occupy conquered enemy territory.

Our attempt to discern how much of this view depended upon the hard characteristics of the ghetto reaction to the police, and how much was due to the perceptual screens which the policemen brought with them to their task was made difficult by the absence of hard data on black perceptions and actions toward the police. However, we can judge that not more than 8.7% of the variance among individual policemen—and probably much less—can be accounted for by variation from city to city. This is much less than we might expect from the known variation in militancy among black communities in major cities. Particularly, we have noted that black policemen, presumably more in tune with ghetto reality than are whites, do have perceptions which differ much more from city to city.

By far most of what a white policeman anticipates from black citizens is determined by factors other than the actual level of hostility in a city. A good deal of the perceived antagonism appears to be a projection of the policeman's own fears and prejudices—although a high level of acquaintance with community residents, leaders, and other individuals tends somewhat to mitigate a highly prejudiced policeman's projection of his hostility. It is not completely clear from the analysis presented whether the perception of hostility by the more prejudiced policeman is a result only of his own interpretations, or a result of actual experiences that he may generate day to day by his own overreactions—though both processes presumably would go hand in hand.

What we should be particularly disturbed about are those policemen who are both highly prejudiced and out of touch with the community. They are most like an occupying army, and are most likely to generate increased antagonisms through their overreaction to, and lack of realistic differentiation among, black residents. Particularly alarming was the finding that among the policemen interviewed, thirty-one percent reported that they did not even know one important teenage or youth leader in their precincts well enough to speak with whenever they saw him. It would be difficult to imagine how these policemen could formulate realistic judgements about the actions of ghetto youth—the source of the most militant actions.

We have presented what is only one side of an interactive system. The behavior of blacks and their perceptions of the hostility of policemen are also parts of a system which interact with the characteristics of policemen, the structure of police departments, and the nature of public opinion to produce what we experience as police-ghetto relationships. The end result, in any case, is a tangle of mutual suspicion and hostility.

We might extend the findings based upon variation within police departments to argue that decreasing the prejudice of policemen, and increasing their acquaintance and experience, might somewhat reduce the apprehensions of the otherwise more insensitive police. But this is valid only to a certain point. There is no assurance that reducing the average prejudice level, for example, will substantially change the nature of police-black relations, as the source of conflict extends far beyond the personalities of those involved. It arises from the general discriminatory treatment in unemployment, in education, in legal norms, in housing, and in most other aspects of daily life that blacks face. And police are stuck, regardless of their level of prejudice, with a most difficult task of maintaining social control in the face of blacks reacting to continuous substantive injustice. Even if the police, and the blacks, were realistic about their perceptions of each other, we would have little reason to believe that the general level of tension would be reduced as long as there is a substantial conflict of goals and norms between the black community and the police departments. This is especially true when police are asked to maintain order for city governments which lack sufficient funds, and will power, to eradicate the economic and social causes of black protest.

NOTES

1. The report was uncovered and summarized by Robert Walters in the *Washington Star*, March 4, 1968.

2. Fact and fancy are close together in situations of this sort. At the same time that this photograph was being circulated from hand to hand, an authentic police atrocity was being committed in the Algiers Motel. See Hersey (1968).

3. Interviews with policemen were part of a larger study in which surveys were made of frontline personnel in major community institutions which dealt with their black ghettos, including educators, social workers, ghetto merchants, political party workers, and personnel managers of large employers. The major findings of the study relating to differences among these groups are reported by the National Advisory Commission on Civil Disorders (1968).

4. Note that in three of the five "nonriot" cases, riots soon broke out in Spring 1968, shortly after most of our interviewing was completed. Pittsburgh, Washington, and Baltimore suffered major riots in response to King's assassination.

5. For the analysis we used a linear model in which the thirteen cities were coded into twelve "dummy" variables. See Bottenberg and Ward (1963) for a good explanation of the use of a general linear model.

6. "Prejudice" in this case was a measure of how apprehensive the individual was about blacks gaining ground in areas not directly related to police work. The index is the sum of answers (coded 2, 1, and 0) to five items: One question about whether Negroes have tried to move too fast in gaining what they feel to be equality, and four items about whether "you are very disturbed, slightly disturbed, or not disturbed at all about": "Negroes draining resources through welfare payments," "Negroes taking over political power," "Negroes moving into areas that, until recently, were occupied only by whites," and "Negroes socializing with whites." These items were interrelated with gammas (γ) at least .45. Thus our index does not entail negative stereotypes of blacks held by whites, but reflects a general antagonism toward or fear of blacks getting "out of place."

7. The level of acquaintance is measured by the sum of the number of persons in six categories whom the policeman reported he knew well enough to "speak with whenever you see them." The categories were: shop owners, managers, clerks; important adult leaders in the neighborhoods; residents in general; important teenage and youth leaders; people from various government and private agencies who work in the neighborhoods; and the continual troublemakers. This index gave us a generalized level of community acquaintance for each patrolman.

REFERENCES

BOTTENBERG, R. A. and J. H. WARD, Jr. (1963) Applied Multiple Linear Regression. Technical Documentary Report PRL-TDR-63-6. Springfield, Va.: U.S. Department of Commerce.

HERSEY, J. (1968) The Algiers Motel Incident. New York: Bantam Books.

National Advisory Commission on Civil Disorders (1968) Supplemental Studies. Washington, D.C.: U.S. Government Printing Office.

WALKER, D. (1968) Rights in Conflict. Report Submitted to the National Commission on the Causes and Prevention of Violence. New York: Bantam Books.

Police Officers as Boundary Personnel

Attitude Congruence Between Policemen and Small Businessmen in Urban Areas

HOWARD ALDRICH
Cornell University

ALBERT J. REISS, Jr.
Yale University

Organizational roles that bring incumbents into contact with members of other organizations where the boundaries of organizations intersect have been labeled *boundary-spanning roles* (Thompson, 1962). These roles provide a connecting link through which information flows among organizations. Beliefs and attitudes should be affected by contact with personnel in the boundary roles of an organization, and the boundary role perspective provides a way of explaining how contact between groups changes attitudes. Traditionally, attitude change resulting from intergroup contact has been dealt with either in the framework of intergroup relations or that of balance theory, as will be discussed in this paper. Using the boundary-personnel perspective, this paper reports a study of factors making for a high degree of similarity in the attitudes policemen and small businessmen in metropolitan areas hold toward their city governments. We will examine the effects of exposure to common environmental pressures and personal contact between policemen and businessmen on attitude congruence between the two groups, using data from three large urban areas.

METHOD OF STUDY

Two studies conducted for the President's Commission on Law Enforcement and the Administration of Justice are used to separate the

Authors' Note: *We wish to acknowledge the helpful comments of David Segal and Larry Williams.*

effect of contact and assumed exchange of information from the effect other environmental pressures may have in making for congruence of attitudes between small businessmen and policemen (Aldrich and Reiss, 1969; Reiss, 1967b). Interviews were taken in the summer of 1966 with 800 small businessmen and 203 policemen of less than lieutenant rank who operated within high crime-rate areas of Boston, Chicago, and Washington, D.C. We will examine the attitude of each group toward a third party—the city government. The city government's crime-fighting ability was chosen as an issue because of its direct relevance to the daily concerns of each group. The same question was asked of both groups: "What about the city government? Do you feel they are doing a very good job, a fairly good job, or not too good a job when it comes to fighting crime in this city?" The dependent variable in our analysis is the degree of similarity between the distribution of the policemen's responses and those of the small businessmen.

There are two approaches that might lead us to expect similarity in the attitudes of two groups whose members are interacting. The first is from the literature on interethnic or interracial contacts, while the second approach comes from the work of Heider and others on balance theory. The inadequacies of these two approaches, when applied to interorganizational contact, caused us to reject them in favor of Thompson's boundary-role perspective. We will discuss the two approaches and their limitations, and then move to a consideration of Thompson's work.

INTERGROUP CONTACTS

Research on intergroup relations has found that, in most cases, personal contact between members of two different racial or ethnic groups leads to more favorable attitudes toward the group that previously was stereotyped or viewed negatively. Much of the research on intergroup contacts has been conducted in public housing projects. Jahoda and West (1951) found that personal contacts resulted in a reduction in stereotyping and an increased acceptance of Negroes by whites. Wilner et al. (1952) report similar results. In a summary of more than thirty studies on the attitudinal outcomes of contact between members of different groups, Cook and Selltiz (1955) found that approximately half reported favorable changes, with the rest reporting qualified results, with favorable change taking place only under certain conditions. Conditions for favorable attitude change include contact in a nonhostile setting, a low degree of competition, and some minimal degree of similarity between the groups.

A study by Brink and Harris came to similar conclusions—whites having previous social contact with Negroes were less prejudiced and had fewer stereotypes than whites without such contact (Brink and Harris, 1963: 138-153). All these studies differ from the present one in that they are concerned with a *dyadic* relationship. The dependent variable is the attitude of one group toward the other, not toward some third object. However, these studies are useful to the present investigation for two reasons. First, they provide evidence that relationships between two groups can be influenced by the amount of contact between them. Second, in all these studies, amount of interaction is the independent variable and degree of attitudinal change is the dependent variable. As we will point out in the next section, this causal ordering is an important precedent.

BALANCE THEORY

Balance theory has gained wide popularity as a theory of attitude change based on a triadic view of the social world. As summarized by Curry and Emerson (1970: 217), the core of the theory

> concerns two persons, A and B, and their joint relation to some object, X, as that relation is perceived by one of them. With A as ego, there are three basic variables: (1) A's attraction toward B; (2) A's attitude toward X; (3) A's perception of B's attitude toward X. The object, X, can be any object of human awareness, including A himself, provided that X is somehow *relevant* to the A-B relation. Given such relevance, there is then a 'strain toward symmetry' or balance among the above three variables.

The active force in such a three-variable system is the desire of persons to avoid situations that are unbalanced, since they are tension-provoking. "Any attitudinal or perceptual change which removes the incongruity removes the tension" (Curry and Emerson, 1970: 218).

As Davis (1963) has pointed out, in the theory as formulated by Heider and modified by Newcomb, the direction of causality between similarity and liking can be hypothesized to go either way. Thus in Homans' work, similarity between the attributes of two individuals is hypothesized to lead to friendship (Homans, 1950), whereas in Festinger's research, friendship is hypothesized to lead to similarity in attitudes (Festinger, 1957). Newcomb found little change in the attitudes of the individuals he studied during a four-month period (Newcomb, 1961). What he did find was that "as individuals acquired more information about each others' attitudes, their high attraction preferences tended to change in favor of individuals with whom they were more closely in agreement" (Newcomb, 1961: 254).

Although balance theory is a quite parsimonious explanation for a wide variety of social phenomena (compare with Davis, 1963), it is difficult to use in research on attitude change because it only specifies that a balancing change will occur without predicting the type of change. Curry and

Emerson's recent replication of Newcomb's study of the acquaintance process represents an attempt to specify more precisely *which* type of change occurs. The results call into question the current formulations of balance theory as a theory of interpersonal attraction. They state that

> We find no empirical support in our study for an AB-X explanation of attraction as a dependent variable. What we do find is: (1) a tendency to perceive those to whom one is attracted as having . . . values more similar to one's own, even when in fact they are not; (2) a tendency for A to perceive B's attraction to C as similar to his own attraction to C . . . and (3) a very strong tendency for social relations to become reciprocally attractive in a manner easily understood through simple exchange theory [Curry and Emerson, 1970: 235].

The authors state that their findings should lead to a reformulation of balance theory:

> We recommend that interpersonal attraction . . . be removed from the status of a dependent variable in AB-X theory. With this change, balance theory is not a theory of group structure and structural change. Rather, it is a theory of attitude formation and change, and it can then make more specific predictions. When applied in an interpersonal context, it is closely akin to, if not identical with, reference group theory, consensual validation, etc. [Curry and Emerson, 1970: 235].

Curry and Emerson's revision of balance theory is in accord with Davis' appraisal of the types of variables that are ignored by balance theory. Davis' criticism has direct relevance to the police-small businessman transaction structure under consideration in this paper. He states that balance theory "ignores differentiation and the effects of a division of labor . . . the benefits that accrue to *Person* from exchange and division of labor are precisely the forces that serve to compensate for or offset tendencies toward balance" (Davis, 1963: 448).

In terms of the policeman-businessman transaction structure, it is clear that the relationship is entered into by the small businessman because of the services the police offer. The differentiation of the labor force in urban areas has left the city police department responsible for the protection of businesses against crime. Businessmen enter into relationships with the police to obtain this service, especially if they are in a high crime-rate area.

Therefore, in this study, the *relationship* between the policemen and small businessmen studied will be taken as given, i.e., as something that is not affected by whether the businessman shares the policeman's view of the city government's crime-fighting ability. Moreover, to ensure that a drive toward balance is not affecting our results, we will control for the businessman's general orientation toward policemen in his area. It is our contention that the businessman's attitude toward city government is affected by information given to him by area policemen, and this attitude is unaffected by the businessman's *liking* for the police.

There are several reasons for the rejection of intergroup contact theory and balance theory as less helpful than boundary-role theory in explaining police-businessman attitude congruence. The first reason was given above—i.e., balance theory ignores the division of labor between police departments and small businessmen that causes a businessman to seek aid from a policeman regardless of his attitudes. Second, the intergroup contact literature is not specific enough to make useful predictions. Third, both approaches are interpersonal, not organizational theories.

In contrast, Thompson's hypothesis about boundary roles has to do with contact between representatives of organizations. As such, it links role theory with organization theory by treating interorganizational relationships as contacts between persons acting in organizational roles. Finally, the rejected approaches treat similarity between persons in contact as an explanatory variable, whereas it is precisely similarity which we wish to make problematic.

BOUNDARY-SPANNING ROLES

Thompson (1962: 309) discusses boundary-spanning roles in the context of open-systems theory:

> Complex purposive organizations receive inputs from, and discharge outputs to, environments, and virtually all such organizations develop specialized roles for these purposes. *Output roles*, designed to arrange for distribution of the organization's ultimate product, service or impact to other agents of the society thus are boundary-spanning roles linking organization and environment through interaction between member and non-member.

Persons in such roles are called *boundary personnel* and are given the responsibility for transacting business with the organization's environment of customers, suppliers, creditors, and so forth. Boundary roles often are defined in reference to reciprocal roles, e.g., salesmen or social workers. Thompson points out (1962: 309) that "Because output roles exist in structures that span the boundaries of the organization, they may be important sources of organization adaptation to environmental influences." Clearly, one way in which boundary personnel fulfill the function of adapting the organization to the environment is by *interpreting it* to nonmembers. Boundary personnel can serve as publicists for the organization, disseminating a desired image of the organization and its policies. This function is especially important when the activities of the organization involve publicly sensitive issues, such as "law and order," in the case of police departments.

Output roles and reciprocating nonmember roles are encompassed in *transaction structures,* i.e., structures of mutually reinforcing norms and expectations surrounding the interaction between members and nonmembers. As with most organization-environment transactions, "the organization cannot predict in advance . . . just what desires, attitudes, or actions the non-member will bring to the transaction structure" (Thompson, 1962: 310). However, two dimensions of the encounter can be predicted: (1) the extent to which the role provides routines of interaction, and (2) the extent to which nonmembers are compelled to participate in the relationship. The first, labeled *specificity of control over member,* ranges from standardized, "programmed," unvarying procedures to general guidelines for behavior. In this latter case, there is high discretion for role incumbents unless they are interacting with persons in boundary roles with programmed procedures. The second dimension, labeled *degree of nonmember discretion,* ranges from mandatory to optional interaction on the part of nonmembers.

Four types of transaction structures are derived by dichotomizing and relating the two dimensions: Type I, member programmed and mandatory nonmember participation; Type II, member programmed and nonmember participation optional; Type III, member heuristic and mandatory nonmember participation; and Type IV, member heuristic and nonmember participation optional. From the standpoint of police organizations, policemen have general regulations to guide them. The types of situations they encounter are so diverse that the department has only a low degree of specificity of control over their behavior. Small businessmen in the inner city have only the police to protect them against crime and so their participation is, in general, nondiscretionary.

Police-businessman interaction generally takes place within a Type III structure; this fact, combined with predictions from the two perspectives discussed in previous sections, leads us to predict that small businessmen will attempt to get to know policemen in their area, and that businessmen who know policemen will adopt the attitudes of the police in matters that are relevant to "law and order." The police officer the small businessman sees on the beat or the detectives who investigate reports of crimes against his business are generally the only links he has to the law enforcement agencies of the city. Business personnel are dependent upon the police not only for protection, but also for much of their information about law enforcement, particularly that beyond their immediate area.

Business personnel see policemen much more often than they see judges or other law enforcement-related individuals. Indeed, frequent contact seems high, as thirty percent of all businessmen in our survey claim they talk to a police officer at least once each day and another thirty percent claim they do so several times each week. A third report helping the police by giving them information, and at least a fourth report doing favors for them (Reiss, 1967b: 10-18). Given that police officers in a city police department develop a shared set of beliefs with regard to their city government, as will be shown in this paper, we would expect them to communicate this view to the citizens with whom they come in contact. A small businessman's view of the entire law enforcement process should be influenced by his relationship with the police.

Police officers thus act as boundary-spanning agents in the police precincts of the city, linking the law enforcement system with small businesses. Many police chiefs are aware of this function, as is shown by the use of "human relations training" and other preparations designed to turn police officers into organizational assets in the field. We do not maintain that the picture conveyed to the small businessman on an officer's beat is necessarily the one publicly held by the police department. What we are hypothesizing is that when a businessman enters into transaction structures with a policeman, the police officer's role as boundary-spanning agent serves as a communication channel through which the shared attitudes of officers are transmitted. For example, our observations in the field show that almost every small businessman has one or two "horror stories" about crimes in his neighborhood which he has learned from local policemen, and which he uses to illustrate his point about the perils of doing business in high crime-rate areas.

ENVIRONMENTAL PRESSURES

Before testing our prediction about the effect of police-businessman contact, we will consider the common impact that environmental pressures have on both the police and the small businessmen. Crime is an occupational hazard for both groups. For policemen, crime is a part of the job definition—combatting crime is something the policeman cannot avoid. We would expect policemen to be highly sensitive, therefore, to the perceived or actual support given them by their city governments. For small businessmen, losses from crimes against their stores are a cost of doing business. Since losses from crime fall disproportionately upon small business in the inner city (Reiss, 1969: 96), we would expect small businessmen to be especially sensitive to the protection against crime given them by the city government.

Surveys for the President's Commission on Law Enforcement and the Administration of Justice (Black and Reiss, 1966; Reiss, 1967b) and for the National Advisory Commission on Civil Disorders (Rossi et al., 1968) provide evidence that small businessmen operating in the inner city perceive the problem of crime and neighborhood characteristics in much the same terms as do police officers. This congruence of perceptions contrasts sharply with the perceptions held by other groups. The commission on civil disorders found, for example, that educators and social workers tend to take positions rather different from those of policemen and businessmen.

The commission on civil disorders asked policemen in twelve cities whether particular groups considered them enemies or friends or were indifferent toward them (Rossi et al., 1968: 103-114). "Storekeepers" ranked second behind "old persons" as the group most often seen as being "on their side." Approximately eighty-three percent viewed storekeepers as friends, with the proportion dropping to thirty-four percent for Negroes and sixteen percent for adolescents. When these policemen were asked about how many people in particular groups they knew well enough to speak with whenever they saw them, eighty-nine percent mentioned six or more shopowners, managers, or clerks. Only three percent reported knowing no businessmen well enough to casually speak with. The portrait of police-businessmen relationships emerging from these studies is that of relatively harmonious cooperation between the groups, at least from the policeman's perspective.

One implication of the above discussion is that businessmen and policemen in each city should resemble one another fairly closely in their crime-relevant attitudes. Table 1 presents the information necessary to test our prediction. Businessmen and policemen in Boston share a relatively negative view of their city government's capacity to combat crime. Washington, D.C., respondents also have a rather negative view of their city government, whereas respondents in Chicago have a relatively positive opinion of their city government. The absence of statistical significance for the chi-squares for Boston and Chicago in Table 1 lends support to the hypothesis that the pressures of facing a common environment and the same city government operate to produce a high degree of similarity in the attitudes of businessmen and policemen.

In Washington, D.C., policemen and businessmen are relatively dissimilar in their attitudes. This difference arises because policemen in Washington, D.C., are the most negative in their attitudes of all policemen in the three cities. There is some evidence that the lack of home rule for the District affects the attitudes of police toward their "local" government. We are inclined to give weight to this evidence because of the special circumstances that characterized police-government relations at the time of our survey. The President had appointed a special crime commission for

TABLE 1
A COMPARISON OF THE ATTITUDES OF POLICEMEN AND SMALL BUSINESSMEN IN BOSTON, CHICAGO, AND WASHINGTON, D.C. TOWARD THE JOB THE CITY GOVERNMENT IS DOING IN FIGHTING CRIME

City		Very Good	Fairly Good	Not Too Good	x^2	Δ^a	n
		Evaluation of City Government					
Boston	policemen	10.9	39.1	50.0			46
	businessmen	14.8	41.6	43.6	.354 $p > .80$	6.4	149
Chicago	policemen	41.5	39.0	19.5			41
	businessmen	36.2	48.7	15.1	.736 $p > .70$	9.7	152
Washington, D.C.	policemen	3.6	46.4	50.0			56
	businessmen	17.5	48.9	33.6	7.817 $p < .05$	16.4	223

a. Index of dissimilarity.

the District of Columbia. At the time of our survey, this commission was issuing reports that were sharply critical of the District police. One would expect that the effects of such releases would make the police more negative toward the city government than the businessmen who were not under attack, particularly in reducing the proportion of the police who see the relationship with city government as "very good." Such is the case.

This explanation is consistent with a more general presumption underlying this paper—that a third party, city government, acting independently of businessmen or the police, constrains the attitudes of those subject to its activities. The city government of Chicago, through a reorganization of the police department and some other highly publicized innovations, has succeeded in winning the confidence of a substantial proportion of the officers in its police department. Both the Boston and District of Columbia departments were under sharp attack from government sources, community leaders, and the local media during this period, and this is reflected in police officers giving city government much less support. For another discussion of attitudinal differences between the residents of different cities, see Schuman and Gruenberg (1970). Their analysis also shows that actual differences between city governments lead to corresponding attitudinal differences between residents of the cities they studied.

A TEST OF THE BOUNDARY PERSONNEL HYPOTHESIS

In testing our predictions, we need to take account of the fact that businessmen's attitudes toward the city government's capacity to fight crime are related to their attitude toward policemen in their area, as shown in Table 2. This is to be expected, since one basis for evaluating the city's battle against crime is how well the police are doing. Of businessmen holding a highly positive evaluation of the job area police are doing, 32.9% also rate the city government as "very good" and only 22.8% rate it as "not too good." These differences are even larger among those business-men holding a negative view of area policemen. As we pointed out in the section on balance theory, it is possible that a businessman who knows a policeman would be influenced in his attitudes toward city government by his evaluation of area policemen. Therefore, when the impact of personal links with the police is investigated in the following analysis, businessmen's attitudes toward area police are controlled.

Our measure of personal links between businessmen and police officers is whether or not a businessman knows any police officers who work in his area well enough to talk with them. This measure of contact is related, of course, to police department policies and practices that affect contact between officers and businessmen. Traditionally, police officers were assigned to small beats they could cover on foot, a fact that facilitated contact with members of the business community, particularly since business areas were patrolled more regularly and frequently. The more modernized police departments today operate without foot patrol, relying almost exclusively on radio-dispatched mobile patrol that covers a large territory. The possibility of regular and frequent contact with businessmen is thereby reduced. Indeed, it becomes less likely that businessmen will know any officer in a modernized department since contact depends more

TABLE 2
ATTITUDE TOWARD AREA POLICE AND ATTITUDE TOWARD CITY GOVERNMENT

Attitude Toward Area Police	Attitude Toward City Government				
	Very Good	Fairly Good	Not Too Good	%	n
Very good	32.9	44.3	22.8	100	246
Fairly good	13.6	53.8	32.6	100	184
Not too good	6.0	34.0	60.0	100	50
All respondents	22.7	46.9	30.4	100	480
X^2 = 47.636	$p < .01$				

on unofficial encounters than on routine patrol. There may be other department policies and practices that affect contact between police officers and businessmen. In our study, the Boston police department facilitated work contacts between businessmen and off-duty police officers. Any Boston businessman may employ an off-duty police officer to protect his place of business, the contract for such employment being made with the department. Both Boston and Washington, D.C., are more given to foot patrol than Chicago, and their mobile patrol is less modernized.

We would expect, therefore, that businessmen in Chicago would be less likely to report contact with police officers than would those in Boston or Washington, D.C., a prediction upheld by our data. Only 53.7% of the businessmen in Chicago reported knowing policemen in their area, as compared with 69.9% in Washington, D.C., and 70.8% in Boston.

To restate the main hypothesis of this paper in terms of the data to be presented: When businessmen's attitudes toward area police are controlled, businessmen who report knowing police officers in the area are more likely to resemble the police in their attitudes toward city government than are businessmen who report they do not know officers in the area.

The data necessary to test this hypothesis are presented in Table 3. A chi-square is obtained for each line of the table by comparing the distribution of the line with the distribution for the police officers in that city. Because the expected value for some cells is fewer than ten cases, all chi-squares have been corrected by continuity. Note that our interest is not in the absolute values of the chi-squares but in the relative value of the "yes" (know policemen) line versus the value of the "no" (do not know policemen) line. Whenever the chi-square for the former is smaller than that for the latter, our hypothesis is supported. The index of dissimilarity, a measure that is one-half the sum of the absolute values of the differences between the distributions, is also reported for each comparison.[1]

Table 3a includes all respondents who believe that policemen in their area are "doing a very good job." In all three cities, businessmen who report knowing policemen in their areas resemble city policemen more closely than do businessmen reporting not knowing any area policemen. Table 3b includes all respondents who feel that area policemen are "doing a fairly good job." In two of the three cities, the hypothesis is again supported. (In Boston the chi-square is smaller for those not knowing any policemen, although the difference is extremely small.) Finally, Table 3c includes all respondents who stated that area policemen are "not doing too good a job." Only five respondents in Chicago chose this alternative, so that part of the table has not been percentaged. In Boston and Washington, D.C., the hypothesis is again supported.

TABLE 3

EFFECT OF PERSONAL RELATIONSHIP WITH POLICEMEN ON
ATTITUDES OF WHITE SMALL BUSINESSMEN TOWARD
CITY GOVERNMENT, CONTROLLING FOR BUSINESSMEN'S
ATTITUDE TOWARD AREA POLICE[a]

		3a. "Police Are Doing A Good Job"					
City	Know Policeman?	Very Good	Fairly Good	Not Too Good	x^2	Δ	n
Boston	Yes	24.4	41.5	34.1	2.516	15.90	41
	No	44.4	33.3	22.2	4.068	33.55	9
Chicago	Yes	45.5	47.6	7.1	1.743	12.35	42
	No	60.0	34.3	5.7	2.758	18.50	35
Wash. D.C.	Yes	22.1	45.3	32.6	8.859	18.50	86
	No	24.2	54.5	21.2	9.974	28.75	33

		3b. "Police Are Doing A Fairly Good Job"					
City	Know Policeman?	Very Good	Fairly Good	Not Too Good	x^2	Δ	n
Boston	Yes	11.6	48.8	39.5	.628	10.45	43
	No	9.5	52.4	38.1	.577	13.30	21
Chicago	Yes	17.9	50.0	32.1	3.084	23.60	28
	No	16.7	62.5	20.8	3.470	24.00	24
Wash. D.C.	Yes	8.3	58.3	33.3	2.180	16.65	48
	No	25.0	50.0	25.0	6.790	25.00	20

		3c. "Police Are Not Doing Too Good A Job"					
City	Know Policeman?	Very Good	Fairly Good	Not Too Good	x^2	Δ	n
Boston	Yes	—	38.5	61.5	.130	11.50	13
	No	—	10.0	90.0	3.140	40.00	10
Chicago	Yes	—	—	(2)	b	b	2
	No	(2)	(1)	—	b	b	3
Wash. D.C.	Yes	—	58.3	41.7	.194	11.90	12
	No	10.0	30.0	60.0	.230	16.40	10

a. A Chi-square was obtained for each line of the table by comparing the distribution of the line with the distribution for the police officers in that city. All values have been corrected for continuity.

b. Chi-square not computed on 5 cases or less.

In seven out of eight possible comparisons, then, the group of businessmen reporting that it knows some area policemen more closely resembles the city policemen's attitudes toward city government than does the group of businessmen who reports not knowing any policemen. While several of the differences are quite small, the consistency across cities and attitudes toward area police gives us confidence in the results. It should be noted that, when an alternative measure of congruence is used, the index of dissimilarity—the differences between the lines in the direction of our hypothesis—becomes much larger and *all* eight comparisons support the hypothesis. We chose not to rest the case for testing the hypothesis on this index, because it cannot be adjusted for the number of cases in a table, whereas chi-square can be adjusted (the correction for continuity).

These findings thus support our hypothesis about the consequences of the boundary-spanning role that policemen play. The results do not support a balance theory interpretation, since the hypothesized differences were found even after attitudes toward area police were controlled. If small businessmen acquainted with area policemen do modify their attitudes toward city government on the basis of their orientation toward area police, then we would expect to find the greatest degree of congruence among those with a favorable orientation and the least degree of congruence among those with an unfavorable orientation toward police. This is not the case, as in Boston and Washington, D.C., where those businessmen most unfavorable toward area policemen have actually greater similarity to city policemen than those favorably oriented to area police. The pattern is obscured in Chicago, because there are only five persons unfavorably disposed to area police. We are therefore left with the boundary personnel or exchange perspective as the most plausible interpretation for our results.

CONCLUSIONS AND IMPLICATIONS

The tests reported in this paper support two positions on the forces making for attitude congruence between groups in a shared environment. The first position argues that when two or more groups are exposed to forces that are highly salient for each and there are similar consequences for each, there is a high degree of similarity in the attitudes of the two groups toward what they share in common. In our study, policemen and small businessmen face a common and in many ways a hostile environment. Crime prevention is a concern of both small businessmen and police officers. Both groups, moreover, are dependent on the city administration for the resources and the policies needed to carry out measures against crime. Thus, crime and the city government's response to crime are salient issues for both groups. As a result, policemen and businessmen in two of the three cities are so similar in their attitudes toward the city government's ability to combat crime that they appear to have been drawn from a common pool. In Washington, D.C., the groups are not as congruent in their attitudes mainly because of the extremely negative view which the District of Columbia officers have of the city's administration.

A second position with regard to attitude congruence asserts that interpersonal contact between representatives of two organizations can lead to the transmission of attitudes from one group to the other. In our study we have treated police officers as acting in the role of boundary personnel for the police department. In this role, police officers interact with the population served by the police force and attempt to establish cooperative relations with them. Of course, much of the initiative for the establishment of personal links may come from small businessmen as they attempt to secure every possible protection against crime for their businesses (Aldrich, 1969; Aldrich and Reiss, 1970).

One consequence of the relationship between police officers and businessmen is that the officers' attitude toward law enforcement in the city gets transmitted to the businessmen. The greater such contact, the more businessmen come to resemble the officers in their attitudes toward such things as crime and the city government's role in crime prevention. When policemen have a rather negative view of what the city administration is doing on the crime front, this attitude is passed on to, and reflected in, the attitudes of small businessmen in the city. This seems to have occurred in Boston and Washington, D.C. When the officers have a positive view, the opposite is the case. Chicago police officers hold a highly positive view of the city administration. Small businessmen in Chicago also have a highly favorable attitude toward the police force.

The above findings have some implications for the current issue of "law and order." Our findings suggest that policemen are related to this issue in a number of ways. First, crime as a political issue seems to affect policemen, who work to prevent losses, as much as it does small businessmen who must suffer the losses. The same pressures that point toward the city government's role, perceived or actual, in fighting crime affect both groups. Second, the effectiveness of the police force in the various precincts of the city appears to have an impact on the attitudes that small businessmen have toward government. When businessmen are satisfied with the job that area police are doing, or the police they meet report satisfaction with city government, the businessmen also are satisfied with the city government's role, and vice versa.

Third, and perhaps most important, if our assumption is correct that businessmen are heavily dependent upon policemen for "inside" information about law enforcement, then the police through their contact with businessmen have within their power the capacity to turn "law and order" into a local issue. Our findings allow us to do no more than show that policemen do influence the attitudes of small businessmen. Yet, the findings are consistent with other evidence that policemen may create "local support" for the police.

NOTES

1. Note that we are using chi-square for a purpose different from the ordinary usage. We know that the two groups come from different populations, since they were sampled from two different universes. We are comparing two populations to see to what extent they depart from complete similarity. Rather than using chi-square to derive a level of confidence concerning whether the two populations are similar enough to treat as coming from the same universe, we are treating the magnitude of the chi-square itself as an indicator of the degree of similarity of the two distributions. Therefore, our interest lies not in a level of confidence, but in the raw chi-squares and the differences between them. A difficulty that usually arises in the use of chi-square is that there is a strong positive relationship between the size of the sample and the size of the chi-square. In our analysis, the size of the samples is not a problem because in every case the subgroup with the larger number of cases is the group predicted to have the smaller chi-square by our hypothesis. The size factor thus goes against our hypothesis. If the chi-square for the group knowing a policeman is smaller than for the group not knowing a policeman, we know it is not because of a bias in the computation of chi-square. Moreover, the fact that another indicator of similarity—the index of dissimilarity—also supports our hypothesis gives us added confidence in our results.

REFERENCES

ALDRICH, H. (1969) "Organizations in a hostile environment: a panel study of small businesses in three cities." Ph.D. dissertation. University of Michigan.
——— and A.J. REISS, Jr. (1970) "The effect of civil disorders on small business in the inner city." J. of Social Issues 26 (Winter): 187-206.
——— (1969) "A 1968 follow-up study of crime and insurance problems of businesses surveyed in 1966 in three cities." Crime Against Small Business: A Report of the Small Business Administration to the Select Committee on Small Business, United States Senate, Ninety-First Congress, First Session, Document 91-14: 145-176.
BLACK, D. J. and A. J. REISS, Jr. (1966) "The evaluations and images of owners and managers of businesses and organizations toward the police and police service." Report to the President's Commission on Law Enforcement and the Administration of Justice.
BRINK, W. and L. HARRIS (1963) The Negro Revolution in America. New York: Simon & Schuster.

COOK, S. and C. SELLTIZ (1955) "Some factors which influence the attitudinal outcomes of personal contact." International Social Sci. Bull. 7, 1: 51-58.

CURRY, T. and R. EMERSON (1970) "Balance theory: a theory of interpersonal attraction?" Sociometry 33 (June): 216-238.

DAVIS, J. A. (1963) "Structural balance, mechanical solidarity and interpersonal relations." Amer. J. of Sociology 68 (January): 442-462.

FESTINGER, L. (1957) A Theory of Cognitive Dissonance. Evanston, Illinois: Row, Peterson.

HOMANS, G. (1950) The Human Group. New York: Harcourt, Brace.

JAHODA, M. and P. WEST (1951) "Race relations in public housing." J. of Social Issues 7 (Winter): 132-139.

JAMES, H. E. O. (1955) "Personal contact in school and change in intergroup attitudes." International Social Sci. Bull. 7, 1: 66-70.

JEFFRIES, V. and H. R. RANSFORD (1969) "Interracial social contact and middle-class white reactions to the Watts riot." Social Problems 16 (Winter): 312-324.

NEWCOMB, T. (1961) The Acquaintance Process. New York: Holt, Rinehart & Winston.

REISS, A. J., Jr. (1969) "Field survey of crime against small businesses," in Crime Against Small Business: A Report of the Small Business Administration to the Select Committee on Small Business. U.S. Senate, Ninety-First Congress, First Session, Document 91-14: 53-143.

——— (1967a) "Public perceptions and recollections about crime, law enforcement and criminal justice," in Studies in Crime and Law Enforcement in Major Metropolitan Areas, Field Studies III, Vol. I, Section II, Washington, D.C.: Government Printing Office.

——— (1967b) "Career orientations, job satisfaction, and the assessment of law enforcement problems by police officers," in Studies in Crime and Law Enforcement in Major Metropolitan Areas, Field Studies III, Volume 2, Section II, Washington, D.C.: Government Printing Office.

ROSSI, P. H., et al. (1968) "Between white and black: the faces of American institutions in the ghetto," in Supplemental Studies for the National Advisory Commission on Civil Disorders, Washington, D.C.: Government Printing Office.

SCHUMAN, H. and B. GRUENBERG (1970) "The Impact of City on Racial Attitudes." Amer. J. of Sociology 76 (September): 213-261.

SEGAL, B. (1965) "Contact, compliance and distance among Jewish and non-Jewish undergraduates." Social Problems 13 (Summer): 66-74.

THOMPSON, J. D. (1962) "Organizations and output transactions." Amer. J. of Sociology 68 (November): 309-324.

WILNER, B. M., WALKEY, and S. COOK (1952) "Residential proximity and intergroup relations in public housing projects." J. of Social Issues 8 (Spring): 45-69.

PART FOUR

The Emergence
of Police Professionalism

The Emergence
of Police Professionalism

While the interaction between policemen and citizens may comprise one of the most critical features of law enforcement activities, police officers long have tended to display a sense of isolation or estrangement from the community. As a result, police attitudes not only have been shaped by police encounters with civilians, but they also have been molded by the internal values and perspectives of police organizations. For many years, law enforcement officers seemed to share a common subculture that separated them both from the community and from other public employees. Increasingly, however, as law enforcement practices became the subject of mounting controversy, an important movement was initiated within the ranks of police departments. Law enforcement personnel began to propose higher salaries, increased educational requirements, greater training, and growing powers of self-regulation as a remedy for their problems. In short, they advocated that police work should become a profession rather than merely a job. The accelerating trend toward police professionalization, therefore, probably has represented one of the most significant new developments in the field of law enforcement.

Although the drive toward professionalism threatens to introduce many radical and potentially disruptive changes in police practices, the powerful informal norms that permeate most law enforcement agencies can still exert a major impact upon the orientation of police recruits. In his article on police socialization in Philadelphia, Leonard Savitz focuses upon the attitudes of both rookie and experienced officers toward traditional law enforcement standards such as secrecy, mutual assistance, and loyalty to the force. While the implications of this study seem to suggest that the strength of some of those values has diminished slightly, many police customs may continue to impede the implementation of uniform and impartial rules within police organizations. As a result, the propensities acquired by policemen through the processes of socialization also may hinder the effective supervision of police conduct by responsible public officials.

Although the transmission of informal values from experienced officers to recruits could promote a reluctance to adopt organizational changes, the expanding influence of professionalism also might provoke serious divisions within law enforcement agencies. The effects of professional strivings upon police attitudes and behavior are assessed by James Leo Walsh. While the findings of this study indicate that professionalization is associated with police perceptions of political events, minority groups, and criminal suspects, they also reveal that relatively professional law enforcement officers manifest a strong dislike for certain types of offenders viewed as interfering with the fulfillment of their responsibilities. Hence, the emergence of professionalism might alter law enforcement values and beliefs, but it may not totally eliminate the influence of the implicit norms that guide police action.

Unlike most government agencies, police departments not only are formally responsible to the public and elected political leaders, but they also occupy a close official relationship to the judiciary. In a study of four police departments, Neal Milner finds that the acceptance of increased legal restrictions upon law enforcement procedures is related to the degree of professionalization in those departments. By reducing police resistance to the directives of judicial and political authorities, the movement to professionalism could facilitate the approval of major policy changes or innovations within police forces. Yet, the ultimate need to gain enhanced public confidence also might require the consideration of further alternatives. While professionalism appears to offer the prospect of improving some aspects of police conduct, it may not provide a panacea for all of the problems that beset law enforcement agencies.

The Dimensions of Police Loyalty

LEONARD SAVITZ
Temple University

In 1967, we began a continuing longitudinal investigation of how a series of norms and beliefs which define appropriate and inappropriate systems of role behavior are informally acquired by a cohort of police recruits during their first three years in the Philadelphia Police Department. It seems unarguable that inevitable occupational socialization will, in time, result in values and behavior which render the novices indistinguishable from older, more experienced (perhaps more "professional") officers. The 226 recruits were examined initially during their first week of training at the Police Academy (hereafter referred to as T1); the same population was re-examined after they had completed the full 12 weeks of training at the Academy (T2) and then after the remaining 197 members of the cohort had been "in the field" for 6 months (T3). Interest was focused not merely on the fact of change but also on the *direction* of attitudinal and behavioral change, so that the questionnaire given to the recruits at T3 was simultaneously administered to a convenience sample of 197 "experienced" patrolmen (who had been in rank for an average of over 5 years and who had minimal expectations about upward mobility within the department) and to 233 detectives (a rank to which most policemen aspire). It was important to determine whether the novice officer came to acquire some of the more "cynical" beliefs of the older patrolmen with whom they necessarily worked in close contact, or the more conventional norms characteristic of the detective population.

THE NATURE OF LOYALTY

This paper will deal only with some tentative conclusions derivable from the study about the components and dimensions of police loyalty. It is important, however, to first of all indicate the manner in which loyalty is a direct consequence of the peculiar nature of police-public interaction. Westley (1951) conclusively demonstrated that the police-citizen relationship was the most distinctive feature of the policeman's job. He concluded that the police tended to view civilians with suspicion, as aliens, and, not infrequently, as enemies, the public systematically failing to grant the police the respect such a vital and central occupation is entitled to as a matter of course. Failing to secure the deference which they feel they are owed by the public has resulted in numerous instances of hostile or brusque officer responses in observed police-citizen transactions (Black and Reiss, 1967) or even a stated desire on the part of an appreciable percentage of members of some northern urban police departments to resign from the force because of public disrespect and apathy (Reiss, 1967).

A frequent reaction to this social rejection may take the form of social isolation. Skolnick (1966) forcefully argues that police isolation arises from a constant sense of danger (which isolates the officer from both the criminal and noncriminal populations) and authority associated with the policeman's job (enforcing minor statutes which generates resentment and hostility in so far as he directs, restrains, and regulates public morality). Niederhoffer (1967) along similar lines finds much evidence of police anomie which he defines as a loss of faith in people. Other researchers have noted extreme police isolation (Wilson, 1963; Fogelson, 1968) and it has even been persuasively suggested that the law enforcement community is beginning to perceive itself as a minority group, discriminated against by the public (Campbell et al., 1969).

An inevitable concomitant of occupational isolation is the rise of high occupational solidarity. Skolnick (1966, 1969), Banton (1964), and McNamara (1967) all suggest that while all occupations have some elements of inclusiveness and identification, the police are unusually high in job solidarity. Reiss' (1967) extended investigation of police behavior in Boston, Washington, and Chicago found that 95% of the officers would defend the department or a fellow officer who had been slurred. Niederhoffer (1967) notes the dilemma of ideal police practice in conflict with practical patrol operation, resulting usually in closer dependence and greater reliance on fellow officers. Wilson (1963) believes that there may develop a police subculture predicated on a "code" quite at variance from that operating within civilian populations. In any event, a view of the research in the field reveals the truth of Skolnik's (1969) conclusion that "students of the police are unanimous in stressing the high degree of police solidarity."

As it is generally used, the concept of police loyalty is an uneasy amalgam of two independent and unequal behavioral components: (1) dangerousness of job plus isolation from the public increases the need for mutual assistance (maximum priority of response given to any police officer requiring assistance). (2) Secrecy (deliberate failure to reveal illicit, illegal, or simply uncomplimentary bits of information about police practices to a hostile citizenry or unsympathetic police superiors). As early as 1930, an eminent authority in the field of law enforcement concluded in one of the Wickersham Commission reports, "It is an unwritten law in police departments that police officers must never testify against their brother officers" (Vollmer, 1930). When Westley (1956) asked several officers in his midwest police department whether they would "report" or "testify" against a theft committed by a fellow officer, eleven of fifteen would not report and ten of the fifteen would not testify. Anyone who would inform was a stool pidgeon and would, as a matter of course, be ostracized. Secrecy was a shield against the attacks of outsiders. Westley (1951) postulated the presence of three primary police norms; secrecy, being the most important, was consciously taught all rookies by older officers. Skolnick (1966) and Wilson (1963), among others, conclude that "secrecy" was present within the departments they had studied and was perceived as being extremely functional and necessary for the continued operation of the forces.

It would be absurd to deny the *presence* of deep ties of loyalty among members of the Philadelphia Police Department. What is worthy of investigation are the several possible recipients of police loyalty (the public, the department, or fellow officers), and a determination of the furthest reaches, the limits of secrecy, and the code of mutual aid and assistance.

EXTERNAL LOYALTY

It is possible the police officer may still retain an idealized conception of his role performance, inculcated during his Police Academy days, so that his primary obligation is to the public which has created his position, delegates to him rather extraordinary amounts of power, indirectly judges his performance, and offers him some material rewards for the adequate performance of his occupational role. Crucial here is the perceived need for concealing information from this audience and the dependability of public support and aid in times of crisis. If the public is thought to be unsympathetic or even hostile, a group which permits, even demands, the use of deadly force and yet inexplicably fails to grant the respect and awe which normally accrues to positions exercising such power, external loyalty is a dubious commodity. A large percentage of the police in this study held this view of the public. A bare majority of the recruits at T1 (fifty-three percent) and T3 (fifty-one percent) and detectives (fifty-two percent) and far fewer experienced patrolmen (thirty-two percent) felt that the "public's view" of the police was favorable or very favorable. Expectedly, the "*Negro* public's view" was considered more negative, with only twenty-eight percent of the recruits at T1 and twenty-two percent at T3, sixteen percent of the detectives and eight percent of the experienced officers finding them to be equally favorable or very favorable. (Indeed, seventy-seven percent of the experienced officers judged the Negro community's attitude to be unfavorable or very unfavorable.) Beyond this, one-third of the rookies (T3) but over sixty percent of the older patrolmen and the detectives agreed that "most civilians think people join the police force because they can't get a better job." Concerning public cooperation with the police, contradictory results were found. While seventy-three percent of the recruits at T2 (without any field experience) though "civilians generally cooperate with the police officers in their **work**," almost fifty percent, *at the same time*, nevertheless said that, "Patrolmen almost never receive cooperation from the public that is needed to handle police work properly" and sixty-nine percent thought that, "It was usually difficult to persuade people to give a patrolman the information he may need." Under conditions where a policeman is most dependent upon others, sixty-five percent of the recruits at T2 and fifty-eight percent at T3, but only forty-eight percent of the detectives and forty-three percent of the experienced patrolmen agreed that, "Most people will somehow help a patrolman being attacked." In this study the public fails on both issues: it is unsympathetic and hostile and not infrequently contemptuous, while one cannot rely upon them in times of greater emergency.

INTERNAL LOYALTY

Perhaps then the police are really a big brotherhood, demanding complete dedication and operating as a closed, semisecretive body. One must now maintain the best possible posture vis-à-vis the public, even if this requires manipulating or concealing organizational malpractices. Internal loyalty is most likely to occur if the actual operation of the organization is held in high regard by its personnel. A favorable self-appraisal would imply fewer occasions arising which would require concealment and secrecy. Perhaps also involved is a somewhat inchoate, seldom articulated belief that there must (or should be) some quid pro quo between officer and department; complete fealty to the organization by an officer should perhaps be reciprocated by deliberate if informal systematic indifference to minor infractions of administrative or legal rules, and the application of minimal sanctions for the violations of more serious regulations governing appropriate police behavior. Given the high frequency of temptations to corruption that are a normal occurrence in the life of a police officer, organizational liberality might be conceived of as partial compensation for officer secrecy. The Philadelphia Department was very highly rated by the subjects; ninety-three percent of the recruits at T1 and T3, eighty-two percent of the detectives, and seventy-four percent of the older officers rated it as the best or one of the best in the country. On specific items, however, evaluations are less enthusiastic. Generally the actual operation of the department was most highly regarded by the rookies and least favorably viewed by experienced policemen. Thus sixty-nine percent of the recruits (T3), forty-four percent of the detectives, and forty percent of older officers agreed that "as one gets to know the department from the inside, it is a very efficient, smoothly operating organization." Yet seventy-five percent of all three populations indicated that "it is impossible to always follow all departmental rules and regulations and still do an efficient job."

Concerning the issue of leniency within the department, Table 1 reveals a consistent tendency by the recruits (from T2 to T3) to suggest lesser punishments for inappropriate or illegal police behavior. For six of the seven acts, a shrinking percentage believed the offending officer should be dismissed or arrested. Taking a $10 bribe not to issue a traffic ticket would be severely punished by only thirty percent of the recruits (at T3), whereas fifty-six percent of the same subjects had previously recommended dismissal or arrest six months before at T2. Similarly, a policeman stealing a few bottles of liquor from a guarded store should be heavily punished according to forty-seven percent of the recruits at T3, nine percent less than those holding the same view at T2. As they respond to the "reality shock" of actual patrol work, recruits tend to become more permissive towards inappropriate police action and, by and large, more closely approximate the values of experienced patrolmen rather than the more critical judgments of the detective population. Cowardice is a condition which is difficult for police to "take seriously." They indicate that it is a condition that is as unlikely to occur as a surgeon who cannot stand the sight of blood. Excepting only cowardice, Table 1 shows the older officers are always most lenient and detectives most severe. The question arises whether Table 1 represents a range of *desired* punishments or is an

TABLE 1

PERCENTAGE OF AGREEMENT AMONG RECRUITS (at T2 and T3), DETECTIVES, AND OLDER EXPERIENCED POLICEMEN FOR ACTS FOR WHICH POLICEMEN SHOULD BE DISMISSED OR ARRESTED

Acts	Recruits		Detectives (n=223)	Officers (n=197)
	T2(n=220)	T3(n=197)		
An officer takes a few bottles of liquor from a state store which he is guarding after it has been burglarized.	56	47	74	36
An officer takes $10.00 a week from a "numbers banker."	77	54	70	38
Cowardice.	63	72	85	75
An officer takes $100.00 from the operator of a "still."	82	61	70	45^a
An officer takes $500.00 not to arrest a burglar.	92	81	94	64
An officer burglarizes a gas station.	95	92	97	83
An officer takes $10.00 not to issue a ticket to a driver of a car.	53	30	52	27

a. Fifteen of the 197 older officers indicated that policemen guilty of such corruption should not be punished at all.

estimate of actual departmental punishment policies and practices. A significant percentage of all subjects believed that "patrolmen are frequently found guilty of violation of departmental rules and are penalized severely," (the percentages were: T2 - twenty-five percent, T3 - twenty-two percent, detectives - twenty-eight percent, experienced patrolmen - forty-two percent) while at the same time an even larger percentage felt that "disciplining a patrolman usually has the effect of making him a less active and efficient officer" (the percentages were: T2 - forty-one percent, T3 - twenty-five percent, detectives - thirty-eight percent, experienced patrolmen - fifty-one percent). Very striking is the fact that forty-four percent of the recruits at T2, forty-eight percent at T3, sixty-four percent of the detectives, and seventy percent of the older patrolmen believed that a patrolman at a departmental hearing (he "goes to the front") will not get a fair, impartial trial. Indeed, twenty-eight percent of the detectives and forty-two percent of the experienced officers contend that "even with a good defense, an officer would be found guilty" by the departmental tribunal. Thus there exists probably a considerable discrepancy between what many officers describe as "fair" penalties for illegitimate police practices and the "unfairness" of punishments meted out at departmental hearings. In conclusion, the department is generally well regarded but is thought excessively severe in penalizing inappropriate police behavior.

What are some of the limits to internal loyalty? Is a "good cop" one who gives his commanding officer unquestioned obedience? Only fifty-four percent of the recruits (T3), forty-two percent of the detectives, and forty-three percent of the experienced officers thought so. "Informally told by his supervisor not to be 'too concerned' with the numbers racket, the officer should comply with such informal directives" according to only twenty-six percent of the recruits (T3), twenty-one percent of the detectives, and thirty-eight percent of the older officers.

Nevertheless, most officers believe that "the police department is really a big brotherhood" and the organization would automatically dispatch all necessary aid whenever an officer requested it so that internal loyalty would be rewarded by the assurance of maximum material assistance in times of crisis.

INTERPERSONAL LOYALTY

With a capricious, uncooperative, and unreliable citizenry, with a bureaucratic structure which does not always properly protect its own, there arises the possibility that latent structures develop which place the highest premium on loyalty among fellow officers. Secrecy is defined as personal and conscious concealment of information not only from the public but also from supervisory and administrative levels within the organization. Mutual aid means one assumes maximum response of all individual officers to any other officer in trouble; such a system of reciprocal aid means that the officer is less dependent upon the possibly vague supervisory directives regarding the allocation of scarce resources (vehicular and personnel) or the unpredictable and often arbitrary variables which go into the decision of the dispatcher regarding the disbursal of police facilities during the time of an emergency. This is replaced by a firm belief in the reliable presence and appropriate reaction of officers sent to an embattled officer as well as the voluntary response of nondispatched police who become aware of the trouble.

Despite the previously indicated consensus among researchers on the existence and power of police secrecy, Table 2 clearly demonstrates that interpersonal bonds of secrecy are not highly developed within this subject population. A very considerable percentage of all officers stated that they felt it would be appropriate to inform a supervisor about a partner who was a grafter, an incompetent, a disgruntled agitator, an alcoholic, or who was excessively violent. It is important to recognize initially that the five proscribed modes of behavior in Table 2 deliberately did not include the most reprehensible forms of police misbehavior, e.g., an officer who is a serious criminal or who "frames" an innocent person, or who becomes involved in more extreme forms of corruption ("continually on the take" from some criminal organization, or being "bought off" by a felon). The recruits generally would inform on a partner who was brutal, or an alcoholic, or a "disgruntled agitator." Detectives were more likely to reveal to their superiors all inappropriate acts, excepting only agitation. The experienced officer, consistently, is most committed to a policy of silence. The questions were difficult for the subjects to deal with and were often described as "rough" or "rotten" because they did not permit simple or conventional responses. A completely conventional set of responses would be for the subject to inform for all five acts; complete interpersonal loyalty would be to remain silent on the same five acts. In point of fact, a very small percentage of respondents gave totally conventional or totally loyal responses. Also the general pattern of informing that emerged was rational, consistent, and easily explicable. Minor graft is a real and constant threat to the incorruptability of policemen "in the street" so that the inability to resist such temptation is, from the point of view of rookies and older patrolmen, understandable as is their reluctance to inform on

TABLE 2

PERCENTAGE OF RECRUITS (nine months on the force), DETECTIVES, AND EXPERIENCED PATROLMEN WHO WOULD INFORM THEIR SUPERIORS ABOUT A PARTNER'S IMPROPER BEHAVIOR, BY TYPE OF BEHAVIOR

Partner's Behavior	Recruits (n=197)	Detectives (n=223)	Officers (n=197)
He is a "grafter" (takes money not to issue traffic tickets).	35	54	30
He is incompetent.	35	42	38
He is a disgruntled agitator.	54	47	45
He is continually drunk on duty.	59	73	49
He is excessively violent and brutal when making arrests.	56	75	60

such behavior. Incompetence is a notoriously spongy term, capable of a wide range of individual definitions; therefore, as one would not like to be judged by someone else's possibly eccentric notion of competence, one in turn should not condemn others except in the most severe and unarguable situations. A disgruntled agitator is a problem because he will ultimately provoke serious trouble within the department so that it is in one's own best interest to inform a superior about him. A drunken cop is simply a bad officer, lacking the most important characteristic of a "good cop": dependability; his unreliability may well put his partner at considerable disadvantage under certain patrol conditions. Excessive violence, beyond its moral implications, raises the distinct possibility of eventual internal departmental investigations of acts of alleged brutality which may result in condemnation and punishment not only for the perpetrator but also perhaps for a partner who has previously failed to notify supervisors about such prior behavior. On the final measure of secrecy, in great contrast to Westley's findings, only sixteen percent of the recruits (T3), five percent of the detectives, and twenty-seven percent of the experienced officers agreed that "A policeman should never testify against a fellow officer in court regardless of what he has done." It would seem then that secrecy, maintenance of mutual confidences among fellow officers, is perhaps not an integral part of a policeman's occupational role.

Regarding mutual aid to officers in trouble, the entire population (with only three exceptions) agreed that if they were out-of-uniform and off duty, they would immediately go to the aid of any officer who required assistance. If an arrested suspect was identified as someone who had killed a policeman, the police would be justified in "roughing him up" in the view of forty-two percent of the recruits at T1, forty-four percent at T2, and fifty percent at T3, as well as fifty-five percent of the experienced patrolmen, but only twenty-four percent of the detectives. The recruits at T2 were overwhelmingly (ninety-five percent) in agreement that an officer can always count on getting aid from other policemen when he needs it. Yet fully twenty-seven percent of the same recruits (T2) thought that "there are a significant number of policemen who will try to get out of doing anything to help other officers."

As a measure of the totality of commitment to rendering aid to fellow officers, the recruits at T1 and T3, the detectives, and older officers were asked to imagine a patrolman walking a beat, far from a police phone box, when two people come up to him and each tells him about two separate acts occurring simultaneously, each of which requires *immediate* police action; he can, of course, respond to only one of them. To which act should the officer respond? One of the acts in each pair involves a policeman requiring some form of help: he has broken his leg; he is simply described as being "in trouble"; he is being "pushed around" by a group of hoodlums; or he is being shot at by burglars. The other act in each pair represents a "good pinch," being a serious offense with a strong possibility of apprehending the offender: a shopkeeper has been murdered and the killer is still in the store; a child has been sexually assaulted and the criminal is still in the area; a robbery has taken place and the robber can still be arrested. Additionally, the crimes are politically clear and would very likely result in much favorable publicity for the arresting officer as well as the entire department. The forced pair choices meant that the respondents were once more faced with selecting between unattractive alternatives. The officer could go to the felonies (thereby jeopardizing a fellow officer) or he could respond to the threatened policeman (which might well result in a serious and dangerous criminal going free). As Table 3 shows, when informed that an officer has broken

TABLE 3

PERCENTAGE OF RECRUITS, DETECTIVES, AND EXPERIENCED PATROLMEN RESPONDING TO ANOTHER OFFICER IN TROUBLE RATHER THAN TO A SIMULTANEOUSLY OCCURRING "GOOD PINCH," BY TYPE OF OFFICER TROUBLE AND BY THE NATURE OF THE OTHER CRIME

Type of Trouble (v. the "Good Pinch")	Rookies T1[a] (n=226)	Rookies T3[b] (n=197)	Detectives (n=223)	Officers (n=197)
Officer falls and breaks leg				
(v. Murder)[c]	23	31	28	49
(v. Child Molester)[d]	25	56	56	58
(v. Robber)[e]	59	60	53	63
Officer simply in trouble				
(v. Murder)	36	37	21	44
(v. Child Molester)	50	60	52	56
(v. Robber)	75	76	62	75
Officer being pushed around				
(v. Murder)	37	58	53	56
(v. Child Molester)	53	76	71	75
(v. Robber)	73	80	74	81
Officer being shot at				
(v. Murder)	65	74	63	80
(v. Child Molester)	72	89	87	90

a. The recruit population during its first week on the police force.

b. The recruit population during its ninth month on the police force.

c. The act reads, in full: A store keeper has been killed by a robber who is still in the store.

d. The act reads, in full: A child has been sexually molested and the criminal is still in the area.

e. The act reads, in full: A man has been held up and the robber may still be caught.

his leg, most police will go instead to the scene of a simultaneously occurring murder, but (excepting only the recruits at T1) a preponderance of the same officers will respond to the injured officer in preference to arresting a child molester. When the officer is described simply as being "in trouble," the same pattern emerges, with the police in the main," responding to a homicide but, once more, choosing to aid the officer rather than investigate a sexual molestation. An officer being manhandled clearly commits most police to his defense (except for the "untutored" recruits at T1) in preference to a murder, sexual assault, or robbery. An officer who has been shot at receives the immediate support of most policemen regardless of whatever else might have claims upon their attention.

Thus the only situation when *most* police will not automatically assist a fellow officer is when an extremely serious felony (murder) has just taken place *and* the officer is in relatively little jeopardy. Recruits increasingly gave highest priority to officers in distress so that by T3 their responses were very similar to that of older officers and detectives. Experienced officers are most likely and detectives least likely to render aid to an endangered officer regardless of setting. Also one is struck by the remarkable similarity in responses of the three, somewhat dissimilar, police populations. Significant is that even in instances of greatest peril to a fellow officer, twenty to thirty-seven percent of the police subjects would not go to his aid but would respond to a recent murder, and over ten percent would pursue a child molester.

CONCLUSIONS

Some tentative conclusions regarding police loyalty would be:

(1) The two components of loyalty, secrecy, and mandatory mutual assistance are of differential importance. Our subject population seemed barely constrained by any norm of interpersonal secrecy (an officer could and should appropriately inform on his partner under a variety of conditions) while, at the same time, they were strongly (but not uniformly) impelled to immediate and unquestioned response to an injured or threatened officer.

(2) There exist countervailing circumstances which negate, for a significant percentage of the police, the highest priority normally assigned to the rendering of maximum mutual aid.

(3) The experienced patrolmen consistently demand (and perhaps reciprocally offer) maintenance of secrecy and loyalty and mutual assistance

in almost every setting, while detectives are least committed to the same norms of loyalty.

(4) As the recruits are rather quickly socialized into their complex occupation, a large proportion internalize *selected portions* of the value systems of experienced officers with whom they work on an intimate daily basis.

REFERENCES

BANTON, M. (1964) The Policeman in the Community. London, England: Tavistock.

BAYLEY, D. H. and H. MENDELSOHN (1969) Minorities and the Police. New York: Free Press.

BLACK, D. J. and A. J. REISS, Jr. (1967) "Patterns of behavior and citizen transactions," in Studies in Crime and Law Enforcement in Major Metropolitan Areas, Vol. II. Washington, D.C.: U.S. Government Printing Office.

CAMPBELL, J. S., J. R. SAHID, and D. P. STANG (1969) Law and Order Reconsidered. Staff Report 10 to the National Commission on the Causes and Prevention of Violence. Washington, D.C.: U.S. Government Printing Office.

FOGELSON, R. M. (1968) "From resentment to confrontation: the police, the Negroes and the outbreak of the nineteen-sixties riots." Pol. Sci. Q. 83: 217-247.

McNAMARA, J. N. (1967) "Uncertainties in police work: the relevance of police recruits, background and training." in D. J. Bordua (ed.) The Police. New York: John Wiley.

NIEDERHOFFER, A. (1967) Behind the Shield. Garden City, N.Y.: Doubleday.

REISS, A. J. Jr. (1967) "Career orientations, job satisfaction, and the assessment of law enforcement problems by police officers." in Studies in Crime and Law Enforcement in Major Metropolitan Areas, Vol. II. Washington, D.C.: U.S. Government Printing Office.

SKOLNICK, J. H. (1969) The Politics of Protest. New York: Ballantine Books.

――― (1966) Justice Without Trial. New York: John Wiley.

VOLLMER, A. (1930) Report on the Police. United States National Committee on Law Observance and Enforcement. Washington, D.C.: U.S. Government Printing Office

WESTLEY, W. A. (1956) "Secrecy and the police." Social Forces 34: 254-257.

――― (1951) "The police: a sociological study of law, custom, and morality." Ph.D. thesis. University of Chicago.

WILSON, J. Q. (1967) "Police morale, reform and citizen respect: the Chicago case," in D. J. Bordua (ed.) The Police. New York: John Wiley.

――― (1963) "The police and their problems: a theory." Public Police 12: 189-216.

Professionalism and the Police

The Cop as Medical Student

JAMES LEO WALSH
Oberlin College

The role of the police in modern life has attracted considerable attention in recent years.[1] Both social scientific research and ideological pronouncements have sought to explain police behavior in terms of such variables as ethnicity, social class, religion, role conflicts, age, rank, and organizational differences in police departments.[2] Others have examined the police from a more psychological vantage point stressing factors such as authoritarianism, childhood socialization experiences, and the personality syndromes of violently inclined police officers.[3]

THE OCCUPATIONAL SETTING

More recently, however, students of police behavior have begun to examine the occupational settings within which police officers work. These research efforts have sought to explain the attitudes and behavior of policemen in terms of the theoretical framework of the sociology of the

Author's Note: *This is a revised version of a paper, "The Professional Cop," presented September 4, 1969 at the meetings of the American Sociological Association, San Francisco, California.*

professions. With one modification, the research reported here fits into this latter approach.

Specifically, concepts and propositions advanced by Hughes (1958, 1959, 1963), Hall (1961), Wilson (1963) and others[4] concerning the impact of professionalism on members of an occupational grouping form the theoretical base of this study. On the basis of other research in the professions, sociologists can argue that variations in professional stature and position lead to variations in attitudes and behavior.[5] Those who view their work as being highly professional should, therefore, express different attitudes toward it and behave differently in fulfilling occupational roles than those in the same occupation whose conception of the work is that it is located further down the occupational prestige ladder.

Policemen do differ considerably in their conceptions of the social position of their work. Some view themselves as professionals, highly trained to provide service in meeting and solving problems the community cannot itself handle (Hughes, 1958: 139-144). On the other hand, many policemen consider their work simply a job involving relatively little more commitment than putting in the time demanded by any other eight-hour factory shift. The initial emphasis of this paper is focused on attitudinal and behavioral differences between the highly professional police officers and those classified as low-professionals. But, to deal adequately with an examination of professionalism and the police requires an expansion of the theoretical perspective of the sociology of the professions to include the process of professional striving.

A rich body of theory and research exists to lend credence to the argument that police officers who are professional strivers differ significantly in their attitudes and behavior from those policemen who place less value on the quest for higher professional stature.[6] Indeed, in many ways, the professionally striving policeman is not unlike a jazz musician or a medical student and the sociological factors explaining their attitudes and behavior also hold promise for explaining attitudinal and behavioral variations among policemen.[7]

In his analysis of the factors leading jazz musicians to harbor less-than-favorable attitudes toward the music-consuming public, Becker described the turmoil created when the artist-musician faced the dilemma of "going commercial" and playing what the fans want in return for status and financial reward, or of sticking by their artistic principles and contenting themselves with status among other musicians only (Becker 1951, 1953). When forced to make such a choice, the jazz musician felt embittered toward society. His occupational self-image as an artist and a creator did not coincide with the public view of him solely as an entertainer.

A similar process has been reported in studies of medical students. Hughes has listed the student criteria for desirable patients as including, among other things, the effect of the patient on the physician's career, income, reputation, and development of further skills (Hughes, 1958: 124-125). Becker and Geer have extended this to point out that student ideas and expectations of patients include in great measure attitudes drawn from the medical culture in which the concept of medical responsibility "pictures a world in which patients may be in danger of losing their lives and identifies the true work of the physician as saving those endangered lives" (Becker and Geer, 1958: 70-71). To lack this sense of medical responsibility is to lack the essence of physicianhood, and medical students come to value those patients who can be cured over those who cannot. Those who are not organically ill in the first place—the hypochondriacs of "crocks"—are the worst of all. Becker and Geer go on to point out that the student physician worries a great deal about managing his interaction with his patients so that they will be pleasant and cooperative. The most difficult scenes come about when patients have no respect for the doctor's authority. Physicians resent this immensely.[8]

So it is with the police officer and the professionally striving police officer in particular. He is involved in the quest for occupational identity (Fisher, 1969) and part of that quest is the management of his relationships with his "clients," the citizens with whom he comes into contact.[9] Managing this relationship is a difficult task for the police for, unlike the continuous excitement and successful arrest records of heroic television policemen, boredom and lack of tangible results are a part of police work (Reiss and Bordua, 1967: 35-37). Similar to the physician, the essence of the police vocation is seen as crime prevention and detection, but the demands placed on the police frequently run counter to this view. The professionally striving officer is the one most likely to feel this and to value experiences in which he "really did some police work."[10]

Further, as was the case with the aspirant professionals in the medical schools, the professionally striving police officers were those who most resented attempts by their clientele to question their authority or balk at their demands (see Freidson, 1968: 33). Fully seventy percent of the striving police officers listed their most unpleasant experience as a policeman as having been a situation in which their authority had been challenged.[11] One of the results of such resentment has been pointed out by Fisher. She argued that one reaction open to an "agent group" (in this case the police) encountering challenge from its clientele may be to depart from efforts to enlighten and woo and, instead, either to discredit clients' motives and knowledge or to use direct coercion. (Fisher, 1969: 430).[12]

HYPOTHESES

Examining the police from the perspective of the sociology of the professions led to the formulation and testing of five hypotheses in this research. These include:

Section I:
(1) Police officers classified as low-professional are more likely to support political candidates of the right and to have voted for George Wallace more frequently than those police officers who were classified as highly professional.

(2) Highly professional police officers differ significantly from low-professional policemen as to when they think it appropriate "to rough a man up."

(3) Highly professional police officers differ significantly from low-professional policemen in attitudes toward racial and economic minorities.

(4) Highly professional police officers differ significantly from low-professional policemen as to the types of people with whom physical force is used differently.

Section II:
(5) High professional striving levels among policemen lead to significantly different attitudes toward the use of physical force with certain types of citizens than do lower levels of professional striving.

METHOD

The data for this study were gathered in personal, largely open-ended interviews conducted by the author in four police departments in small and medium-sized cities in the Middle West during the winter and spring of 1969. The police departments were located in communities ranging from suburban bedrooms for nearby cities to ethnically-diverse mill towns.

A total of seventy-nine police officers were interviewed while on duty. Analysis was limited to uniformed police officers. Interviews were conducted on all three turns or shifts and observational data on the routine of the police stations and the behavior of the police officers while on duty were recorded. Prior to the actual interviewing, several months were spent visiting, calling, and writing the police departments studied so as to explain the purposes of the research and answer questions in advance. Cooperation was excellent and only three policemen refused to be interviewed. One of these later changed his mind.[13]

Seemingly endless arguments often result when efforts are made to define precisely the meaning of the term "profession" (Carr-Saunders, 1937: 491-492; Faunce and Clelland, 1967; Wilensky, 1964). Becker (1962: 33) has offered perhaps the most helpful solution to the problem of definition, arguing that any work group that succeeds in getting itself called such is a profession. Extending Becker's argument somewhat, it can be argued with Vollmer and Mills (1966: vii-viii) that the concept "profession" be used to refer to an abstract model of occupational organization. Professionalism, on the other hand, refers to a dynamic process, an ideology, used by members of an occupational group whose members aspire to professional status. There is clear evidence that many policemen are seeking this recognition and whether they are "real" professionals or not does not affect the fact that policemen vary on both subjective and objective measures of "professionalism." Though side-stepping the difficult definitional problems involved with the concept "profession," suffice it to say that police officers do respond readily, if differently, to questions concerning the professional stature of their work and that variations in attitude related to such variations in professional level provide useful sociological insights. In sum, whether they have "made it" or not, or even whether they ever will achieve the coveted status of a profession, does not seem to affect the efforts of the police to garner this elusive goal, and it is this quest and not so much the success or possibilities of success which is of interest in the formulation of the research reported here.

The respondents to this study were classified into categories based on their responses to seven items from the interview schedule.[14] These items had all proven useful in other research (Walsh and Elling, 1968; Walsh, 1969). This seven-item "professionalism score" facilitated categorizing the respondents into highly professional, medium-professional, and low-professional categories.

Following the collection of the data, social class, rank, age, organizational differences between the departments, ethnicity and, finally, authoritarianism were utilized as independent variables insofar as all have been used in other studies of the police. Neither significant differences nor consistent trends appeared in this analysis and emphasis was placed on testing the importance of level of professionalism and professional striving in differentiating and explaining police attitudes and behavior. Chi-square tests of significance were utilized in testing these relationships. The results of these tests are reported below.

FINDINGS: PROFESSIONAL STATURE
AND POLICE ATTITUDES

VOTING BEHAVIOR

Voting behavior of police officers has been considered in several studies and generally the argument has been that they tend to vote conservatively (Lipset, 1969; Skolnick, 1966; Niederhoffer, 1969; Vega, 1968). However, measures of voting behavior in this research indicate that police officers vary in their voting practices and that the professional stature of a policeman is helpful in explaining that variation. Specifically, the low-professional police officer was the policeman most likely to have voted for George Wallace in the past presidential election while Hubert Humphrey and Richard Nixon were supported more frequently by the more professional police officers.

Considering the data presented in Table 1, further insight into the voting behavior of the policemen interviewed comes into view. Two questions were asked dealing with voting behavior in this study. The first asked if the respondent generally voted as a Republican, a Democrat, or an Independent. Later, the respondent was asked which of the three presidential candidates he had voted for in 1968. As the data indicate, the low-professional policemen were those most likely to bolt from traditional Democratic voting practices and to vote for George Wallace. One-half of the low-professional policemen voted for Wallace in 1968 whereas forty-five percent of these low-professional officers said they usually voted for Democrats. Only fifteen percent of the low-professional policemen voted for Hubert Humphrey.

Moving up the professional stature index, the data in Table 1 indicate that the more professional police officers also frequently altered their usual practices but that most of them voted for Richard Nixon, not George Wallace. Indeed, in the case of the highly professional policemen, the Democrats remained Democrats in all cases while twenty-six percent of those highly professional policemen who were usually independents voted for Nixon, not for Wallace.

If voting for George Wallace for President in 1968 is a good operational definition of right-wing political behavior on the part of the police, then it is clear that most policemen are not reactionary politically and that the professional stature of a policeman helps to predict voting behavior. While in general the Democrats lost seventeen percent of their traditional supporters among the police in the 1968 presidential election, the highly professional Democratic policemen remained in the fold. At the other end of the continuum, however, thirty percent of the low-professional

TABLE 1

COMPARISON OF USUAL VOTING PRACTICES WITH ACTUAL VOTING BEHAVIOR IN 1968 PRESIDENTIAL ELECTION BY PROFESSIONAL LEVEL OF POLICEMEN

(in percentages)

a Usual Voting Practice	b How Actually Voted in 1968	Level of Professionalism											
		Low			Medium			High			Total		
		a	b	Change from a to b	a	b	Change from a to b	a	b	Change from a to b	a	b	Change from a to b
Democratic	Hubert Humphrey	45	15	-30	43	33	-10	28	29	+1[a]	38	21	-17
Republican	Richard Nixon	15	35	+20	10	37	+27	14	39	+25	13	37	+24
Independent	George Wallace	40	50	+10	47	30	-17	58	32	-26	49	36	-13
	Total	100	100		100	100		100	100		100	100	
		n=20	n=20		n=30	n=30		n=29	n=28[a]		n=79	n=78[a]	

a. One policeman did not vote.

policemen deserted the Democrats. And, only among the low-professional policemen did the defections go to George Wallace more readily than to Richard Nixon. Thus, the first hypothesis tested in this study seems to be supported by the data.

ATTITUDES TOWARD ETHNIC AND ECONOMIC MINORITIES

A second finding of this research relates to an observation made in a recent work by Bayley and Mendelsohn (1969: 148) who observed, "Very little credence is given by policemen to charges that policemen treat minority people unfairly or improperly." To test this notion and to examine further the dynamics of police-minority interactions, respondents to this research were asked a series of nine questions concerning the position and treatment of ethnic and minority groups in the society. On the basis of the responses to these nine items, an "orientation score" was calculated on which respondents were compared by level of professionalism.[15] Table 2 reports these data where orientations toward minorities are classified either as negative, mixed or positive.

The efficacy of utilizing this multi-item measure was suggested in other research wherein it was argued that if racial or economic characteristics were of no importance to professionals in dealings with a variety of citizens, most respondents would list problems germane to the nature of the professional-client interaction, not concentrate on social class or ethnic factors in describing problems with clients (Walsh and Elling, 1968). But the police, like other professionals, did list ethnic and social class factors as being important considerations in their dealings with some persons. Again, the professional stature of a police officer appears as a critical variable in explaining which policemen are most likely to approach ethnic and economic minorities negatively and which are positive in their orientations.

TABLE 2

ORIENTATION SCORE BY PROFESSIONAL LEVEL

Orientation Toward Ethnic and Economic Minorities	Level of Professionalism							
	Low		Medium		High		Total	
	n	%	n	%	n	%	n	%
Positive	1	5	10	33	11	38	22	28
Mixed	7	35	14	47	12	41	33	42
Negative	12	60	6	20	6	21	24	30
Total	20	100	30	100	29	100	79	100

NOTE: X^2 = 13.261, 4 degrees of freedom, significant at .02.

The differences between the three groupings of police officers on the orientation score are statistically significant as predicted. The low-professional policemen were most likely (sixty percent) to harbor negative attitudes toward minority groups. For example, one such policeman argued, "A Negro in the community has more opportunities to get something for nothing that I do. It's their fault if they don't get good treatment. Hell, everyone has the same opportunity" (interview thirty-six).

The professional policemen, on the other hand, appeared much more empathetic toward minority groups and scored positively on the orientation score. These police officers frequently argued that no small proportion of the difficulties between the police and the minority groups developed because of inadequate training or insight on the part of policemen working with such groups. The need for training for the police, not repression of the minorities, was stressed by the professionals. The second hypothesis of this research, then, seems to be verified.

THE POLICE AND PHYSICAL FORCE—I

Data concerning the role of professionalism in explaining attitudes toward the use of physical force provided the impetus to introduce a modification of the more traditional theoretical statements of the sociology of the professions. At first glance it would appear, as the data in Table 3 indicate, that the more professional a police officer is, the less likely he is to condone the use of physical force in situations other than defending himself or making an arrest. But, as Table 4 will indicate, a more complicated explanation for the differential use of force by the police is needed.

TABLE 3
WHEN DO POLICEMEN THINK A POLICE OFFICER
IS JUSTIFIED IN ROUGHING A MAN UP?

	Level of Professionalism							
	Low		Medium		High		Total	
	n	%	n	%	n	%	n	%
To make an arrest	5	25	10	33	15	52	30	38
To defend myself	6	30	14	47	12	41	32	41
When they look or talk tough	9	45	6	20	2	7	17	21
Total	20	100	30	100	29	100	79	100

NOTE: $X^2 = 11.370$, 4 degrees of freedom, significant at .05.

In Table 3 the evidence is clear that low-professional police officers differ significantly from their professional counterparts in their responses to a question asking, "When do you think a policeman is justified in roughing a man up?" (Westley, 1953: 38).

On this question, it is interesting to note, none of the low-professional police officers questioned the use of the term "roughing up" or asked if it meant using sufficient force to make an arrest. The professionals, on the other hand, frequently objected to the term "roughing up" and asked that the wording be changed to mean using sufficient force to defend myself or make an arrest.

Almost one half (forty-five percent) of the low-professional police officers interviewed argued that a policeman was justified in roughing a man up if he "looked rough" or "talked tough."[16] One low-professional policeman explained that he thought a man should be roughed up in order to defend himself and, he added, "I'm defending myself when someone calls me a son-of-a-bitch and means it" (interview 38).

The data in Table 3, then, seem to indicate again that professional policemen differ significantly from their low-professional counterparts and that the third hypothesis tested in this study is borne out. The professional police officer is far less likely to condone the use of force in dealing with citizens. This finding, however, is confounded somewhat when the data presented in Table 4 are considered.

THE POLICE AND PHYSICAL FORCE—II

When asked, "From your experience does it seem that physical force is something a policeman finds he uses differently with different kinds of people?" both low-professional and professional police officers responded

TABLE 4

IS PHYSICAL FORCE USED DIFFERENTLY BY THE POLICE
WITH DIFFERENT KINDS OF PEOPLE?

Force is Used Differently by...	Level of Professionalism							
	Low		Medium		High		Total	
	n	%	n	%	n	%	n	%
Race and class	11	55	8	31	5	21	24	34
Animals	9	45	18	69	19	79	46	66
Total	20	100	26	100	24	100	70[a]	100

NOTE: X^2 = 6.497, 2 degrees of freedom, significant at .05.

a. Seven did not answer this question and two gave "unclassifiable" responses.

affirmatively. But the kinds of people they labelled as the likely recipients of such differential uses of force varied! Racial and social class differences were cited by the low-professional policemen much more frequently than by the professionals. But, a novel category of citizens, "animals," appear as those with whom the professionals use force more frequently.

To explain this difference between professional and low-professional policemen, several propositions from studies of professional-client interaction in nonpolice settings provide insight into the findings reported in Table 4. This explanation follows.

FINDINGS: PROFESSIONAL STRIVING AND POLICE ATTITUDES

Considering the policeman as a jazz musician or a medical student proved to be a fruitful perspective in analyzing the data for the second section of this paper. A nine-item professional striving score was utilized in this research to separate the respondents into "low," "medium," and "high" striving categories.[17]

Effective statistical controls are difficult to impose in studies involving small numbers of cases but several were attempted in the analysis of these data. Of specific interest is the finding that the data in Table 4, when professional striving was used as a control variable, indicate that the highly striving segments of the low, medium, and highly professional categories were those who specified "animals" as citizens with whom force was used differently.

Classifying the respondents in terms of their professional-striving levels led to the finding that the professionally striving police officer expressed attitudes considerably different from those of his less-actively striving counterparts. These differences appear to result from similarities in the role of the police officer and those of the jazz musician and medical students as outlined earlier.

CITIZENS AS "ANIMALS"

Police officers have their own term for those whom Becker's medical students would have labeled "crocks." The police have their "crocks" also but call them "animals." An understanding of their perceptions of such citizens sheds further light on the use of physical force by the police.

To the police officer the concept "animal" covers a variety of sins; but generally animals are those persons with whom very little likelihood of a positive outcome faces the officer as he sets out to handle a family dispute, to face a mentally disturbed citizen,[18] a belligerent drunk, a neighborhood quarrel in which the police must play the role of middlemen, or the known cop fighter.

The "animal" is frequently known to the police officer and often when interviews were interrupted and respondents were called to take care of citizens they characterized as animals, the officer stated before leaving that the chances were very high that a physical encounter would take place with the person in question. The police dislike such citizens intensely and for reasons similar to the medical students' dislike of the crock or the noninteresting patient.[19]

The animal is seen as putting the police officer in a "damned if he does, damned if he doesn't" position. If, for example, a police officer battles a citizen, he faces criticism for the use of force and frequently enhances the standing of the animal in the eyes of the latter's peers. If he doesn't, he must subject himself to the insults of the animal and lose respect both with the animal and his friends and with his fellow police officers (Whyte, 1943: 138; Bordua, 1967: 65-68).

It is interesting, in continuing this analogy between policemen and medical students, that those police officers who most actively seek higher professional stature are also those who are most likely to view the animal as problematic to police work. In fact, as the data in Table 5 indicate, the animal is set apart as the type of citizen with whom physical force is most likely to be utilized by eighty percent of the highly striving police officers interviewed. The willingness to use force against animals by professionally striving policemen resulted from, I think, many of the same reasons the medical student resents the hypochondriac.

To the professionally striving police officers, engaging in barroom brawls or street fights is seen as being detrimental to the stature of the

TABLE 5

WITH WHAT KINDS OF PERSONS DO YOU FIND THAT A POLICE OFFICER MUST USE FORCE DIFFERENTLY?

Force is Used Differently by. . .	Level of Professional Striving							
	Low		Medium		High		Total	
	n	%	n	%	n	%	n	%
Race and Social Class	12	57	10	33.3	4	20	26	37
With Animals	9	43	20	66.6	16	80	45	63
Total	21	100	30	99.9	20	100	71[a]	100

NOTE: X^2 = 6.285, 2 degrees of freedom, significant at .05.

a. Seven policemen did not answer this question and one response was unclassifiable.

police in the eyes of the general public (Sutherland and Cressey, 1966). Such behavior is seen by the striving policeman as opening the way to charges of police brutality, and it is seen as engaging in dangerous duty for little, if any, reward. The animal is expected to be back on the streets after a brief time and the police officer must face him again and again. Parenthetically, the police-animal relationship is perhaps one of the chief causes of police resentment of the public and the courts (Sutherland and Cressey, 1966). And, as Reiss and Bordua (1967: 33-37) have spelled out, may in fact lead to further use of force against animals. It is frustrating to the police officer to face the same animals time and again when they see the courts dispensing what they view to be lenient treatment. They interpret this as a sign that their efforts have not been appreciated and that justice has not been served (Reiss and Bordua, 1967: 33-37).

Comparing the policeman's animal with the medical student's crock, does seem to shed some light on the use of violence by the police. The analogy begins to break down when pushed further, however. The reason for this breakdown suggests that police perceptions of animals may be of even greater importance to their interaction than the crock's impact on the medical student's relations with his patients.

One of the textbook steps in the process of professionalizing has been to shed "dirty-work," and many professionalizing occupational groups have included shedding or altering relationships with those clients seen as being akin to dirty work (Walsh and Elling, 1968; Walsh, 1969). Such a step, however, is far more difficult for the police. They, too, view dealing with animals as dirty work, and the professional strivers in particular resent their inability to shed such duties to persons lower on the professional prestige ladder. Wrestling with drunks and dealing with animals remain firmly entrenched in the occupational duties of policemen, and, instead of being able to shed dirty work, the police are convinced that such tasks will continue as a major part of their responsibility. Cynicism toward the public is one result.[20] Increased willingness to use excessive force with some citizens is another.

DISCUSSION

Utilizing the theoretical perspective of the sociology of the professions, then, has utility in efforts to understand better the dynamics of the role of the police. Verification of the five hypotheses tested in this study indicates that the impact of professionalism does play a major role in explaining variations in police attitudes and behavior.

In this research, variables such as social class, ethnicity, age, rank, authoritarianism, and the like did not explain the variations noted in this paper. For example, the interesting work of Niederhoffer (1969), Lipset (1969), and Bayley and Mendelsohn (1969) emphasizing the role of police authoritarianism as a variable affecting police attitudes, was not substantiated in this research.[21] Nor did any consistent or significant differences in attitudes and behavior appear to result from the other, more traditional variables.

This is not to say that these are not important factors to consider in studies of the police; rather, these variables appear to play a significant role in determining which police officers come to consider themselves as high versus low professionals and also which policemen become professional strivers.[22]

While occupational conceptions do appear to separate professional police officers from their nonprofessional colleagues, such occupational prestige differences did not seem to divide the police forces studied into hostile or even separate camps. Indeed, the data seem to indicate that some highly striving police officers come to hold attitudes analogous to those of the nonprofessional policemen.[23]

The attitudes and behavior of policemen, therefore, are not the result of any one set of factors. Several social variables combine to produce occupational self-conceptions and levels of professional striving. And, in turn, those police officers who strive with confidence are, it seems, different from those who also strive but do so with awareness of Wilson's glum prediction that the police probably face more severe obstacles in their quest for recognition than do most other occupational groups (J. Wilson, 1963). Frustration, discontent, cynicism, and a continuation of the feeling that the police are set apart from other work groups (Lipset, 1969; Niederhoffer, 1969) and asked to play incompatible roles as stern defenders of the law in some cases and, somehow, also be able to use professional discretion and insight in handling still other situations with widely variant meanings to diverse sets of persons, are likely to continue.

The feeling for policemen and police work gained through this study suggests that a better understanding of the impact of the policeman's professional stature and of the results of professional striving on police attitudes will provide a useful inroad for better theoretical understanding of the sociology of the professions in general, and the police in particular.

Three final comments need to be made. The first is to emphasize that the findings reported in this paper are based on measures of the attitudes of policemen, not their behavior.[24] Numerous social scientists have cautioned against making the leap from studies of attitudes to predictions of behavior by those expressing such attitudes (see Deutscher, 1966; deFleur and Westie, 1958; Ehrlich, 1969; Tittle and Hill, 1967; and LaPiere, 1934).

Deutscher (1969) has raised this issue once again in a recent discussion. He (1969: 40) concludes, "Validity poses a serious problem when we use instruments designed to provide estimates of hypothetical behavior. If, instead, our data consist of direct behavioral observations, the problem of validity becomes negligible."

Clearly the data presented here tapped hypothetical behavior and must be interpreted as such. But, far from being as valueless as Deutscher would have us believe attitudinal data to be, such findings seem to me to be of value in paving the theoretical ground for future behavioral studies of the police—or other professions for that matter.

Secondly, the "last gospel" of many sociological reports needs to be emphasized strongly here. The findings reported in this article were based on a limited number of interviews and can claim to be representative only of the policemen interviewed. To generalize these conclusions further without first testing the theoretical perspective of this study on a more ambitious level would be inappropriate.

Finally and despite these cautions, it does seem apparent that the results of research such as this have bearing upon the selection and training of police officers. It also has implications for those with the task of administering police departments and consulting with policemen. If the social scientists have only recently embarked upon serious efforts to trace the impact of social variables upon police behavior, consider the need for policemen themselves to comprehend the subtle social factors affecting themselves, their work, and their "clientele."

NOTES

1. See for example Banton (1965), Chevigny (1969), Cray (1967), Fox (1966), Grimshaw (1963), Hopkins (1931), Jacobs (1966), Lane (1967), Piliavin and Briar (1964), Atlantic (1969), Issues in Criminology (1968), Stoddard (1968), Turner (1968), Van Allen (1968), Wiener (1960), and O. Wilson (1964).

2. See for example Bordua (1967), Ehrlich (1959), Goldstein (1960), Koenig (1960), Levy (1968), Niederhoffer (1969), Skolnick (1966), Stinchcombe (1963), and J. Wilson (1964).

3. See for example Knupfer (1947), Lipset (1969), Rankin (1959), Toch (1969), and Zimbardo (1968).

4. See for example Becker (1962), Goode (1961), New (1965), Niederhoffer (1969), Wilensky (1964), Zola and Croog (1968), Walsh (1969).

5. See for example Becker (1952), Davis (1968), Fanshel (1959), Gold (1952), and Hughes (1958).

6. See for example Eaton (1962), Bucher (1962), Bucher and A. Strauss (1961), Elling (1967), Goode (1960), G. Strauss (1964), Walsh and Elling (1968).

7. Comparisons of medical students and policemen are not novel to this paper. The only difference here lies in the interpretation of the data based on that analogy. For a different approach see McNamara (1967: 221-222).

8. The police resent attacks upon their authority in a manner analogous to the medical community. See Reiss and Bordua (1967: 48). Also, see Becker (1951-1952: 459), and Westley (1951: 30).

9. Reiss and Bordua (1967: 30) argue that the police are essentially a service without clients. In a different light, J. Wilson (1963: 201) has pointed out a major difference in the efforts of the police to professionalize when he wrote "professionalism among policemen will differ from professionalism in other occupations in that the primary function of the professional code will be to protect the practitioner from the client rather than the client from the practitioners."

10. The professionally striving police officers interviewed in this study were those who consistently named their most pleasant experiences as police officers as having actually solved crimes or done "something to help." Fifty-six percent of the professional strivers responded this way while only 30.6% of the low-striving policemen saw their most pleasant experience as having been a crime-solving or "professional" police task.

11. These data were drawn from an unstructured question, "What would you say your most unpleasant experience as a police officer has been?" Unlike the striving officer, only thirty-six percent of their low-striving counterparts described such an experience as having been a situation in which their authority had been challenged.

12. See also Cumming et al. (1965). Jacobs (1966) has argued that the police often view the public as the enemy.

13. In light of intervening events in two departments in terms of local-level political furor involving the police, it was thought that such factors could effect the results of the study and the remaining policemen were not interviewed. An additional twelve officers would have been added to the sample.

14. The professionalism score was based on the following items: (1) rank, (2) membership in professional police organizations, (3) reading of professional police publications, (4) the number and frequency of journals read, (5) "cosmopolitan" versus "local" role identity, (6) self-adjudged professional status, and (7) academic training in police work. Code categories were numbered low to high on each item and the professionalism score was obtained by adding the codes of the seven items.

15. The orientation score consisted of nine items, the responses to which were coded so that the highest code categories indicated the most negative orientation toward minorities and the lowest codes the least negative. The nine items included: perceptions of public hostility from minority groups toward the police, specifying minority groups as the "greatest problem" facing the police, specifying minority group members as those with whom it is most difficult to work, arguing that physical force is a necessity in minority areas, anticipating trouble from minority group members, blaming lazy minority group members for any discrimination in existence today, and specifying past dealings with minority group members as having been among a policeman's most unpleasant experiences as an officer. These items and codes can be obtained from the author.

16. McNamara (1967: 222) has reported similar findings and argued that experience in the field lead to such attitudes. Field experience, however, did not

seem to be a major factor in this research while the professional level of the police interviewed did. All of the respondents were involved in similar field experiences.

17. This professional striving score was developed in earlier research (Walsh and Elling, 1968: 21) and includes measures of the following characteristics: (1) delegating or shedding menial or unpleasant tasks to less highly trained persons; (2) attempting to assume more responsibilities on a higher level, such as seeking more voice in setting policy or undertaking new and novel activities; (3) seeking to become better known among professional colleagues in order to advance or gain professional respect; (4) developing or expressing willingness to join professional associations whose purpose is to advance the professional status of the police.

18. "Mentals" was another concept used frequently by the police to categorize persons with mental instabilities. They disliked mentals for they were thought to be unpredictable and often violent. Mentals are, however, a subgroup of animal.

19. One important difference between the medical students' "crocks" and those of the police did appear in this research. While the medical students resented uninteresting, nonenriching cases and sought to avoid them, the police officer often reacts to calls to provide assistance or solve problems not necessarily within the realm of law enforcement as at least enhancing the status of the police in the community and, therefore, does not seek to debunk or avoid them. It could be hypothesized that the police officers viewing their work as a job would be more likely to view such calls as coming from "crocks" than would the professional strivers and therefore be more likely to become involved in unsavory confrontations with citizens than would be the strivers. No such data were gathered in this study but findings indicating the utility of such a hypothesis were obtained from a question asking the police if they thought it appropriate for the police to become involved in health and welfare activities. The professional strivers overwhelmingly thought they should, the nonstrivers said no.

20. A recent excellent discussion of police cynicism can be found in Niederhoffer (1969: 95-108). Another perspective that seems to have application to the police is Levitin (1964).

21. In the pretest of this research an effort was made to utilize measures of authoritarianism employed in other studies. Bayley and Mendelsohn (1969) used the five-item F scale developed by Leo Srole (1956). Koenig (1960) used a similar measure, as did Niederhoffer (1969: 129).

The questions did not work, however, partially because some of the police involved in the pretest had had college training and recognized the items immediately and partially because, as one officer said, "Those questions are dumb." I think he was arguing, as most of the respondents would, that the police are exceptionally sensitive to criticism these days and that these questions were threatening.

An alternative measure of authoritarianism based on Milton Rokeach's work was utilized in this study. This consisted of a ten-item rigidity-flexibility score. Thus, the claim that authoritarianism is not a major factor in police attitudes may be a function of the measures employed.

22. These data are presented in an unpublished paper available through the author.

23. It is interesting to note, for example, that the highly striving police officers were those who were more likely to vote for George Wallace in the last presidential election. Earlier, data were presented to demonstrate that low-professional policemen were most likely to vote for Wallace. Those data were reported in Table 1 and the similarities between the voting behavior of the highly striving and low-professional police officers indicates the validity of the argument that the two types of policemen do share attitudes if for divergent reasons.

VOTING BEHAVIOR BY PROFESSIONAL STRIVING LEVEL

| | Striving Level | | | | | | | |
| | Low | | Medium | | High | | Total | |
	n	%	n	%	n	%	n	%
Humphrey	5	20	9	29	7	32	21	27
Nixon	12	48	11	35.4	5	23	28	36
Wallace	8	32	11	35.4	10	45	29	37
Total	25	100	31	99.8	22	100	78	100

24. It could be argued that the voting data are behavioral but insofar as they are based on self-reports, many of the pitfalls of attitudinal data are also involved.

REFERENCES

Atlantic (1969) "The police and the rest of us." 223 (March): 74-135.

BANTON, M. (1965) The Policeman in the Community. New York: Basic Books.

BAYLEY, D. and H. MENDELSOHN (1969) Minorities and the Police. New York: Free Press.

BECKER, H. (1962) "The Nature of a profession," pp. 27-46 in Sixty-First Year-Book of the National Society for the Study of Education, Part II, Education for the Professions. Chicago: Univ. of Chicago Press.

——— (1958) Boys in White. Chicago: Univ. of Chicago Press.

——— (1953) "Some contingencies of the professional dance band musician's career." Human Organization 12 (Spring): 22-26.

——— (1952) "The career of the Chicago public school teacher." Amer. J. of Sociology 57 (March): 473-477.

——— (1951-1952) "Social class yariations in the teacher-pupil relationship." J. of Educational Sociology 25: 459.

——— (1951) "The professional jazz musician and his audience." Amer. J. of Sociology 57 (September): 136-144.

——— and B. GEER (1958) "Student culture and medical school." Harvard Educational Rev. 28: 70-71.

BORDUA, D. (1967) The Police: Six Sociological Essays. New York: John Wiley.

BUCHER, R. (1962) "Pathology: a study of social movements within a profession." Social Problems 10 (Summer): 40-51.

——— and A. STRAUSS (1961) "Professions in process." Amer. J. of Sociology 46 (January): 325-334.

CARR-SAUNDERS, A. (1955) "Metropolitan conditions and traditional professional relationships," pp. 279-314 in R. M. Fisher (ed.) The Metropolis in Modern Life. New York: Doubleday.

CHEVIGNY, P. (1969) Police Power. New York: Pantheon Books.

CRAY, E. (1967) The Big Blue Line—Police Power vs. Human Rights. New York: Coward-McCann.

CUMMING, E., I. CUMMING, and L. EDELL (1965) "Policeman as philosopher, guide and friend." Social Problems 12 (Winter): 276-286.

DeFLEUR, M. and F. WESTIE (1958) "Verbal attitudes and overt acts: an experiment on the salience of attitudes." Amer. Soc. Rev. 23: 667-673.

DAVIS, F. (1968) "Professional socialization as subjective experience: the process of doctrinal conversion among student nurses," pp. 235-251 in H. Becker et al. (eds.) Institutions and the Person. Chicago: Aldine.

DEUTSCHER, I. (1969) "Looking backward: case studies on the progress of methodology in sociological research." Amer. Sociologist 4 (February): 35-41.

——— (1966) "Words and deeds; social sciences and social policy." Social Problems 13 (Winter): 235-254.

EATON, J.W. (1962) Stone Walls not a Prison Make. Springfield, Ill.: Charles C. Thomas.

EHRLICH, H. (1969) "Attitudes, behavior and the intervening variables." Amer. Sociologist 4 (February): 29-34.

——— (1959) "The analysis of role conflicts in a complex organization: the police." Ph.D. dissertation. Michigan State University.

ELLING, R. H. (1967) "Occupational group striving and administration in public health," in M. Arnold, V. Blankenship, and J. Hill (eds.) Public Health Administration. New York: Atherton Press.

FANSHEL, D. (1959) "A study of caseworkers' perceptions of their clients." Social Casework 39 (December): 543-551.

FAUNCE, W. and D. CLELLAND (1967) "Professionalization and stratification patterns in an industrial community." Amer. J. of Sociology 72 (January): 341-350.

FISHER, B. (1969) "Claims and credibility: a discussion of occupational identity and the agent-client relationship." Social Problems 16 (Spring): 423-433.

FOX, V. (1966) "Sociological and political aspects of police administration." Sociology and Social Research 51 (October): 39-48.

FREIDSON, E. (1968) "The impurity of professional authority," pp. 25-35 in H. Becker et al. (eds.) Institutions and the Person. Chicago: Aldine.

GOLD, R. (1952) "Janitors vs. tenants: a status income dilemma." Amer. J. of Sociology 57 (March): 486-493.

GOLDSTEIN, F. (1960) "Police discretion not to invoke the criminal process." Yale Law J. 69 (March): 543-594.

GOODE, W. (1961) "The librarian: from occupation to profession?" Library Q. 31 (October): 306-320.

——— (1960) "Encroachment, charlatanism and the emerging profession: psychology, sociology and medicine." Amer. Soc. Rev. 25 (December): 902-914.

GRIMSHAW, A. D. (1963) "Actions of police and the military in American race riots." Phylon 24 (Fall): 271-289.

HALL, O. (1961) "The place of the professions in the urban community," pp. 117-134 in S. D. Clark (ed.) Urbanism and the Changing Canadian Society. Toronto: Univ. of Toronto Press.

HUGHES, E. C. (1963) "Professions." Daedalus 92 (Fall): 655-668.

——— (1959) "The study of occupation," pp. 442-460 in R. Merton et al. (eds.) Sociology Today. New York: Basic Books.

——— (1958) Men and Their Work. Glencoe: Free Press.

HOPKINS, E. (1931) Our Lawless Police. New York: Viking Press.

Issues in Criminology (1968) "Race and the Police." 4 (Fall).

JACOBS, P. (1966) Prelude to Riot. New York: Random House.

KNUPFER, G. (1947) "Portrait of the underdog." Public Opinion Q. 11: 103-114.

KOENIG, M. (1960) "Congruency, satisfaction and attitudes: a study of the police." M.A. thesis. Oberlin College.

LANE, R. (1967) Policing the City. Cambridge: Harvard Univ. Press.

LaPIERE, R. (1934) "Attitudes vs. actions." Social Forces 13 (March): 230-237.

LEVITIN, T. E. (1964) "Role performance and role distance in a low-status occupation: the puller." Soc. Q. 5 (Summer): 251-260.

LEVY, B. (1968) "Cops in the ghetto: a problem of the police system." Amer. Behavioral Scientist 2 (March-April): 31-34.

LIPSET, S. (1969) "Why cops hate liberals—and vice versa." Atlantic 223 (March): 76-83.

McNAMARA, J. (1967) "Uncertainties in police work: recruits' backgrounds and training," pp. 221-222 in D. Bordua (ed.) The Police: Six Sociological Essays. New York: John Wiley.

MILLER, W. (1958) "Lower class culture as a generating milieu of gang delinquency." J. of Social Issues 14.

NEW, P. K. (1965) "Communication: problems of interaction between professionals and clients." Community Mental Health J. (Fall): 251-255.

NIEDERHOFFER, A. (1969) Behind the Shield. Garden City: Anchor Books.

PILIAVIN, I. and S. BRIAR (1964) "Police encounters with juveniles." Amer. J. of Sociology 70 (September): 209-211.

RANKIN, J. (1959) "Psychiatric screening of police recruits." Public Personnel Rev. 20 (July): 191-196.

REISS, A. and D. BORDUA (1967) "Environment and organization: a perspective on the police," in D. Bordua (ed.) The Police: Six Sociological Essays. New York: John Wiley.

SKOLNICK, J. H. (1966) Justice Without Trial. New York: John Wiley.

SMITH, A., B. LOCKE, and W. WALKER (1968) "Authoritarianism in police college students and non-police college students." J. of Criminal Law, Criminology & Police Sci. 59 (December): 624-631.

STINCHCOMBE, A.L. (1963) "Institutions of privacy in the determination of police administrative practice." Amer. J. of Sociology 69 (September): 150-161.

STODDARD, E. (1968) "The informal 'code' of police deviancy: a group approach to blue-coat crime." J. of Criminal Law, Criminology & Police Sci. 59 (June): 201-213.

SROLE, L. (1956) "Social integration and certain corollaries: an explanatory study." Amer. Soc. Rev. 21 (December): 709-716.

STRAUSS, E. (1964) "Work-flow frictions, interfunctional rivalry and professionalism: a case study of purchasing agents." Human Organization 23 (Summer): 137-149.

SUTHERLAND, E. and D. CRESSEY (1966) Principles of Criminology. Philadelphia: J. B. Lippincott.

TITTLE, C. and R. HILL (1967) "Attitude measurement and prediction of behavior: an evaluation of conditions and measurement techniques." Sociometry 30: 199-213.

TOCH, H. (1969) Violent Men. Chicago: Aldine.

TURNER, W.W. (1968) The Police Establishment. New York: Putnam.

VAN ALLEN, E. (1968) Our Handcuffed Police. Mineola, N.Y.: Repertorial Press.

VEGA, W. (1968) "The liberal policeman: a contradiction in terms." Issues In Criminology 4 (Fall): 15.

VOLLMER, H. and D. MILLS (1966) Professionalization. Englewood Cliffs, N.J.: Prentice-Hall.

WALSH, J. L. (1969) "Nurses, professional striving and the poor—a case of incompatibility." Social Sci. and Medicine 3 (forthcoming).

——— and R. H. ELLING (1968) "Professionalism and the poor-structural effects and professional behavior." J. of Health and Social Behavior 9 (March): 16-28.

WESTLEY, W. (1953) "Violence and the police." Amer. J. of Sociology 59 (July): 34-41.

——— (1951) "The police: a sociological study of law, custom and morality." Ph.D. dissertation. University of Chicago.

WHYTE, W.F. (1943) Street Corner Society. Chicago: Univ. of Chicago Press.

WIENER, N. (1950) "The grand privilege: a scholar's appreciation." Saturday Rev. 43 (March 5): 54.

WILENSKY, H. L. (1964) "The professionalization of everyone?" Amer. J. of Sociology 70 (September): 137-158.

WILSON, J. Q. (1964) "Generational and ethnic differences among career police officers." Amer. J. of Sociology 69 (March): 522-529.

——— (1963) "The police and their problems: a theory." Public Policy 12: 189-216.

WILSON, O.W. (1964) "Police authority in a free society." J. of Criminal Law, Criminology & Police Sci. 54 (June): 175-177.

ZIMBARDO, P. (1968) "Coercion and compliance: the psychology of police confessions," pp. 550-570 in R. Perrucci and M. Pilesuk (eds.) The Triple Revolution: Social Problems in Depth. Boston: Little, Brown.

ZOLA, I. and S. CROOG (1968) "Work perceptions and their implication for professional identity." Social Sci. & Medicine 2 (March): 15-28.

Some Common Themes in Police Responses to Legal Change

NEAL A. MILNER
Grinnell College

This essay focuses on police perceptions of and attitudes toward changes in criminal law and procedure. It initially reviews the literature concerning police perceptions of social and legal change, as well as the literature concerned with police attitudes toward such change. Some common themes about police attitudes toward present changes in criminal law are identified on the basis of this review. These themes are more systematically investigated by analyzing police officer response to the United States Supreme Court's *Miranda v. Arizona* decision.[1]

Those who investigate police-court conflicts typically view them as emanating from police disapproval of increased judicial supervision of their activities. While not denying the importance of this explanation, this essay seeks to broaden the scope of such analyses by relating police responses to the courts to their more general responses to social change.

Focusing on attitudes toward law is useful for understanding the relationship between police and society, because the law is probably the most important bridge connecting societal values and police behavior. Laws reflect the values of the dominant groups in the community and, by embodying and personifying the law, the police personify these dominant

Author's Note: *Some of the data for this paper appear in a different form in Chapter 9 of my book,* The Court and Local Law Enforcement: The Impact of Miranda *(Beverly Hills: Sage Publications, 1971).*

values (Alex, 1969: 3-5). The criminal law and, presumably, its enforcement exemplify this nexus between police behavior and societal values.

In the past few decades, the degree of legal change, particularly the proliferation of procedural and substantive laws, has profoundly affected the policeman's view of society. The increase in substantive law has led to a broadening of the police definition of deviance and criminality, while the proliferation of procedural law has at the same time increased police awareness of attempts to place constraints upon the enforcement of substantive law. Because of the debate over the priority of substantive versus procedural law, competing legal ideologies have been institutionalized (McNamara, 1967: 163-164; models of criminal justice administration are best presented in Packer, 1964; 1968).

This debate greatly affects the police officers' views of social change. The police find themselves in an ambiguous position. Society asks them to enforce more laws, while at the same time placing greater constraints on police behavior. Consequently, the police regularly and strongly condemn those in society who act to increase this uncertainty (McNamara, 1967: 164). This tension between law enforcement and due process of law is certainly not new. Indeed, it is part of an inherent tension in a political system that both espouses democratic ideals and is concerned with the maintenance of social order. But the proliferation of substantive and procedural law has undoubtedly increased the tension and made it more salient.

The police officer reacts to the often conflicting forces of social change by adopting a highly defensive ideology exaggerating the correctness of the police organization's conception of its role in society. Police develop a contempt both for those they consider the criminal and for those they consider the hypocritical, noncriminal elements of the population (Wilson, 1967: 161).

Social reformers are commonly branded as among the hypocritical elements. Because the police attribute their job difficulties primarily to the defects of the individuals and groups which they encounter, rather than to the limits of their own organizations, both crime and social protest are seen as emanating from the evil intentions of individuals. Thus, the police officer has little regard for explanations of crime which stress social or institutional causes. The Skolnick report to the National Commission on the Causes and Prevention of Violence calls this police view the "rotten apple" view of man.

This belief is especially important because it profoundly affects the regard police have for social and legal reformers. Because these reformers usually emphasize social conditions, the police perceive them as at best misguided idealists and at worst coddlers of criminals (Skolnick, 1969:

194-201). Thus police defensiveness, plus their distaste for social reform-ers, leads police to take a rather negative view toward the present direction in criminal law reform and toward those who advocate these changes.

In fact, this emphasis on the correctness of the police department's own view of its problems and of their solutions is also apparent in the literature which more specifically discusses law enforcement attitudes toward criminal law. The police commonly stress their own special abilities in determining guilt or innocence. Consequently, they consider the rules based on due process to be rather arduous and unnecessary job constraints imposed by outsiders who not only have minimal understanding of police work, but also prevent police from doing the job expected by society (Skolnick, 1966: 196-202; compare with Wilson, 1968: 38-41). Once again the perceived threat to job effectiveness is important.

Indeed, according to Skolnick (1966: 197), the police seem to make a moral distinction between constraints placed on an individual (the substantive law, whose enforcement they see as their paramount task) and constraints on authority (procedural law, which they typically see as an unnecessary constraint on performing this paramount task). They do not recognize the legitimacy of the view that both of these constraints are possibly equally important aspects of the criminal law. Thus they oppose the views of the judges and lawyers whom they see as proponents of the procedural (or due process) point of view. To them, the regulations emanating from the socially distant appellate judiciary constitute "a type of government—by the courts—without consent of the governed—the police" (Skolnick, 1966: 228).[2]

Police departments also attempt to protect themselves from the increasing dilemma resulting from tension between substantive and procedural law by emphasizing overly literal interpretations of police authority. Training programs stress that "police be prepared to defend themselves from outside criticism through knowledge of the letter of the law rather than its spirit" (McNamara, 1967: 250). This emphasis may limit amenability to change in both substantive and procedural criminal law because it leads police to view the law as fixed and immutable (McNamara, 1967: 250-251). Niederhoffer (1966: 164) suggests that legal change imposed by outsiders further increases police cynicism and distrust of these authorities because "each new reversal of hallowed legal principles upon which the code of police work rests, strips away some of the majesty from the body of the law."

The ideology of police departments which is most frequently empha-sized by the police reflects their views toward criminal law and reforms imposed by outsiders. This ideology, professionalism, stresses the special competence of a police officer, his high level of training, as well as his ability to perform his task efficiently and objectively.[3] This is not to say that police departments are highly professionalized. But professionalism is certainly a common ideology used to defend police behavior, and professionalization is the most frequently emphasized goal of police officers. Advocates of greater police professionalization are most likely to seek rigorous training and admissions policies, a high degree of specialization, and the adoption of organizational incentives, such as high salaries, in order to achieve these goals (Milner, 1970a).

There are two contradictory assumptions concerning the relationship between a police department's professionalization and its members' attitudes toward the trend in the development of criminal law and procedure. Most advocates of police reform at least implicitly assume that professionalization increases a department's amenability to such changes. Others claim that professionalization reinforces police distrust of outside influence and thus limits willingness to accept such legal changes (these hypotheses are discussed in Milner, forthcoming). But all agree that there is a relationship between organizational characteristics and attitudes toward criminal law.

On the basis of this summary of the literature, we can cull the following propositions about police attitudes toward court-initiated changes in the legal constraints on a police officer's job:

Proposition 1. Police officers are likely to disapprove of such changes.

Proposition 2a. In their disapproval, they stress their own expertise and the Supreme Court's lack of perspective about police work.

Proposition 2b. As a corollary, they are not likely to accept the legitimacy of due process constraints on their jobs.

Proposition 3. In their disapproval, they stress the Supreme Court's deviation from fixed legal principles.

Proposition 4. The characteristics of police organizations, particularly the degree of their professionalization, is related to their attitudes toward such changes. As suggested earlier, the literature differs over the nature of the relationship between professionalization and attitudes.

These propositions reflect a consideration of both perspectives of the individual police officer and the organizational structure in which he operates. They can be seen as intervening variables which at least partially determine the relationship between the formal written law and its implementation (Skolnick, 1966: 219-220).[4]

MIRANDA AS A CASE IN POINT:
METHOD AND ANALYSIS

In the *Miranda* opinion, the Court adopted a set of formal rules which the police must follow if a subsequent confession or any incriminating statement is to be considered admissible as evidence. Prior to questioning, the police officer must inform the suspect that he has the right to remain silent or to stop talking at any time. He must warn the suspect that anything he says may be used against him. The officer must further tell him that he has the right to a lawyer and that he can have one appointed at public expense. A suspect may waive these rights, but the waiver is accepted in court only if it is given in an intelligent and competent manner. At the minimum, a competent waiver can only follow a clear presentation of the *Miranda* rules.[5]

Though by no means a treatise on police reform, Chief Justice Warren's majority opinion certainly considered police reactions to those who attempt to bring about changes in police procedures. The Chief Justice sensed that the police would be very concerned about an increase in outside supervision, and consequently he emphasized the advantages of greater cooperation and understanding between law enforcement officers and others in the legal community.[6]

The information about police reactions was obtained from mail-back questionnaires administered in late 1966 and early 1967 to all policemen in four Wisconsin cities. Two hundred seventy officers responded; the total response rate was 45%. The response rate for the last open-ended question on the questionnaire, which will be discussed below, was twenty-seven percent.[7] The cities vary in their economic bases and in their political culture, but, compared to all of the American cities with a 1960 population of over 10,000, they are relatively similar in their population (varying from 70,000 to 150,000), and in their small minority-group population (ranging from less than one percent to less than six percent). The crime problem varied from being almost nonexistent in one community to moderately significant in the others (for more details on the characteristics of these four cities, see Alford and Scoble, 1969; Jacob, 1969: 87-96; Milner, 1970b).

In order to investigate the previously discussed propositions, we can use two items from this questionnaire. To measure the degree of police approval of the decision (proposition 1), each officer was asked to state simply whether he approved or disapproved of *Miranda*. To test the other propositions, which required more sophisticated analysis, we can analyze the responses to an open-ended question which attempted to elicit more fully police perceptions and views of the decision. The question read as follows:

If you so desire, please make any other comment about the *Miranda* rule. Why, for example, do you think the Supreme Court decided the case the way that it did?

The contents of the responses were analyzed. The 163 officers who answered this question offered 236 codable responses.

ATTITUDES TOWARD THE DECISION (PROPOSITION 1)

As anticipated, few of the 270 officers (twenty percent) approved of the decision. Neither the amount of time served on the force nor the degree of formal education seemed to be important factors associated with these attitudes. Of these 270 officers, those who had attended some college were most likely to approve of the decision (twenty-nine percent), but this was only a slightly larger number than the twenty-four percent who approved among those who had not even graduated from high school. Indeed, those men who had graduated from high school but had no further formal education—the largest group by far—were least likely of all to approve of *Miranda*. The type of knowledge obtained on the job seemed a slightly better indicator of attitudes. Detectives, the officers who have the most experience in using interrogation procedures, were more likely (twenty-nine percent) to approve of *Miranda* than were superior officers who were not detectives (twenty-two percent), or patrolmen (sixteen percent). These detectives had no greater degree of formal education than did the other officers.

Table 1 states the frequency of themes apparent in the content analysis of the officers' responses to the open-ended question. Even though the police responded to a question which did not explicitly encourage criticism of the Court and its decision, it is particularly interesting to note that an overwhelming majority of the responses are critical. More important for the purposes of the present analysis, however, is the fact that these responses are consistent with propositions 2a, 2b, 3, and 4 suggested below. Indeed *all* of the responses contained themes which are quite easily related to these propositions.[8]

REASONS FOR DISAPPROVAL: POLICE PERSPECTIVES AND JOB CONSTRAINTS (PROPOSITIONS 2a AND 2b)

Proposition 2a suggests that police will be critical of a decision like *Miranda* on the grounds that the justices lack a correct or realistic perspective of the police officer's tasks. Table 1 shows that this questioning of Supreme Court expertise is one of the two most frequent

TABLE 1
RESPONSES TO AND VIEWS OF *MIRANDA*

Theme	% of Officers
Questioning Supreme Court expertise in supervising police activities	36
In *Miranda* decision the Supreme Court has unduly emphasized the rights of the criminal over the rights of the rest of society	36
Decision is a response to illegitimate political pressure	11
Decision was an illegitimate change in law and procedure	20
Explanations consistent with typical advocates of police reform[a]	33
Other	5[b]
	n = 163

a. See the explanation accompanying the discussion of proposition 4a, below.

b. Total greater than 100% because as many as three responses per officer were coded.

responses. Many of these officers specifically emphasize the Court's lack of understanding of the police officer's perspective and problems. In the words of a young patrolman,

> It is obvious that some of our Supreme Court Justices are not familiar with the complexities of everyday police work.

> We should put our nine Supreme Court Justices in a few police departments to show them a few problems of common everyday police work.

The Court is also accused of operating with a presumption of guilt against the police officer. The officers insist that the justices overemphasize the extent of police brutality and underestimate the obstacles found by the police officer in performing his public duty. Because of this lack of "realism," these police claim, law enforcement officers cannot do their job effectively. These officers have no doubt that greater exposure to police departments would change the Court's perspective.

The decision raises particular resentment among those who claim that it punishes many police departments because of the misdeeds of one or two:

> As a professional, well trained police officer, I strongly resent being hand-cuffed by the Supreme Court for the misdeeds of my fellow officers.

This resentment is related to the view that most interrogations should not operate under such considerations. "Good," "efficient" police work suffers at the hands of this misguided decision because of its proscription of the use of indispensable tools. An experienced detective put it this way:

> I believe a man's right should be protected, however, I believe the police should be able to question a person without advising him of rights. Police work has been mostly bluff in the past and now you have nothing. The very good aspect of being a detective was to match wits with the criminal. Now that can't be done.

The resentment against outside regulation is forceful and pervasive. The latter two quoted statements, for example, show the relationship between a sense of confidence in police expertise and a feeling that the Court is unreasonably meddling in affairs it knows little about. Certainly the officers see themselves as the experts in administering justice in a manner they think most people in society want it to be administered.

Proposition 2b suggests that the police will not easily accept the legitimacy of due process constraints. Certainly in their denial of the Court's expertise the police are implying that such legitimacy is limited, but this is even more apparent in the second of the most frequent categories of responses in Table 1. Thirty-six percent of the officers feel that the *Miranda* rules harm both the police officer and society by aiding the criminal at the expense of the majority. Clearly the officers see the Court as placing obstacles in the way of what the community legitimately wants, as the following comment by an upper-echelon officer demonstrates:

> The Courts should be more aware of the rights of the community also. Courts are bending over backwards to help the criminals. If a person is competent enough to commit criminal acts why must the police advise subject of all the rights other than to remain silent and to the right of an attorney? What rights are the Courts giving the victim? Voluntary confessions should be admitted without trouble and honored by the courts. The police are of the opinion that the Courts are being too lenient with criminals.[9]

Although due process is not explicitly rejected, the rhetoric of the police officers in this category reflects a rejection of important assumptions made by advocates of due process. Guilt is assumed; the word "suspect" is never used. Only two of these responses even used the comparatively generous phrase "the accused" to describe the suspect. "Criminal" and "guilty party" are the predominant words. The decision "lets the criminals go free." It "makes it easier for the criminals." Again, the words of an officer (an inspector with twenty-five years of experience) best express the stark differences between the Court's view and the officers' view. After stating quite explicitly that all officers must obey the decision, he summarized what he considered to be the dominant police viewpoint:

> They [the police] feel that most of the protection is being afforded to the criminal without any regard for the rights of the innocent. *Certainly only the criminal would take advantage of the Miranda decision, the innocent need not worry* [italics added].

Taken together, the emphasis on expertise and the presumption of guilt reflect the acceptance of what Packer (1968: 162) calls the Crime Control Model of the criminal justice process. This model, the opposite of the due process model,

> has no truck with the presumption of innocence because of the probability that ... the preliminary screening processes operated by police and the prosecuting officials contain adequate guarantees of reliable fact-finding. Indeed the model takes an even stronger position. It is that subsequent processes, particularly those of formal adjudicatory nature, are unlikely to produce as reliable fact-finding as the expertise administrative process [involving the screening by the police].

The officers' responses fulfill most of the criteria of this model, particularly in regard to the emphasis it places upon the necessity of police determination of guilt or innocence and the related lack of importance of the presumption of innocence which is so crucial to due process. The views of these officers are reinforced by their belief that the Court's acceptance of due process is contrary to the views of the majority.

FURTHER REASONS FOR DISAPPROVAL: ILLEGITIMATE CHANGE IN CRIMINAL LAW AND PROCEDURE (PROPOSITION 3)

Twenty percent of the responses question the legal or procedural grounds forming the basis of the *Miranda* decision. The officers in this group seldom explicitly discuss the dilemmas arising from the changing basis of their legal authority, but their comments clearly emphasize the view that the law is certain and quite immutable (proposition 3).

The justices are criticized because, in making the decision, they made law rather than interpreted it. As one detective said critically, "I feel that the Supreme Court is trying to make legislation by judicial decree." As a corollary, the Court is accused of destroying the certainty of the law so clearly established by the founding fathers. In the words of a young patrolman:

> For as long as our land has been, we have lived by the constitution and the bill of rights of man. Now we must live by what someone thinks it means. This is done by adding words and ideas that our Supreme Court inserted.

Some officers question the legitimacy of a legal decision, like *Miranda*, which is the product of a divided Court. Each of these men mentions that the outcome of the decision was only by the barest of margins and that a single vote should not be decisive in legal matters. If the justices cannot agree on the interpretation, surely the interpretation must be suspect. For example,

> I feel any Supreme Court decision which is based on a 5 to 4 decision leaves much to be desired! When 9 learned men can't agree, the rule is open to debate.

This view of the law leads some officers to view changes in defense attorneys' procedures as attempts to circumvent the "true meaning" of the law by taking advantage of what the police disapprovingly call "technicalities" or "loopholes." In the opinion of these officers, the attorney has two reasons for this behavior: first, to free "guilty" clients, and second, to make money for selfish reasons at the expense of the public.

Some officers explicitly relate the Supreme Court's illegitimate change in the law and their own distrust of attorneys. The following comments of an experienced detective offer a good example:

> The Supreme Court has forgotten or chose [sic] not to acknowledge its function—to interpret law not to make law. Soon a lawyer will be necessary for so many things they will be as lice on society.

These comments further suggest that many of the officers are extremely reluctant to accept some basic operating rules of due process. In their opinion, the decision was an illegitimate breach of the Constitution. This breach was doubly damaging because it further limits reliable fact-finding on the part of the police. These views again reflect an acceptance of the previously discussed crime control model.

VIEWS CONSISTENT WITH DUE PROCESS-ORIENTED REFORM

The following views are especially important, because they must be included in our analysis of proposition 4, which posits a relationship between organizational characteristics and individual views. Due process-oriented police reformers commonly view *Miranda* as a necessary attempt to protect the suspect from the coercive atmosphere of police interrogation. They typically see the decision as at least an inevitable, if not a necessary, change in the constraints placed upon police behavior. Though all of these reformers may not agree on the *degree* of validity of the due process model of criminal justice, all would agree necessarily that police departments "upgrade" themselves to cope with the decision.[10]

The views of thirty-three percent of the officers suggest that these men had opinions and perceptions of the decision which were either consistent or at least empathetic with those who attempt to impose criminal law changes from the outside. This category is generously inclusive. These officers did not always approve of the decision. Their responses were also placed in this category if the officers perceived that the Court made the decision because it desired stricter guidelines, or because it desired to improve police behavior. If they mentioned the Court's desire to protect citizen rights without attributing the latter goal to a lack of realism, they were also put into this category.

The greatest number of these officers comment that the Court acted because of the need for stricter guidelines for police behavior. These men usually mention police abuses without criticizing the Court for taking general action to protect individuals from such abuses. In the words of a patrolman, the Court acted because "too many police departments in the country were operating in a manner that deprived a citizen of a right to counsel."

Others are more explicit in their emphasis on the Court's desire to protect the rights of all individuals, whether the individual is guilty or not. The Court is not condemned for this desire. Moreover, the distinction is made between a guilty party and a suspect. The following comments serve as good examples:

> The Court made the decision to protect the average citizen who is usually unaware of his full rights, when arrested.

> . . . so a person's rights would not be violated. As a rule some people are not aware of their rights and also the rich and poor would have equal rights as well as the educated and uneducated.

Some others relate the decision to the need for a more highly professionalized police department. Not all of these completely approved of the immediate results of the decision, as the comments of a young patrolman show:

> I think they [the justices] did it to protect the right of everyone and not to make it hard for us. But it has hurt some but in the long run I think it just makes for better and more complete police work.

ORGANIZATIONAL CHARACTERISTICS (PROPOSITION 4)

The previously considered propositions relate primarily to the attitudes of the individual officer. It was also suggested that organizational characteristics, particularly the degree of professionalization, are related to views toward change in criminal law. This hypothesis can only be tested in a very exploratory fashion. There are many other possible variables related to views of the criminal law. With only four cities, it is statistically impossible to distinguish how much variation is explained by organizational characteristics because useful techniques like multiple regression analysis cannot be used. Yet there are some important reasons for emphasizing professionalization. For example, in his study of the same four cities, Alford finds that characteristics closely related to professionalization are important determinants both of the difference in a community's political culture and of the nature of its governmental services. This alone tells us nothing directly about the police officer's attitude toward criminal law, but the general importance of the variable—coupled with the fact that other studies of the four cities have found a relationship between legal and police behavior and professionalization—further emphasizes its importance (see Alford and Scoble, 1969; Jacob, 1969: 87-96; Milner, 1970a).[11] Moreover, interdepartmental attitudinal differences are not related to other nonindividual variables such as city size, crime rate, or social composition of the city. There is thus at least some indication that organizational variables are important and that professionalization may be the most important of such variables.

In order to test this relationship between organizational characteristics and individual responses, the four departments were ranked according to an index of professionalization (for a discussion of construction of the index, see Milner, 1970a). Professionalization was directly related to the frequency of views which were most consistent with those of outside reformers. In the larger sample of 270 officers, approval of the decision was directly related to professionalization. Eleven percent of the officers in the two least professionalized departments approved of the decision, as compared to seventeen percent and thirty-six percent in the second most and most professionalized departments, respectively.

Table 2 shows that departmental professionalization is also directly related to the frequency of perceptions which are consistent with the way typical police reformers view *Miranda*. The responses of ten percent of the officers in the least professionalized, fifteen percent of the second lowest, twenty-two percent of the second highest, and twenty-eight percent of the most professionalized departments were consistent.[12] We might expect that the frequency of criticisms of Court emphasis on the rights of criminals (earlier interpreted as a denial of the importance of due process) is inversely related to professionalization. That pattern is roughly followed in Table 2. We might also expect the same inverse relationship between questioning of expertise and professionalization. Although the two most professionalized departments are slightly less likely to question the expertise, the difference is very small.

TABLE 2

VIEWS OF *MIRANDA* (by degree of professionalization
of police department; in percentages)

Responses[a]	Degree of Professionalization			
	Lowest	Second Lowest	Second Highest	Highest
Responses consistent with those of reformers	10	15	22	28
Criticism of Supreme Court's emphasis on rights of criminals	38	22	24	18
Questioning Supreme Court expertise in police matters	25	25	22	23
Other[b]	28	38	33	31
Total %	101	100	101	100
n =	61	55	46	74

a. Unlike Table 1 this table uses the total number of responses rather than respondents. This is done in order to control for multiple responses and to facilitate interdepartmental comparison which is not necessary in Table 1. As a result, of course, the totals in Table 2, unlike those in Table 1, approximate 100%.

b. This category includes the "other" category in Table 1, plus the categories dealing with the immutability of law and illicit political pressure.

One might thus interpret that professionalization is related to what in a general sense may be considered a more positive attitude toward the trend in criminal law and procedure. As proposition 4 suggested, however, we might expect some contradictory evidence. There are, in fact, other factors which limit such conclusions regarding such a positive relationship. Only a minority of police officers, even in the most professionalized department, either approved of the decision or discussed it in terms suggesting more amenability to outside influence. Furthermore, the degree of higher education, usually considered an important criterion of professionalization, was not positively related to the frequency of approving the decision (the relationship between professionalized ideology and the professionalization of these four departments is discussed in Milner, 1970b: ch. 9).

CONCLUSION

Probably no one is surprised at the degree or intensity of police opposition to the *Miranda* decision. What is more interesting is the similarity between the way a majority of the police view the decision and the way other studies suggest they view outside attempts to impinge upon police behavior. The police are, for the most part, unconvinced that decisions like *Miranda* can be reconciled with good police work. Their statements generally suggest that the police distrust outsiders' attempts to make basic changes in police behavior or in the standards of police efficiency. Most officers distrust those who see *Miranda* as a legitimate and necessary means of protection just as they distrust those who counsel the need to understand the broader causes of crime and violence.

Reactions to the *Miranda* decision are perhaps a microcosm of police views toward the outsider who advocates change in police behavior, and police attitudes toward criminal law seem to reflect many of the characteristics of their general attitudes toward outsiders. Common components include an emphasis on police expertise, an emphasis on the legitimacy of the police organization's own criteria for successfully fulfilling its goals, and a distrust of those who attempt to influence police procedures by advocating other goals. Perhaps this is not surprising. After all, the decision was indeed a further attempt by those who are not police officers to routinize and regularize police behavior. The majority opinion in *Miranda* made an obvious attempt to legitimate such outsiders' attempts to regulate and supervise law enforcement activities. Certainly there is a similarity between these actions and the attempts to get the police to adopt civilian review boards and other forms of supervision by civilians. Finally, as in other issues involving outside control, the Court tried to intervene in an area where the police claim a special competence.

There are, of course, important differences between the *Miranda* decision and other attempts to impose innovations on police departments. For example, the decision did not directly involve issues of race or neighborhood control. Yet the similarity of the reaction to these types of innovations and their reactions to *Miranda* suggest that police views of that decision are a consistent and direct part of a more encompassing and pervasive view concerning pressure for change in the legal constraints on their authority.

NOTES

1. *Miranda v. Arizona*, 384 U.S. 436 (1966).
2. This view emphasizing the social distance of the judiciary may be related to the limited utility of legal guidelines for many, if not most, common police activities. In typical order maintenance work, like handling a family quarrel, the patrolman uses the law as only one of many resources. In these situations, the law and its advocates pose two particularly vexing problems. First, the law is often not very helpful in telling the officer what he should do. It is far clearer in proscribing behavior. Second, partially because of the law's limitations, the officer will arrest only as a last resort,

i.e., when the other remedies seem inappropriate. Thus he sees himself as a lenient person who "goes by the book" only when he determines that leniency is not the answer. He is, of course, confident in the fairness and accuracy of his interpretation. Judges, however, are much more likely to use formal legal criteria to evaluate police behavior and much less likely to sympathize with the police officer's situation-oriented rather than formal rule-oriented behavior (see Wilson, 1968: 30-31, 34-35, 52).

3. Compare with Alex (1969: 59): "While the policeman may be criticized by the public, he can still justify his official role on the basis of his professional know-how in maintaining and restoring social order." See also Wilson (1968) and Skolnick (1969: ch. 7).

4. Skolnick aptly summarizes this hypothesis when he says that "the language of courts is given meaning through a process mediated by the organizational structure and perspectives of the police."

5. 384 U.S. 436, 444-445, 467-476.

6. 384 U.S. 436, at 480-481.

7. In the two departments having mailboxes for each individual officer, the questionnaires were placed in these mailboxes. In the other two, they were distributed by a police sergeant. The response rate by department was as follows: fifty-eight percent and thirty-nine percent for those departments with mailboxes, and fifty-four percent and thirty-seven percent for those that did not have them.

Because of the lack of randomness, no tests for sampling error could be used. I can, however, check for sample representativeness by rank, since official department statistics furnish the actual rank breakdown. Detectives were generally disproportionately represented in all departments.

Because the bulk of the analysis in this study involves the smaller subsample of men who answered the open-ended question, I made some rough comparisons between this and the larger sample. They are quite similar, as shown by the departmental breakdown below:

	% of larger sample	% of coded responses on open-ended question
Dept. A	26	26
Dept. B	24	23
Dept. C	21	19
Dept. D	29	31

8. For a discussion of the use of themes in content analysis, see Berelson (1952: 138-140). As Berelson points out, thematic analysis is both one of the most useful and one of the most unreliable methods of content analysis.

To limit the reliability problem caused by coding complex statements as a reflection of a simple theme, I coded as many as three themes per statement. Berelson (1952: 139) also states that full illustration of the theme helps to improve reliability. In the present study, the propositions themselves helped furnish such illustrations.

9. This criticism of the Court's concern with minority views may be related to the fact that eleven percent of the officers accuse the Court of bowing to illicit political pressures (Table 1). Usually the justices are accused of succumbing to the pressure of "militant" civil rights groups and organized crime, both of whose views they see as contrary to views of the majority.

10. This is obviously only a suggestive analysis of the rhetoric and ideas of police reformers. For some typical statements about responses in *Miranda*, see More (1967);

Moenssens (1967); President's Commission on Law Enforcement and the Administration of Justice (1967: 94). For a discussion of the due process model, see Packer
(1968, 1964) and the majority opinion in *Miranda v. Arizona,* 384 U.S. 436 (1966).

 11. Jacob is similarly cautious in his use of somewhat similar variables to explain
intercity differences in the use of the courts for garnishment remedies and
bankruptcy.

 12. Furthermore, there did not seem to be any distinction between interrogation
behavior of the officers, regardless of the professionalization of their respective
departments. See Milner (1970a). In fact, the present essay has said little about the
way in which institutional or individual values affect *behavior* as opposed to
attitudes. An identification of perceptions and attitudes is only a preliminary step.

REFERENCES

ALEX, N. (1969) Black in Blue: A Study of the Negro Policeman. New York:
   Appleton-Century-Crofts.
ALFORD, R. with H. SCOBLE (1969) Bureaucracy and Participation. Chicago: Rand
   McNally.
BERELSON, B. (1952) Content Analysis in Communications Research. Glencoe, Ill.:
   Free Press.
JACOB, H. (1969) Debtors in Court: The Consumption of Governmental Services.
   Chicago: Rand McNally.
McNAMARA, J. H. (1967) "Uncertainties in police work: the relevance of police
   recruits' background and training," in D. J. Bordua (ed.) The Police: Six
   Sociological Essays. New York: John Wiley.
MILNER, N. A. (forthcoming) "Pluralism, professionalism, and police reform," in E.
   S. Greenberg et al. (eds.) Black Politics—The Inevitability of Conflict: Readings.
   New York: Holt, Rinehart & Winston.
––– (1970a) "Comparative analysis of patterns of compliance with Supreme Court
   decisions: *Miranda* and the police in four communities." Law & Society Rev. 4
   (August): 119-134.
––– (1970b) The Court and Local Law Enforcement: The Impact of Miranda.
   Beverly Hills: Sage Pubns.
MOENSSENS, A. (1967) "Police law reviews." Police 11: 42-45.
MORE, H. [ed.] (1967) "Professional periodical review." Police 11: 51.
NIEDERHOFFER, A. (1966) Behind the Shield: The Police in Urban Society.
   Garden City, N.Y.: Doubleday.
PACKER, H. (1968) The Limits of Criminal Sanctions. Palo Alto: Stanford Univ.
   Press.
––– (1964) "Two models of the criminal process." Univ. of Pennsylvania Law Rev.
   113 (November): 1-68.
President's Commission on Law Enforcement and the Administration of Justice
   (1967) The Challenge of Crime in a Free Society. Washington, D.C.: Government
   Printing Office.
SKOLNICK, J. (1969) The Politics of Protest: A Staff Report to the National
   Commission on Causes and Prevention of Violence. Washington, D.C.: Govern-
   ment Printing Office.
––– (1966) Justice Without Trial. New York: John Wiley.
WILSON, J. Q. (1968) Varieties of Police Behavior. Cambridge, Mass.: Harvard Univ.
   Press.
––– (1967) "Police morale, reform, and citizen respect: the Chicago case," in D. J.
   Bordua (ed.) The Police: Six Sociological Essays. New York: John Wiley.

PART FIVE

Policemen in the Community

Policemen in the Community

In attempting to achieve their objectives, police forces are subjected to many diverse external and internal pressures. As a result, law enforcement officers play a variety of important roles in the community. Although the principal mission of the police frequently is portrayed as reflecting a narrow emphasis upon controlling crime, policemen usually engage in numerous activities that are relatively unrelated to their law enforcement responsibilities. In fact, the largest segment of active police duty may consist of work that does not entail the investigation or arrest of criminal suspects. Hence, the study of police problems also must encompass an examination of the entire range of their actions. The net effect of police practices upon urban society not only might be influenced by police ability to combat crime, but it also may be determined by the many other tasks that they perform.

Perhaps one of the most important duties that police officers must fulfill is represented by their role in providing community service. Data compiled by Thomas E. Bercal from calls received by the police in New York, St. Louis, and Detroit disclose that the largest proportion of requests from citizens for police assistance involve community services rather than violations of the law. Public demands for police aid, therefore, suggest that many persons perceive non-law enforcement duties as a salient and significant function of police departments. In addition, however, they also appear to signify the existence of a widespread public need for the type of services that policemen can provide. Perhaps the explicit public recognition of the obligation of government agencies to respond immediately to personal or family emergencies would require a major expansion of prevailing concepts of political responsibility. The granting of formal approval to this function of the police by placing increased emphasis upon the provision of community services, however, also might provide law enforcement agencies with a relatively stable and enduring source of public support and respect.

As Marvin Cummins notes in his participant-observation study of police patrolling, however, law enforcement officers frequently tend to deemphasize their community service activities. Not only do many policemen regard service work as unwelcome interference with their primary goal of curtailing crime, but they also may be ill-equipped by resources and training to meet the needs of local residents. Perhaps methods must be developed to improve communication and cooperation between police departments and other relevant government agencies. In addition, attention might be devoted to the possibility of integrating specially prepared and skilled community service workers into the ranks of police organizations.

Although the many responsibilities assumed by police officers constitute a vital extension of government services to the public, policemen also play a critical role in the community in their own capacities as citizens and voters. In fact, the increasing militancy of law enforcement officers in local politics appears to represent an important new development affecting the relationship between the police and urban residents. In the final essay, Eugene Eidenberg and Joe Rigert probe the election of a former policeman as a "law and order" candidate for mayor of Minneapolis in discussing the general problem of maintaining adequate supervision of police conduct by responsible civic and political leaders. Although the problem of ensuring democratic control of police forces is a highly complex and sensitive issue, it may be one of the most fundamental challenges confronting American cities and their law enforcement agencies.

Calls for Police Assistance

Consumer Demands for Governmental Service

THOMAS E. BERCAL
Southeast Michigan Council of Governments

The principle thesis of this paper is that metropolitan police departments should be viewed as service agencies which are involved in dispensing a wide and diversified variety of services, both to the individual and to society.[1] Traditionally, police departments have thought of themselves as quasi-military organizations which "enforce the law." This is reflected by James Q. Wilson (1968) who takes the position that police activities can be classified as the functions of law enforcement, order maintenance, and public service and then goes on to say: "The service functions of the police—first aid, rescuing cats, helping ladies and the like—are omitted from the study because, unlike the law enforcement functions, they are intended to please the client and no one else." Is not the mere knowledge that these services exist and are available as beneficial to society as the actual service to the individual? Is not society then just as much the "client" as the individual recipient of the service?

However, Wilson has contributed significantly to the recognition that the police do more than "crime prevention and control."[2] This paper seeks to reinforce this recognition by providing an orientation which views all police functions as "services." It is believed that this orientation will provide a new framework within which the police system may be dissected, studied, and restructured to fit the needs of a changing and enlightened society.

SERVICE ROLE OF THE POLICE

The service orientation allows us to break with the traditional concepts of police action that equate calls for assistance with the appearance of a patrol and with the notion that it is responding to "crime." As Table 1 indicates, of the 1,027,000 calls received by the Detroit Police Department in 1968 via their police emergency number, 370,000 (36%) were terminated in ways other than the dispatch of a patrol. In addition, the research indicated that only 166,000 (16%) of all calls were "crime"[3] related. As these data indicate, to study the police in the context of a para-military organization primarily concerned with the control and prevention of crime focuses attention on but a small portion of police

TABLE 1

RESPONSE OF POLICE COMPLAINT OPERATORS TO CITIZEN CALLS FOR ASSISTANCE

(as opposed to the response by the officer at the scene of the incident)

	Detroit	New York	St. Louis
Number of Telephone Calls for Assistance Received Via Police Emergency Number in 1968[a]	1,027,000	5,200,000	461,000
Disposition of Calls (service provided) by Police Complaint Operator[b]			
SERVICE I—call handled without dispatch of patrol[c]	370,000 (36%)	2,080,000 (40%)	98,000 (21%)
SERVICE II—dispatch of patrol to scene[d]	657,000 (64%)	3,120,000 (60%)	363,000 (79%)
1968 Population Figures[e]	1,570,000	7,964,200	671,700
Requests for Service Index (calls/person)	.65	.65	.67

a. Figures on calls for assistance received and their respective breakdowns were obtained from: in Detroit, Detroit Police Department, Communications Department; in New York, New York Police Department, Communications Department; in St. Louis, St. Louis Police Department, R&D Division.

b. Upon receipt of a call, a police complaint operator must make the following decisions: whether or not to dispatch a car in response to the call; how to respond to those calls in which a patrol car is *not* dispatched.

c. See Table 2 for breakdown of complaint operators' responses to calls handled without the dispatch of a patrol.
d. See Table 3 for breakdown of types of runs responded to by patrol.

e. Estimates from Bureau of the Census ppovisional figures July 1, 1968.

work. Such an orientation has encouraged police to make major policy decisions on the weight of crime statistics and to overlook, and thereby fail to take sufficiently into account, the vast majority of its activities.[4] Conversely, emphasis on the "crime problem" and "social unrest" have hidden the majority of police work from the public's eye.

REQUEST FOR SERVICE

Tables 2 through 4 begin to give an idea of the variety and diversity of requests made upon the police by the public; Tables 2 and 3 present by category the calls handled by police complaint operators which were resolved without the dispatch of a patrol. Table 4 treats the calls which were handled by the dispatch of a patrol. For instance, Table 3 indicates the large role played by police in providing information and/or direction by pointing out that twenty-two percent of all calls received by the Detroit Police Department and eighteen percent of all calls received by the St. Louis Police Department were redirected to agencies outside the department or "solved" verbally. Within this category the police are requested to provide assistance when other services such as gas, electricity,

TABLE 2

POLICE COMPLAINT OPERATORS' RESPONSES TO CALLS IN WHICH A PATROL CAR WAS NOT DISPATCHED

	Detroit[a]	St. Louis[b]
Total Calls Handled Without Dispatch in 1968	370,000	98,000
Police Report Taken via Telephone[c]	—	6,225 (6.3%)
Call Referred to Another Government Agency	35,600 (9.6%)	8,325 (8.5%)
Call Referred and/or Transferred to Another Police Bureau	131,000 (35.5%)	9,700 (9.9%)
Call Referred to Private Agency	8,400 (2.2%)	2,250 (2.3%)
Call Resolved Without Referral	195,000 (52.6%)	71,500 (73.%)

a. Breakdown estimated from one month study taken during June of 1969.

b. Breakdown estimated from figures of calls handled during first eight months of 1969.

c. No phone reports currently taken in Detroit.

TABLE 3

METROPOLITAN POLICE DEPARTMENT REQUESTS FOR POLICE SERVICE RESOLVED
WITHOUT DISPATCH UNDER COMPLAINT EVALUATION PROGRAM (BY CATEGORY)

CATEGORY	Detroit[a]		St. Louis[b]	
	% of All Calls Received	% of Calls Handled Without Dispatch[c]	% of All Calls Received	% of Calls Handled Without Dispatch[c]
Referral to Outside Governmental Agencies Recorder's Court, Board of Health, Fire Department, Dog Pound, Department of Public Works, City Physician, Ambulance Dispatcher,[d] Building Commissioner, Citizen Service Bureau, Street Lighting Section, City Traffic Division, Water Division	3.4	9.1	1.7	8.5
Referrals to Private Agencies Alcoholics Anonymous, Legal Aid Society, Family Service Association of America, Attorney, Michigan Humane Society, Anticruelty Association, Service (gas, light, and the like)	0.8	2.2	0.5	2.3
Referrals to Police Department Units[e] Precinct Detective, Uniform Division Precinct, Youth Bureau, Women's Division	12.2	33.8	2.1	9.9
Resolved Without Referral Caller discontinued conversation, natural phenomenon, miscellaneous information, ordinary sick case (complaint consented to secure own transportation to hospital), resolved through advice by phone	18.0	50.1	15.5	73.0
Police Report Prepared via Phone[f] MDP, minor larceny	1.6	4.8	1.2	6.3

a. Breakdown estimated from one month study, June 1969. Sample size 35,192 calls handled without dispatch.

b. Breakdown estimated from calls received during first eight months of 1969. Sample size 72,557 calls handled without dispatch.

c. Percentages different from Table 2 due to the inclusion of an estimate of reports that could have been taken by telephone by the Detroit Police Department.

d. Applicable only to St. Louis Police Department. Detroit Police provide ambulance service.

e. The large difference between the departments is due to the dispatching of runs in St. Louis for incidents in which Detroit requests that the caller make a report in person at his local precinct station.

f. Estimated for Detroit. No phone reports currently taken.

telephone, and water fail; to provide information when something out of the ordinary happens as in the occurrence of sonic booms, high winds, electric storms, and the like; or just to listen in order that the caller may relieve his tensions.

Even when a patrol is dispatched in response to a call for assistance, the majority of runs are noncrime related, as indicated in Table 4. The police are asked to provide health care through ambulance service and emergency first aid, mediate family and neighbor arguments (these being civil suits and therefore not directly police business) and to handle environmental disturbances, which may or may not be crimes, such as "disorderly

TABLE 4

BREAKDOWN OF TYPES OF RUNS RESPONDED TO BY THE DISPATCH OF A PATROL

CATEGORY	% of Calls Dispatched	
	Detroit[a]	St. Louis[b]
Predatory and Illegal Service Crimes		
Crime, prowler, alarms, recovery of property	38.7	51.0
Public Disorder		
Boys,[c] family trouble, parking complaint, disturbance, missing person, neighbor trouble, tenant trouble, rubbish complaint, strike	34.8	27.2
Crimes of Negligence		
Accidents—vehicles	12.0	9.6
Service		
Health		
Sick person, injury or miscellaneous accident, city physician, animal bites, death, attempted suicide, suicide, ambulance call	10.0	11.7
Safety		
Crossing detail, direct traffic, fire, street defect, tree-pole-wire, animal injured, miscellaneous hazards	4.5	0.5
Total service	14.5	12.2

a. Breakdown estimated from one month study of runs dispatched in Precincts fifteen and sixteen. Sample size 16,531 runs.

b. Breakdown estimated from runs dispatched during first nine months of 1969. Sample size 200,496 runs.

c. This is a general description used to indicate such incidents as "the boys are making noise," "the boys are throwing rocks."

conduct" and "drunkenness." In effect, they are asked to intervene in any situation in which the caller perceives "trouble."

> It is easy to understand why the police traditionally perform such services. They are services that somebody must perform and policemen being the only representative of local government readily accessible twenty-four hours a day, make the police logical candidates. Moreover, it is natural to interpret the police role of "protection" as meaning protection not only against crime but against other hazards, accidents or even discomforts of life [President's Commission, 1967].

However, there exists at this time no consensus, either among police or the communities they service, on the degree and legitimacy of police involvement in the community. A variety of questions are raised, therefore, by each call for assistance: Is the caller asking the police to perform services within recognized police responsibility? How should the call be handled? Should medical assistance be given? If so, to what extent? How prepared should officers be to give advice or other direction?

REDEFINITION OF THE POLICE ROLE

That someone should provide these services is not to be denied. But, the expeditious and unthinking manner in which they become police problems is open to considerable question. As a result of its tendency to "get rid" of its unresolved problems by giving them to the police, society has placed the department in a somewhat awkward position of utilizing resources to perform functions not normally recognized by the public. Consequently, the police find their performance being judged on but one-fifth of their activity, i.e., that activity which is crime related. It is, therefore, submitted that the following set of objectives is more in line with what society asks of its police than the current emphasis on "crime prevention and control":

(1) Minimize personal injury or loss of life by "unnatural and/or avoidable causes."
(2) Minimize damage or loss of property.
(3) Minimize confusion by providing the required authority, information, and/or aid for a given situation.
(4) Maintain the status quo and/or dampen the consequences of change.

This is an impossible set of objectives for the police to fulfill. Impossible, unless there is a reawakening to the fact that the problems faced by the police are not exclusively theirs and that in many areas more effective solutions may be found through an integrated approach by all community organizations pursuing goals related to the provision of services.

Implicit to this integrated approach is the development of a model of the environment in which we live—our societal profile—which defines how we want to live. The development of this model is integral to any successful examination and subsequent restructuring of metropolitan police departments—or of any other urban agency.

The lack of this "model of the environment," this set of "standards" by which to detect and measure deviation, has placed the police in the position of being uncertain as to whether a serious problem exists, and whether or not police action is capable of correcting it. For instance, the department is not presently able to answer such questions as: What probability of being robbed is acceptable? Is it different for different locations? What level of medical services is to be provided to the public? What role does the department play in providing this service? What form of behavior shall be taken as being seriously deviant? What are the "needs" of society?

Metropolitan police departments are, however, in a position to contribute substantially to developing this model. Through their position and role in the dynamics of society, they have access to data which reflect on many aspects of urban life.[5] This paper has attempted to show that one such source is provided through an analysis of calls for assistance. It has also attempted to show that the current emphasis on the "law enforcement" function of the police has caused this source to have been overlooked. As a consequence approximately four-fifths of police activity, as measured by these calls for assistance, has been lost to the policy and decision-making processes of the departments. This situation is currently being remedied in certain police departments. In St. Louis, information on the type and disposition of all calls received for assistance is currently collected as a matter of practice. Detroit is in the process of implementing such a system.

It is suggested, then, that as a first step in developing an understanding of our "societal characteristics" that the information generated by calls for assistance be transformed into a profile of "customer demands for service." With this profile we can begin to identify the services required by the community and for the first time recognize those currently provided in part or in total by the police.

In suggesting this means through which information available to the police may be utilized to begin to develop a model of the environment, it is recognized that the formulation is a simplistic one which does not take into consideration all the internal and external variables which, in varying degrees, affect the structure of this model. This model may ultimately include many of the relevant social, physical, and political aspects of the urban environment. However, for the moment, let us "cop out" and assume that it is society which ultimately defines what the environment is to look like, and that it does this by generating "demands" which are to be serviced. In effect, the environment may be defined in terms of the needs of the community as defined by requests from the community itself.

SUMMARY

It is perhaps a trivial observation that our society is comprised of organized groups of people, each with their own interests and outlooks. What is not so obvious, having been hidden for the most part in the day to day solution of problems, is that the management of such groups is a critical factor in our social order. Executive decisions in government are an especially powerful social force vital to the functioning of our society [Clough, 1963].

This observation is especially true of the decisions of the police executive whose responsibilities encompass the delivery of services in response to a wide variety of societal "needs," the majority of which have been shown to be outside the realm of "law enforcement." Having the ability to directly affect many aspects of urban life, it is important that his current role in the community be identified and understood.

In order to do this, the role of metropolitan police departments in "crime prevention and control" must be deemphasized and placed in a framework which recognizes this activity as being only one of many services with which it is concerned. Utilizing one such framework, it may be seen that policy activities, both crime and noncrime related, may contribute to the realization of the same objective or objectives. For example, within this framework, traffic control may contribute more toward the minimization of personal injury or loss of life than activity in the crime areas of homicide and assault. Several criteria follow:

(1) Minimize personal injury or loss of life by "unnatural and/or avoidable causes": murder, robbery, suicide, ambulance service, first aid, traffic control, fights, family and neighbor arguments, loose manhole covers, missing persons.

(2) Minimize damage to or loss of property: burglary, malicious destruction of property, distribution of crime prevention literature, civil defense procedures, fire runs, rescuing animals.

(3) Minimize confusion by providing required authority, information, and/or aid for a given situation: family arguments, travel directions, telephone information, traffic control, assist in opening locked apartments, crowd control, licensing.

(4) Maintain status quo and/or dampen consequences of change: enforcement of morals, standards of dress, and modes of behavior.

More significant, however, has been the realization of the unique ability police have to determine the "needs" of the community they serve. Due to the broad interpretation by the public of the "protection" role of the police and the ease with which they may be contacted, day or night, metropolitan police departments find that they are able to measure "consumer demands for governmental service" through an analysis of the calls for assistance received by their telephone complaint operators. The analysis of these calls, then, can and will contribute to the description, measurement, and understanding of urban life through the creation of a "model of the environment" based on community "needs" for service.

Metropolitan police departments, therefore, find themselves in a position of being able not only to utilize this information to clarify issues, identify alternatives, obtain relevant facts, and formulate departmental policy, but also to (1) identify problems in the community, (2) stimulate and assist the development of programs aimed at the solution of these problems, and (3) assist in effective performance by other agencies.

Policies based on such information could take many forms, such as the restriction or complete removal of police action and/or the examination of laws which contribute to crime. For example, the police may be removed from enforcing public morals (prostitution and homosexuality) and the licensing of dogs and businesses. Their discretion in handling incidents can, and should, be limited. At the same time they must be provided with a broadened set of "legal" alternatives from which to draw. For instance, the provision of effective rehabilitation programs to which youthful offenders may be referred would be far more beneficial than repetitive police encounters.

Further, alcoholism is now perceived and treated for what it is—a disease and not a crime. Gambling, then, could be looked upon as a "crime" only when its profits are utilized to subsidize acts against society and not as a function of the location or economic level of those engaged in it. Going a step further, laws which contribute to the "creation" of crime such as the two a.m. closing time of bars should be examined and their effects on society weighed.

It is, therefore, submitted that by viewing metropolitan police departments as service agencies, the needs of the community as well as the services provided by the police will be identified. In so doing, the "real" nature of these needs may be determined and the limitations of effective police service in "satisfying" these needs recognized. As a result, it is hoped that such an analysis will lead to a more rational restructuring of the responsibilities of metropolitan police departments within the communities they serve and that it will lead to innovative solutions to what are now defined as "police problems."

NOTES

1. This thesis emerged in March 1968, when work began with the Detroit Police Department to define and make more efficient the operation of its Communications Bureau and field units. In order to make this task manageable, research was restricted to the identification and analysis of the "dispatching function" of the department, i.e., that system through which a citizen is able to call for and receive police assistance. Operationally, this system consists of the public telephone system and the police emergency number, the complaint officer who receives and acts upon the calls in a variety of ways, the dispatch officers who dispatch the patrol cars as required, and the patrols assigned at the direction of the dispatchers. The dispatching function, through both the complaint officer and the patrol officer, does in fact initiate the majority of contacts between the police and the public. It, therefore, provides basic information on (1) the efficiency and effectiveness of current police actions in delivering requested services and (2) the roles played by the police as defined by the public's requests for assistance.

Due to the structure of the study, the data presented herein will include *only* information on those calls received via the police emergency phone number. Activities such as self-initiated street action on the part of the patrols and of other specialized police units and the activities of the remainder of the departments, i.e., detective bureaus, youth bureaus, license bureaus and others, are excluded.

For details of this study, see U.S. Department of Justice (1969).

2. The supposition that the police can prevent and/or control crime is an extremely dangerous one. There is evidence that most crimes, especially those of stealth, are not prevented and most criminals are not caught.

Prevention of crime through police action is based upon the projection of the threat of detection and apprehension. However, once a patrol passes a particular spot, the probability of its or another's appearance is so slim and the speed at which a crime is committed generally is so quick that the probability of apprehension (risk) to the perpetrator is quite low.

3. Crime here is construed as consisting of predatory crimes, acts which have a definite and intended victim. Specifically, these crimes have been designated Part I crimes by the FBI and are listed as: homicide and non-negligent manslaughter, rape-forcible, robbery, aggravated assault, burglary—breaking or entering, larceny—theft and auto theft. Part II crimes are also included in our definition, these being

forgery and counterfeiting; embezzlement and fraud; weapons—carry, possess, and the like; sex offenses; disorderly conduct; arson; malicious destruction of property and other miscellaneous offenses.

4. In 1968, 155,419 "crimes" (122,351 Part I and 33,068 Part II) were reported in the city of Detroit. Compare this with the 657,000 recorded dispatched runs which occurred that year plus an unrecorded number of self-initiated activities on the part of the patrols.

One effect of this disproportionate emphasis on the use of crime statistics has been the formation of specialized crime groups which drain resources required to effectively service calls for assistance.

5. Although we have been addressing ourselves to information obtained through a record of the activity generated by a call for assistance, the department is also able to provide useful information from crime reports, citizen complaint bureau reports, field interviews, and arrest reports.

REFERENCES

CLOUGH, D. J. (1963) Concepts in Management Science. Englewood Cliffs. N.J.: Prentice-Hall.

President's Commission on Law Enforcement and Administration of Justice (1967) The Challenge of Crime in a Free Society. Washington, D.C.: U.S. Government Printing Office.

U.S. Department of Justice (1969) Final Report: Accelerating the Application of Technology to Law Enforcement, Grant 236. Washington, D.C.: Law Enforcement Assistance Administration (June).

WILSON, J. Q. (1968) Varieties of Police Behavior. Cambridge: Harvard Univ. Press.

Police and Service Work

MARVIN CUMMINS
Washington University (St. Louis)

The topical focus on the police for either the social scientist or the general public is essentially issues of law enforcement. Problems of the police are taken to be those that are inherent in the operations of the organizations and their men rather than those problems in the community they service. Such an approach emphasizes the police as the official arm of the legal system rather than the pragmatic agency servicing the general community with problems of its own.

The growth of public information about police departments, an increasing awareness among social scientists about the nature of police work, and more systematic information within police science and police administration have all made it clear that the role of the beat patrolman is much less that of an agent for capturing law violators than that of an agent who mediates personal and community problems. If for no other reason, this is true because of the functional specialization within police organization, a specialization which assigns law violations to particularized bureaus of the municipal police departments, leaving street patrolmen with the tasks of dealing with community problems.

COMMUNITY SERVICE VERSUS LAW ENFORCEMENT

The ratio of contacts that involve legal offenses to those that involve community services is much larger on the services dimension. The recent

Author's Note: *This research was fully supported by the National Institutes of Mental Health under Training Grant 6630.*

"Crime Commission" (President's Commission on Law Enforcement and Administration of Justice, 1967: 91) surmised that "a great majority of the situations in which patrolmen intervene are not, or are not interpreted by the police to be, criminal situations." Analysis of police radio calls (Strecher, 1966) indicates that the traditional criminal functions utilize fifteen percent or less of total police efforts. The evidence is strong that the patrol officer on the street is not involved in the exciting routines of carefully plotted crimes or in volatile, aggressive clashes, but instead his time is devoted to rather routine public order and assistance activities.

To some social scientists and, to a lesser degree, to the legal scholars, this has suggested a duality of police roles. The English sociologist, Michael Banton (1964: 6-7), has suggested that this functional differentiation in police work has led to the development of "law officers" and "peace officers." Similarly Jerome Skolnick (1967: 30) suggests that the part of street policemen in law enforcement is minimal with the comment that "law enforcement is not to be found in its most significant and interesting forms on the streets."

Such a position assumes that law enforcement is truly an independent form of social control, rather than an analytically distinctive arena. The entire recent history of social scientific theory has identified the legal order as a component of the more general order of social control, which includes all social institutions and exchanges. Indeed the basic notions of *consent* in the theories of power are reflections of the concern with the broader social basis for the applications of power. The police, as well as the legal system, are but a part of the general authority structure of the community, the authority structure that combines services and restraints.

The general problems of the street patrolman are situated in immediate social relations, primarily those with his coworkers and with his citizen contacts. At this level, these interactions comprise the "social environment" of enforcement of the law. The remainder of this discussion is an elaboration of responsiveness to service calls in that environment which is work performed by police officers that is not focused primarily on legal violations. Using police response to service tasks allows an examination of duties peripheral to official purpose to see their functionality in central control functions. A final discussion will address the policy implications that can be derived from these observations.

The materials for this study were derived by observational technique. The author spent over a hundred eight-hour shifts in police cars, riding with over sixty different patrolmen. The shifts were varied over all hours of the day and over all the days of the week. The observations were gathered during a time period that extended over sixteen months with a summer's interruption.

Undoubtedly, as with any observer, my presence had an effect on the behavior of the police officers to some degree. Such effect, logically, should only have been biased in the direction of more "favorable" task performance. Rapport generally seemed excellent, and the extended time period apparently reduced some of the obtrusiveness of the observer, resulting in satisfactory acceptance among the patrolmen and a wide exposure to the diversity of situations and of police responses. For the purposes of dealing with responses to service calls, the biases in the observations should have been even less important, since they involve less controversial areas of police work in the minds of the police officers.

The police department in which this study was done is a medium-sized suburban department, which expanded from three hundred to four hundred men during the research period. It is one of the growing number of suburban departments which spans a complex of political units within a single county (International Association of Chiefs of Police, 1968). The department has overarching responsibility for the entire complex, although some areas have full-time or part-time police services of their own. The police department that was researched, then, provides supplementary services for some areas, part-time police services for other areas, and total services for still other areas. The estimated population at the time of the study was just under one million in a physical area of approximately five hundred square miles.

Service work, of course, constitutes a public service function for the police. The types of tasks performed are often available in other sectors of the economy, either under private or public auspices. For the police department, then, service work is said to provide a community relations function; it is a supplement to other public agencies, primarily for good will and effective relationships. Orlando W. Wilson (1963: 229), foremost authority on police administration, describes the situation as follows:

> The patrolman is the ultimate in the decentralization of municipal services. He is a roving city-hall information and complaint counter for the distressed citizen ... The constant availability and mobility of the patrolman make his services useful to other city departments, and he improves both public and interdepartmental relationship[s] by attending more immediately to citizen needs.

At the most practical level the police officers themselves consider service work as essentially "knit-shit stuff." Officers, individually and within their groups, discuss service calls as an added burden that they are called upon to perform, added precisely because such calls go beyond the generalized definition of what they perceive a policeman should do—namely, enforce the law.

In his role as a service worker the beat patrol officer cannot truly extend much in the way of material aid or service. The scope of the police role does not provide much legitimate basis for the utilization of police authority or police resources. There are times when the police officer is willing to use police authority unofficially, even illegally, for the assistance of individuals, just as in the more noticed situations of such usage for apprehensions of law violators. As one policeman commented, "We're not supposed to carry anybody to the hospital in the (police) car, but if (Suburban County) Supervisor Rose were there, you know I'd run him code three (emergency procedure with light and siren)."

One of the more interesting facts of service work for the police officer, then, is that he performs duties which defy the prevalent negative stereotypes of the policeman (Cumming et al., 1965). He does provide comfort, information, and service, sometimes exceeding his own authority in order to do so. The stereotype of the patrolman on streets would be more accurately focused if it centered around the "troubles" of the community instead of the problems of upholding the law. Such behavior is not publicly conceived as a part of police work, perhaps even less so as the "war on crime" spirals. The use of police time and authority for service work is hardly ever referred to as more than the exceptional devotion or courage of individual officers.

This subcultural view of service calls is matched by the view of police departments that police work means law enforcement. The individual patrolman is given a mandate to "handle his beat" (J. Wilson, 1968: 31), an unoriginal and vague directive. But the rewards, both internally and externally, concentrate on law enforcement. Police departments tally numbers of arrests and numbers of citations as indicators of officers' activities, and, naturally enough, so do the officers.

In point of fact, it is a common practice among police officers to report their service calls, and the work performed for them, in a verbal fashion that indicates that it was unworthy of a police report, known as NRN (no report necessary) in the department studied. These cases do not usually involve risk to the organization, and since writing reports is the least favored activity of police officers, service calls are dismissed as routine duty. This means, for all practical purposes, that the position of service work within the department is relegated to a lower status.

SERVICE WORK ROLES

The service work imposition by citizens usually places patrolmen in one of two roles, that of instrumental-negotiator or that of emotional-reassurance agent. The roles are not necessarily exclusive, of course, any more than service work is exclusive of law enforcement functions. The implementation of these service roles is a combination of the demands of citizens on the police beats and the strategies in the police subculture. Variations in statuses of the citizens in the neighborhoods inevitably limit the strategies that policemen can use. Likewise, strategies in the police subcultures provide means to limit the demands that citizens can impose on the police officer.

The instrumental-negotiator role grows out of the facts of conflict in neighborhood life. In proscribing the ability to use conflict to settle interpersonal problems, the legal system thrusts itself as a mediating party into such problems. In the relationships between individuals and the communities, the police can serve as a disinterested party which people try to use as a resource. The legal power of the patrolman is always a potent factor in such cases, even though it is rarely a legally proper resource for civil disagreements. Parties to these controversies attempt to align the police officer to their own side of the conflict, and thereby to gain the leverage of his authority.

One example is the case of a woman who had called the police to complain that a neighbor across the street had harassed her seven year old son by backing his car out of his driveway and bumping her son who was on his tricycle on the curb. The officer began backing away from his involvement by responding, "Police action in cases like these usually makes things worse. Your neighbor's going to feel resentment, even though he might do what I say." And minutes later at the door of the home of the alleged harasser, the officer began the discussion by divorcing himself: "I guess you know why I'm here. . . .police can't really handle a situation like this. . . .Of course, if it gets to where you need to call, then we're glad to come." And in this case the patrolman was successful, for he gained this sympathetic response from the man he was supposed to warn, "I feel sorry for *you* (officer)."

Not all such negotiations even extend to the second party. One woman began her complaint to the police officer: "Look at that car. . . . It belongs next door, and they parked there yesterday, too. He's colored and she's married. I don't know what they're doing over there." The officer refused to act, explaining, "A man's got a right to park in (Suburban County). I'd be exceeding my authority to tell him to move his car when it's legally parked in the street."

The woman cited a two-hour parking restriction which the officer said was not applicable, and then in a last ditch effort she responded, "Then I'll put up my own sign." The policeman backed down the sidewalk and countered, "Then you'll be in violation."

On occasion there is aggressive conflict in the negotiator role. The troubles of marriages, separations, and possession of children seem especially vulnerable to aggression, perhaps because of the high emotional involvement. In one case, a woman called the police to a service station where she complained that she had just been run off her mother-in-law's property with a shotgun and police dog while trying to take her infant son for a holiday visit. The officer drove the woman back to the house where other police officers had since arrived in response to a call from the mother-in-law. At the front door the two women met, argued, and finally began pulling at each other's clothing and hair. The officers separated them, and back in the police car the officer prepared the woman: "I don't know if you'll get busted tonight or not." Finally he drove the woman back to her car in the service station, probed her extensively for additional information, searched her car, and then released her with the additional information (a reward for cooperation): "She's (the mother-in-law) going to get a lawyer to get legal rights on that child, so you'd better hurry to your lawyer to beat her to it."

The subtleties of the instrumental-negotiator role are of considerable concern to the individual police patrolman, for such is the statesmanship that demonstrates the skill of his performance in the police role. Although only a few positive rewards are to be gained through skillful performance of these roles, there are numerous difficulties to be paid for inept handling. The paradigm case of the problems of the negotiator role is the husband-wife dispute, which patrolmen believe to be one of their most dangerous activities (President's Commission on Law Enforcement and Administration of Justice, 1967: 92). Police officers learn early that the best strategy is definitely to avoid taking sides, since, the police lore says, enraged wives easily redirect wrath from the husband onto the policemen. The negotiator role demands the finesse to play a containment role without becoming a participant in the dispute.

The emotional-reassurance role directly demands an alertness to the public relations function for police. The police patrolman becomes aware that the gap between the public and the police leaves the public ill-informed about the enactment of police duties. The impression of a steady and omnipresent police is itself adequate to relieve some of the problems of the neighborhood; indeed sometimes it is more important than actual police services. Thus neighborhood patrolmen must accommodate themselves to promoting that impression. As one police officer commented, "The lieutenant told me long time ago—'You leave 'em with a song and dance.' "

The reassurance performance is illustrated in this case of the police officer's response to a woman who called the police about a "suspicious person." The woman told the officer that a man, whom she did not know, had knocked on her door and "He asked for water, but he didn't have no pitcher or nothing."

The patrolman proceeded through a few additional questions and then finished, "Be sure and call again, if he shows up." Safely back in the police car, the officer announced, "These women get all excited. What are you supposed to do, arrest a guy for asking for water?"

Similarly, a second officer assured a habitual caller that he had told the occupants of a car parked on her property to go elsewhere: "It's okay, Mrs. Lane, we moved them on." And later he ridiculed the action to a fellow officer, adding that the caller was "that dippy old broad."

And a third patrolman took down the details of a teenaged boy's story about other boys yelling at him and shooting at him with a gun as they drove by in a car. The officer was thorough in getting descriptive information, and then he tactfully suggested that the gun might have been a toy and the "shots" might have been firecrackers. As he shelved his notes back in the police car, the officer reaffirmed, "See, they feel better even though we don't do nothing."

The emotional-reassurance role gives the individual police officer the opportunity to maximize citizen contact and to provide the citizens with the sense of comfort and protection. By initiating apparent responsiveness to citizen concern, the policeman can provide direct support for the person involved, as well as reinforce his own role in the police-citizen contact.

FUNCTIONALITY OF SERVICE WORK

Functionally, service work should not be viewed as a supplemental police service, for the facts are that service calls provide the individual police officer with the resources for implementing the rest of his tasks. Service work effectively informs the neighborhood policeman about the structure of social activities and social relationships which exist in his area. The officer takes as much from service work in current information and background materials about the neighborhood as he gives in instrumental or reassuring activity. It is through service work that the officer learns the "social environment" of enforcement.

In a real sense, service work gives the patrol officer the material for the most essential form of control that he has in his department. Patrol officers provide the police organization with the front-line knowledge for police business—the concrete knowledge of the neighborhoods and of the residents. It is the beat patrolman who "knows the territory." The reams of official information lodged in police departments—such as arrest records, fingerprints, modes of operation—are far too abstract for the practical tasks of law enforcement. From that point of view, it is clear that the street knowledge of the individual officer is the most effective leverage in his organization as it currently operates. And much of that street knowledge is built from the experiences of providing service work in the area.

Similarly, the functional operations of the patrol officer in his neighborhoods are derived out of a working relationship with the areas and the residents. The self-image of the beat patrolman is ever refurbished on the claim of intimate knowledge of his area. While the accuracy of any individual patrolman's knowledge is highly questionable, it is usually sufficient for him to foster the impression that he knows what's going on in his area. Service work, then, enables the police officer to build working relationships and practical knowledge of relationships in the area at the same time that he provides services. Although the police officer complains or commiserates with his colleagues about the demands of service work, he readily reassures the citizens that "If you don't call, we don't know what's going on." And this apparent dilemma is literally correct on both counts, for while the officer does not like such tasks, neither would he wish to forego the access that they provide.

The responsiveness of the individual patrolman to public needs provides the officer with the opportunities to build the elements of ready control. The reciprocities with citizens and the knowledge of existing relationships are the staples for the exercise of informal control in the areas. Compliance with police authority—a matter that many analysts take to be the essential problem for the police—is more easily developed when the patrolman can use service work as a complement to legal enforcement. The police department itself argues that "good will" is built by officer involvement. More important than a residual of good will are the benefits of personal maps of the social territory. The most consistently utilized technique of handling a beat is to have indications of its residents, their life-styles, and their problems, for these provide key information for alternative modes of disposing of situations, present or future.

Finally, it should be noted that service calls provide a practical functionality against the bureaucratic demands of the police department. Where officers are requested to account for their task performances in terms of time consumed, service work offers a means of converting cases. Provisions for turning cases, either from law violations to service work or the other way or even back again, is the primary discretionary area for the individual patrolman to use in applying rules or policy. As an illustration, since the patrolman dislikes writing reports, it is a common device to try to reduce "violations" to service calls. This typical strategy is described in the police officer's response to vandalism of a camper-trailer lot. After listening to the owner's story and determining that there would be no insurance claim, the officer concluded: "Well, there's really no reason to make a police report, then, if you're not going to report it to your insurance company. But I'll tell you what I'll do—I'll tell the regular man on this beat and have him stop around as often as he can."

The owner commented, "It's a problem. There's not much you can do about it."

The patrolman agreed, "Yeah. That's right. A report would be useless."

In another case the officer, trying to get an older man walking the street in his pajamas back to bed, threatened, "You're going to have to cooperate now, or I'm going to have to arrest you."

Clearly, such flexibility is highly desirable for the individual police officer, who has few other optional resources to implement his common-sense solutions to problematic situations. Guided by subcultural dictates and experience, he attempts to use what he has at hand to keep the problems within manageable scope, for incompetence to both citizens and superiors is the inability to pacify other people's problems.

POLICY IMPLICATIONS

The policy implications behind this examination of service work extend in several directions. First, it is abundantly evident that the operations of the police departments, especially in the areas of public services, are drastically affected by the character of responses of the various other public agencies. The fact that the police are a twenty-four-hour-a-day, seven-day-a-week, mobile, and free public service results in a residual of problems which the police handle. The structure of community services in general seems to maximize a least-costs principle rather than the application of maximum effectiveness or skill.

In many ways, interagency cooperation on service work in the community offers some distinct possibilities for improvements. It may have the very real consequences of releasing the police from violence or arrest as the only viable resources available for handling problems. Interagency cooperation might indicate a professional acceptance to the police that conceivably could reinforce demands for high performance upon them. But there are corresponding risks that the interagency cooperation might be used for even more excessive surveillance and control over the residents of neighborhood areas (Skolnick and Woodworth, 1967).

Alternative modes of interagency operation are part of the possible ways of handling such problems. Just as current emphasis in police work stresses the analysis of current police operations for locating manpower for maximum law enforcement techniques, so could analysis of current service work performed by the police yield crucial information about the need for personnel from other agencies—child welfare, family counseling, alcoholism council—to be mobilized to work with the problems in their settings.

Even if just police resources alone are still utilized for service work, two options appear worth consideration. First, there is significant need for structural means of channelling tasks through interagency operations with minimal interference. Currently, few policemen give second thoughts to using other public agencies to deal with service work, despite their professional techniques. Indeed too few policemen even seem aware of the realities of other community agencies.

Second, it is possible, as James Q. Wilson (1968: 294) has pointed out, to "offer opportunities for some rather vivid role-playing exercises." There seems to be considerable ambivalence about training patrolmen to deal with the variety of service problems that arise, ambivalence within police work that contends that there is too much complexity in the individual problems. But the police subculture already contains a significant number of common sense strategies for dealing with service work, and through these strategies generalized formulae are already transmitted to new officers, just as is generalized information about arrest techniques. The complexity of the role of the police officer is all the more reason for giving the officer more training, rather than simply abandoning him to his own devices.

The content of such training need not provide abstract information about solving people's problems or giving normative prescriptions. At this stage of development, it seems unlikely that any of the behavioral sciences can provide capsule models for dealing with human behavior. Such training might, however, emphasize the character of the officer's obligations and the potentialities of different modes of involvement.

Another programmatic consideration about service work is its symbolic importance, inside and outside of the police department (Wenninger and Clark, 1967). Obviously, the symbolic position of police service work in the community is marginal. Police departments have typically presented their case for such work as the "community relations" poor relative, relying on law enforcement operations to symbolize the public mandate for police work. This rationalization persists even though the facts of allocation of police time are otherwise. It has reinforced the sharp distinction and segmentation between police services and other community services. In the long run that symbolic position will depend heavily upon the actual relationship to other community agencies, as noted above. In the definitions of public agencies as essentially legal, helpful, bureaucratic, violent, or whatever, the police will tend to suffer.

Likewise, the symbolic aspects of the performance of service work is most often treated as a matter of the extra dedication of individual officers, denying that it comprises normal demands upon police work. The individual officers dismiss its importance, even though, as described above, it seems unlikely that they would be satisfied with the consequences of deleting service work from their duties. The distinction between peace officers and law officers is not effective in the police world, where the occupational identity of all hinges upon being a law enforcement official. Thus, either internally or externally, police departments symbolize the performance of police work as an extra function of policing.

Finally, it could be suggested that the relationship between the police and the public in service work is undefined. Virtually no police department has faced the prospects of professional obligations of policemen as they participate in the lives of their citizenry. The access to personal information and to private relationships is sometimes exceptionally high. What kinds of obligations police officers have to citizens, more than traditional politeness, under the circumstances of service calls is not elaborated. The nature of this citizen-officer relationship seems worthy of consideration. And this also holds for the obligations of police departments to the citizenry. The initiation of service work has primarily come from the neighborhood resident himself. But some departments are now developing policing units whose responsibilities include initiating police activities in problems on behalf of the citizens involved. No doubt, one of the most critical changes in law enforcement has been the slow shift from reactive to initiatory patterns of enforcement (Bordua and Reiss, 1967). That same shift in police involvement in service work may be even more revolutionary, and correspondingly, because of dramatic implications, it should be subject to more careful consideration.

REFERENCES

BANTON, M. (1964) The Policeman in the Community. New York: Basic Books.

BITTNER, E. (1967) "Policing skid row: a study of peace-keeping." Amer. Soc. Rev. 32 (October): 699-715.

BORDUA, D. J. and A. J. REISS, Jr. (1967) "Environment and organization: a perspective on the police," in D. J. Bordua (ed.) The Police: Six Sociological Essays. New York: John Wiley.

CUMMING, E., I. CUMMING, and L. EDELL (1965) "Policeman as philosopher, guide and friend." Social Problems 12 (Winter): 276-286.

International Association of Chiefs of Police (1968) "Workshop: role of county law enforcement—present and future," in The Police Yearbook 1968. Washington, D.C.

President's Commission on Law Enforcement and Administration of Justice (1967) The Challenge of Crime in a Free Society. Washington, D.C.: Government Printing Office.

SKOLNICK, J. H. (1967) Justice Without Trial. New York: John Wiley.

——— and J. R. WOODWORTH (1967) "Bureaucracy, information and social control: a study of a morals detail," in D. J. Bordua (ed.) The Police: Six Sociological Essays. New York: John Wiley.

STRECHER, V. G. (1966) "When subcultures meet: police-Negro relations," in S. A. Yefsky (ed.) Law Enforcement, Science, and Technology. Chicago: Thompson.

WENNINGER, E. P. and J. P. CLARK (1967) "A theoretical orientation for police studies," in M. W. Klein (ed.) Juvenile Gangs in Context. Englewood Cliffs, N.J.: Prentice-Hall.

WILSON, J. Q. (1968) Varieties of Police Behavior. Cambridge, Mass.: Harvard Univ. Press.

WILSON, O. W. (1963) Police Administration. New York: McGraw-Hill.

The Police and Politics

EUGENE EIDENBERG
University of Minnesota

JOE RIGERT
The Minneapolis Tribune

A Task Force of the National Commission on the Causes and Prevention of Violence (Skolnick, 1969) has written that the growing politicization and militance of police make them a force to be reckoned with in the cities. That politicization is now an accomplished fact. In 1969 policemen helped to reelect Mayor Sam Yorty in Los Angeles, worked to elect Sheriff Roman Gribbs as mayor in Detroit, and campaigned against Mayor Carl Stokes in Cleveland.

But in no other city had the police carried their political thrust as far as in Minneapolis, Minnesota. There, at mid-year, an estimated two hundred of them took part in a campaign that elected one of their own to the mayor's office. Charles Stenvig, head of the Police Officers Federation, who vowed to take the handcuffs off the police, rode a sixty-two percent majority vote from the crowded downstairs office of detectives to the upstairs suite of the city's chief executive. The police not only had entered the political process in that city, they had in a sense taken it over.

Deep and troubling questions are raised by this development, questions that have been faced in only a few major cities in the country and certainly have not been resolved in any. Who controls the police? What does it mean when the police organize for political purposes? Can a democratic society afford to permit the one domestic agency of government with the legitimate use of deadly force to gain control of the machinery that contributes to decisions about when and how that force

[291]

will be used? Why are the police less responsive to the normal channels of civilian governance than it is assumed they once were? Are the police actually moving beyond civilian control, becoming a law unto themselves?

Such questions are based on an implicit assumption that the police in the recent past indeed have been responsive to civilian authority. It is a questionable assumption. In Minneapolis and many cities, the police actually have not been effectively controlled by the elected officials to whom they are legally responsible (President's Commission on Law Enforcement and Administration of Justice, 1967: 30). With the decline of the great urban political machines, the police essentially have been rudderless. Their role in the larger criminal justice system has been uncoordinated. Without any tradition of integration into the range of services that municipal government is expected to provide its citizens, the police have been free to develop their own definition of the urban crisis and their own rules for responding to it. In short, the extraordinary politicization and growing militance of the police in Minneapolis and other cities are more a function of the absence of a tradition of civilian direction than a product of the victory of a new law enforcement philosophy itself.

The dilemma, of course, is that to insulate the police from community pressures to a degree that ensures that they will not become an independent, undemocratic political force, also can result in their being effectively insulated from the legitimate and changing needs of the various client groups that rely on police service. The problem for mayors and other civilian officials is to find the proper balance between those two alternatives without provoking open warfare with the police.

The discovery by police rank and file in recent years that the civilian organs of government were either too badly equipped to deal with law enforcement or simply did not make the police a very high priority issue, stimulated the push by police to control their own professional destinies.[1] An aide to a mayor of a major eastern city says that the problem "is getting the mayor to take the initiative in this area. The average mayor doesn't have the criminal justice system at the top of his personal priority list." In Minneapolis, the mayor's office was not provided with budget to employ a staff person to work with the police department until 1968.

The experience in the 1960s with police (Watts, Detroit, Newark, Cleveland, and Chicago, or substitute Berkeley, Wisconsin, Columbia, and Harvard) thrust the law enforcement process, its functions, and its administration onto center stage. Recruitment patterns, training, and command structure became issues of deep concern at the highest levels of government and for serious academic inquiry. While debate and analysis continue, the police rank and file are developing their functions, their command structures, and the uses to which personnel will be put in practices and procedures on the streets. Their function, as many see it, is to enforce the letter of law; their command structure is to be free of "political influences," and the personnel are to respond aggressively to protest or disorder.[2]

To understand why the police arrived at such a view of their role, it should be realized that the police are in every respect a defensive, hostile minority group. They socialize with each other, their wives tend to associate with each other, and generally they constitute a closed society hearing roughly the same account of public events and interpreting them through the same rumor process. They are defensive because they know better than most the low degree of respect for their careers among minorities, liberals, and intellectuals. They appreciate that they are being asked to contain the most violent impulses of a social revolution without being given either prestige for their position or adequate resources for the task (Edwards, 1968: 34-35).

During and after the riots and college busts of the late 1960s, the left had little to offer but criticism of the police, while the right could do little more than provide equally unseeing support through bumper-sticker campaigns. Neither had pay-off for the police, and both helped to polarize an already volatile climate. The result was that the police became part of the "law and order" campaign being waged by the radical right and imperceptibly then became the focus for the reaction of substantial numbers of middle-class citizens frightened by crime, violence, disruption, and their own growing feeling of powerlessness.

The Minneapolis experience is instructive. The police in that city were prepared to exploit the law and order mood of the community in the mayoral campaign of 1969. They were prepared because, over a sustained period of time, they had organized politically and had developed requisite political skills. Thus equipped, they went out and captured the most politically significant office that makes law enforcement policy in the city.

There were, of course, many factors that accounted for the mayoral victory of a policeman in Minneapolis: the fertile territory for a law and order appeal among the city's high proportion of white working-class and elderly residents, the impact of black and student disorders at home and across the nation, a serious split in the city's Democratic-Farmer-Labor Party, and the ineffective campaigning of the Republican candidate. But one of the most significant factors, especially in its implications for other cities, was the politicized tradition of the police department itself. That tradition dates from the days the police were used to help fill the pockets of corrupt politicians, to the 1930s when they were used to break the working-man's strikes, to the 1960s when they aligned themselves with organized labor to build a political power in their own right.

The governmental structure favors police-political involvement in Minneapolis more than in some cities. The reform movement that depoliticized the police in many cities after the 1919 Boston police strike did not reach this midwestern metropolis. Hence, while police commissions, tenure for chiefs, and even gubernatorial appointments of chiefs were established elsewhere, in Minneapolis, except for a brief period in the late 1800s, the police chief has served at the pleasure of the mayor, and until more recent years, at the political use of the mayor. Lincoln Steffens related in *The Shame of the Cities* how a notorious mayor, "Doc" Ames, named his brother as Minneapolis police chief in 1901 and "laid plans to turn the city over to outlaws who were to work under police direction for the profit of his administration." In the 1930s, Minneapolis and St. Paul were described by U.S. Attorney General Cummings as "poison spots of crime and racketeering." Even in the 1940s, a veteran police official says, it was general knowledge in the department that "you didn't rock the boat" on certain illegal activities. Crime-tolerance policies continued until the mid-1940s when then-Mayor Hubert Humphrey put the police to work cleaning up the city of its more pernicious forms of illegal activity.

The end of that era marked the beginning of another—the rise of the police themselves as a major political force in the community, heralding what now is a fact of life in almost every major city in the nation. At first, the Minneapolis police were interested mostly in the mayor's race in anticipation of who would be named chief in the next administration. Police officers who aspired to top command often chose sides between the two candidates and assisted in their campaigns. It was not until the late 1950s, after rigid "Hatch Act" rules were relaxed to permit city employees to engage in politics in off-duty hours, that policemen began to involve themselves in a major way in the politics of the city council. That interest is pecuniary. In Minneapolis, it is the council, not the mayor, that both prepares the budget and sets salaries for city employees. Accordingly, rank-and-file policemen in Minneapolis have helped to elect friendly aldermen, sought to preserve or improve upon—from their standpoint—the structure of city government, and involved themselves in partisan politics.

Bread-and-butter zeal propelled the police into the politics of charter change in the early 1960s. They joined with other city employees and organized labor in 1960 in helping to defeat a proposed charter amendment that would have strengthened the mayor's office at the expense of the pressure-prone city council. They helped win voter approval of a tax-mileage increase to hire more policemen in 1961. And they combined with firemen in a losing campaign to win approval of a ballot proposal to peg their wages to building-trades rates in 1962.

Undeterred by defeat, the rank and file turned to different and even more aggressive leadership in the mid-1960s and plunged directly into partisan politics. In 1966, prodded by an alderman interested in support for his political ambitions, and prompted again by their desire for better wages, the police, their wives, and their allies packed Democratic precinct caucuses to win election as delegates to the 1967 city convention. Together with firemen and other city employees, they dominated that convention, extracted support for their long-sought goal of wage parity with building-trades employees, and provided party endorsement for three friendly aldermanic candidates in contested wards.

This growing militance of the police and firemen also prompted them that same cold winter of 1967 to set up an informational picket line around city hall in a bitter wage dispute with the city council, resulting in a one-day siege of "blue-flu" among policemen and leading to publicly reported pressures on an alderman who had a key vote on their wage demands. There was no doubt at that point that the Police Officers Federation, organized in 1918 as a social group, had become a significant political force with a membership of 850 men (50 to 100 of whom usually attend meetings) in a city of 465,000. The president of the federation during this period was Charles Stenvig, now mayor of the city.

The progressive development of a highly politicized Minneapolis police department in the 1960s, however, was not without its counterforce. In fact, much of the fascination in this story has to do with the profound struggle within police departments over the future of policing. Younger, college-educated, career-oriented officers are pushing and organizing for a basic change in the definition of the law enforcement function, and for change in the personal qualities necessary for entrance into the field.

Their view holds that police provide a vitally important service that can only be effective when it is made an integral part of all city services, when the skills of the men providing the service are substantially upgraded, and when the administration of the delivery of the service is technically up-to-date and professionally bureaucratic. The underlying attitude in this conception of policing is that police must be responsive in enlightened ways to the complex social pressures boiling all around them on the streets they patrol. In order for their service to be functional for the communities in which they work, they must be trained to deal with deviant behavior in its full social context rather than against a rigid set of values and laws that have varying meanings in different neighborhoods of the city. The assumption is that the police officer who defines his role and status in these terms will be creative in dealing with difficult situations and will be willing to take risks for his "clients," confident that his work will be evaluated using qualitative criteria that mean something in the specific social context.[3]

While police have been increasingly politicized, for too long they have been isolated from the rest of the criminal justice system and other agencies of municipal government. Both functionally and often physically separated from city government, the police have been, for all practical purposes, denied full participation in the official life of the community and thereby have been denied the opportunity to adjust to meet the new demands being made of law enforcement. Suddenly they have been confronted with a crisis of their shortcomings, and are being told to make changes in structure, personnel, procedures, and values that will take a generation to develop.[4]

But there have been beginnings. New law enforcement values have been growing in the Minneapolis department in the past five years. A "young Turk" element opposed the police building-trades wage proposal in 1962 and surfaced in 1965 in an unsuccessful effort to commit the federation against absolute veteran's preferences on police promotions. The new guard, now organized into a Law Enforcement Fraternity, has pushed for other measures to widen the department's horizons: code of ethics, an end to gratuities, an education incentive plan, community relations programs, intensive minority recruitment (the department now has only six nonwhite officers) and opposition to partisan political activity.

Because the fraternity was interested in changing standards for hiring, for promotion, and for the administration of the agency, the members were quickly viewed as a threat by the federation, which has a much larger nominal membership and which is the official bargaining agent for the men during contract negotiations. The old guard-young Turk distinction became a real force in the internal operations of the department, as it has in others around the country. One of the characteristics of organizations in crisis is the fragmentation and splintering that occurs within them. The police have their own form of the generation gap, whether it's the old guard versus the young Turks in Minneapolis or the racial antagonisms that are appearing within the ranks of the largest departments (New York Times, 1969).

While the fraternity has been fighting for police professionalism in Minneapolis, the dominant federation traditionalists headed by Stenvig were moving from an assertive posture on working-condition issues to public stands on policies and ways of policing social crises. It is this latter development which poses such a serious threat to the achievement of meaningful accountability of police to the communities they serve. The militant activity on traditional union issues is only a threat to those police administrators and mayors and city councilmen who refuse to acknowledge the legitimacy of many of the demands made by police unions, although financial problems often make it difficult to meet those demands. Still, those administrators who give the proper priority to wage and working-condition issues, and who move toward some form of participatory management involving the rank and file in decisional processes of police departments, can yet forestall some excesses of police unions—the blue flu, slowdowns, and strikes. The 1969 police strike in Montreal shows how militant even a highly rated professional force can become if its bread-and-butter needs are not adequately met.

It will not be so easy to deal with, or neutralize, the tendency of the rank-and-file police to define their posture on complex social issues from a narrow enforcement perspective. In Minneapolis, and elsewhere, this perspective has pushed the police to an involvement in administrative and law enforcement matters related to critical issues of race, poverty, and police-community relations. Some of that involvement has been healthy, but some of it also has undermined discipline, hindered police adminis-tration, harmed racial relations, and slowed the drive for police profes-sionalism. Minneapolis policemen have raised money for fellow officers suspended over improper conduct toward minorities, protested the proposed circulation of pamphlets to inform minorities of their right to complain about police procedures, successfully objected to the presence of an outspoken civil rights advocate on a police-training panel, fought changes in organization, and opposed a civilian-ride-along program.

The corollary to the question of police influence on social policy is the issue of civilian influence on police policy. Some liberals saw in Stenvig's election the end of regular involvement by nonpolice in the making of law enforcement policy and the victory for an undiluted police viewpoint. Indeed, Stenvig had taken the hard line in his campaign and had a mandate from sixty-two percent of the voters. One woman wrote the *Minneapolis Tribune*: "Many of us prefer a 'police state' to one run by hoodlums and weaklings." But others, including former Mayor Arthur Naftalin, predicted that the traditions, pressures, and responsibilities of office would cause the new mayor to exercise restraint. Naftalin saw a danger that some police might feel free to violate constitutional protections. At the same time, he said, the result might be "to remind people that if they are going to have law and order, even from the police point of view, that it will have to follow the traditions of due process." Stenvig's reaction to the speculation was, "The news media are going to have to get this police state out of their minds. It's ridiculous to talk about a police state, because the courts mete out justice, so you could never have a police state."

"Police state" or not, there was a difference in the way the police acted in their first confrontation with young adults in the black community after Stenvig took office. Films of the incident showed the police charging, clubbing, and kicking demonstrators with little or no provocation.

Stenvig's response to the allegation that the police overreacted suggests that the police are well protected from any crass inquiries from the outside. "I don't have to second-guess my police." The police were second-guessed, however, in the courts. Of nine demonstrators arrested on such charges as unlawful assembly and obstruction of traffic, all but one were acquitted in subsequent court action. And the presiding judge issued an unusual statement critical of the police conduct.

Stenvig's view of his role as mayor perhaps was reflected in his handling of Vietnam War Moratorium demonstrations in October 1969. The mayor, who earlier had described his job as that of "police commissioner," took a direct hand in police operations to disperse a group of protestors who had moved from an orderly assembly in front of a federal building to the city's Nicollet Mall. News reports had the mayor telling police to "arrest them" and "clear this street."

For what it is worth, many men in the Minneapolis police department privately share the belief that excessive police conduct was restrained during Mayor Naftalin's administration. But the Naftalin "influence" is gone now and the "traditionalists" clearly have the controlling position in the Minneapolis police department. The Stenvig administration swept out all but one of the top supervisors, installing a number of men who had worked on Stenvig's campaign and others who had been out of favor in the Naftalin regime. The implications of this go beyond the question of police conduct on the street to the question of whether political considerations rather than merit, ability, and education will be basic criteria for advancement in this department and other departments feeling similar pressures from the rank and file. For a mayor who is a policeman, who was elected with the active support of a large part of the police department, the pressures to favor those political supporters might be well nigh irresistible.

Those same pressures exert a strong influence on departmental policies as well. The Stenvig administration has shown no inclination to seek a pay-promotion, college-incentive program, which Naftalin was unable to implement because of objections from the men. The new police command also has catered to "traditionalist" rank-and-file views in decisions on such matters as use of equipment, citizen patrols in poverty areas, and departmental reorganization. It would be unfair to overwork the argument because the administration did set up a separate unit to investigate citizen complaints against policemen, a move in line with recommendations of the President's Crime Commission. The administration also moved ahead on steps to recruit minorities, expand recruit training, and improve police-community relations. It could be argued that the new administration is better able to make changes now because it knows that it has the confidence of the men. But it is not clear whether the changes represent real reforms or mere window-dressing. The investigative unit's work, for example, may be neutralized by the fact that the rank and file will have a two to one majority on a disciplinary review board. The top command decentralized some of its control over discipline to weaken its ability to curb misconduct. And when a firearms policy came under attack after a thirteen-year-old black youth was shot by police in a stolen car chase, the police administration revised the policy in a way that left it more ambiguous than ever.

In theory, the mayor's office in many cities provides the direction and continuous civilian control to keep the police from running themselves as they seem to be doing in many ways in Minneapolis. But in fact police departments and mayors' offices, and the relations between the two, are structured in ways that often make the mayor the last to know what is going on. Police administrators are skeptical about the mayor's intentions in this field and generally take the view of a midwestern chief, "I give policy to the mayor for his edification not for his approval." The harsh fact is that in many cities the mayor, the chief, and the men are caught in a three-way struggle for control of the department.

The mayor is not adequately staffed and does not have enough personal time or expertise to appreciate the special dynamics within the department; the chief is continually walking the thin line between his nominal civilian authority and the cynics in the union waiting for him to prove what they suspect—that he is with the mayor and against them; the rank and file move steadily toward greater militancy as they experience the frustrations of dealing with chiefs desperately trying to hold on to their control of the department while also remaining loyal to their civilian authority, and mayors reluctant to deal with the rank and file for fear of undermining their handpicked chief.

At one level, there is great irony in all this. Many police in Minneapolis hold the view that they were dragged kicking and screaming into politics because of the structure of city government. During the wage dispute of 1967, Stenvig noted that the mayor appoints the police chief and that several key administrative positions in the department are appointive. "How can we stay out of politics if that is the case?" he asked. What Stenvig was saying in 1967 and what is widely believed today in the Minneapolis department and in others is that it would be desirable if the police were removed from all political influence, free to run their own operation. But, of course, there are significant differences between insulating the police from events to such an extent that they can ignore the appeals of politically responsible officials and having them so exposed that they feel their only alternative is to seek precisely the same kind of insularity by controlling the system.

The three-way contest for power, meantime, often results in a paralysis of will to do anything at all. The mayor, anxious to avoid conflict with either his chief or the union, will, for example, side-step complaints about police practices. The mayor is increasingly constrained against moving forcefully on matters of internal department discipline because he runs the risk of losing even his nominal control over the department, and because his chief, subject to intolerable cross-pressures, will in almost every instance defend the men and plead he can do nothing in the absence of overwhelming evidence of wrongdoing. One of the many tragedies of this is that community tensions and conflicts build day by day known only to the officers and citizens involved. It is not until a major crisis erupts that the central administration or the mayor's office gets involved—and then it is for crisis decisions often made with too little information. A former police official under Naftalin says, "We were involved only on controversial issues. . . . He let us run the deal on the street."

The men for their part, asked to do too much with too little, direct their frustration and anger at permissive courts, meddlesome mayors (or their assistants), and indecisive chiefs who fail to get in front of the men to take some of the heat for them in their exercise of an astonishing range of discretionary power on the street.[5] Often the men are neither adequately trained to use this power nor administratively supported when they do. The result is a hostile, defensive, and nonrisk-taking patrol force which by definition is doing little or no experimenting with the way in which it delivers its vital service.

Perhaps it is by the use of discretionary power that the contradictions and the ambivalence of the police officer's position can best be illustrated. On the one hand the police want to be free to make decisions on the street unfettered by the scrutiny of the chief, the mayor, or his staff. In practice, though, the patrol officer is asked to make hurried decisions under highly stressful conditions that, if "wrong," can produce great community crisis. And the officer demands specific guidance and support for his handling of uncertain situations. What is needed is an appropriate mix of independence for the individual officer facing infinitely varied circumstances, with guidance and supervision from superiors (both law enforcement and civilian) who bear the larger responsibility of the community's interest. In the meantime, the question of the use of discretion by police is a continuing obstacle to efficient management of police agencies. An example of this was seen in Minneapolis in the spring of 1968 when an elderly black woman was handcuffed in accordance with a department policy of handcuffing all arrested adults. Demonstrations followed protesting the handcuffing of a woman who clearly was no threat to anyone. After a review of the policy, the chief changed the order to state that arresting officers, "may exercise their own discretion whether to handcuff any prisoner." The then Police Federation President, Charles Stenvig, protested, "The administration once again is throwing the entire decision on the officer's shoulders and they can sit back and second-guess."

The most visible consequence of this hostility and mutual lack of confidence is the mushrooming list of police associations and departments around the country whose leaders are already major political powers in their present roles or are being discussed as candidates for elective office. There are very few mayors in the major cities of the country who do not have to deal with the police department and the union on something approaching an equal footing on an increasingly varied set of issues. Further, the beginning efforts to form a national police union suggest that the local unions will gain even more strength in dealing with civilian authority. For the mayor and his staff, the problems are aggravated by the absence of any shared set of expectations about what the mayor's role ought to be in giving positive direction to the department (see Murphy, 1969 on this point). When the mayor does take an active interest in police issues the cry is instantly taken up in locker rooms in every precinct of the city that the mayor is dictating to the chief. It was, therefore, only a small wonder that when Mayor Naftalin in the spring of 1968 removed the high-powered AR-15 rifle from the Minneapolis police arsenal (because the weapon was inappropriate for use in an urban setting), the chief of police asked for and was granted permission to publicly disassociate himself from the decision. Nonetheless, the chief was the object of considerable anger within the department for "permitting the mayor to disarm us."

The Minneapolis experience is not unique on these vital questions. To lesser or greater degrees, the same forces within police departments are at work in every major city in the country (Skolnick, 1969). And the newly emerged politics of the police is likely to remain, whether for the specific reasons offered to explain the Minneapolis case, or because in every city the intolerable conditions of law enforcement at a time of heightened demand for superior performance produce their own reaction.

For too long, positive control of the police has not been exercised. The structure and procedures of administering law enforcement have prevented it. Decisions about the basic objectives and style of police agencies are not made because of the structural and political conflicts built into and around police, while discretionary choices are made day by day without adequate supervision or guidance. As the function of law enforcement has expanded from narrow rule enforcement to the broader goal of providing general security for the community, the police have been increasingly vulnerable to attack for using their discretionary power to operate dual standards of justice, and as the attacks grow and polar positions are taken in political debate, the police agency itself is less and less capable of maintaining a flexible posture.

The challenge in the cities is to avoid a dangerous politicization of the police and to define an appropriate role for them in this time of social revolution. How can the challenge be met?

First, it seems critically important that the mayors intervene actively in the law enforcement process. Mayors have ignored for too long the plight of their police departments. Using the strength of political legitimacy, the mayor can view law enforcement against the perspective of all city needs. Even in weak-mayor cities like Minneapolis, the mayor can provide a continuous focus for public and official attention on the unmet needs of the police. Further, he can be the catalyst that gets the rest of the city bureaucracy thinking about its services in relationship to law enforcement. It is absurd on the face of it that welfare and relief agencies, for example, make little effort to work with the police in making their agency personnel available twenty-four hours a day. The police have much to contribute to, and much to learn from, other agencies of municipal government, if only they were in regular contact and worked together.

For the mayor to assume this leadership role, he must be provided adequate staff. Assistants with substantive knowledge in the law enforcement and criminal justice fields can begin to give the mayor the resource of reliable information on the status of police issues in his city. Likewise, police officers with sensitivity and political acumen can be detailed to the mayor's office to provide continuing professional liaison with the department.

Second, city administrators must develop career lines in police agencies for highly trained, educated, and motivated professionals. The rigid structure and process of promotion within the police service now makes law enforcement an unappealing career for many idealistic, service-oriented young men. The President's Commission on Law Enforcement and Administration of Justice recommends several specific ways for police agencies to make more effective use of the generalist patrolman while also opening career opportunities for specialists with a variety of special skills. In addition, the personnel already on the streets of the cities must be rewarded, both monetarily and in terms of promotions, for crime-prevention and community-service work, as suggested by the Kerner-Lindsay Commission report (see National Advisory Commission on Civil Disorders, 1968).

Then, experimentation in the structure of decision-making can proceed to define the proper community role for police. In this regard, former Mayor Naftalin says,

> The police department must be brought into genuine involvement in the flow of the community process and community activity. It just isn't police work that is so important. It is getting compliance, getting acceptance that gets the public to become law observant. The police department view is different. They feel there has been too much civilian dominance. But there has not been enough. Not enough resources to bring the police department out of city hall, leading the department into programs that would encourage people to be law observant. The pressures are all the other way because of a low budget, and because of a public view that toughness will control crime.

Without the restructuring of the police to bring in new kinds of professionals and without the healthy involvement of the police in the community's life, there may not be much more time before the Minneapolis experience becomes a widespread phenomenon on the urban scene. Surely change will not occur unless law enforcement and criminal justice are redefined as relevant and important political issues outside of a climate of repression and fear. The issue is currently controlled far too much by radicals on both the left and right.

Finally, police administrators have a major responsibility to give direction to the men and counsel to their civilian authority that will realize the changes necessary to professionalize law enforcement. Regrettably, too many chiefs are mirror images of the most traditional thinking in law enforcement circles. This circumstance will not be altered until civilians and sworn personnel have the opportunity for lateral entry into police agencies in all major cities. This would stimulate, for the first time, serious competition for top-quality law enforcement personnel and would eliminate the inbreeding that is characteristic of many departments.

It may be also that inadequacies in middle-management are a more serious problem than deficiencies at the top posts. Street supervisors are often not trained for their role, have developed a philosophy from years on the beat that is frequently superimposed on the new patrolman at his most impressionable stage of development, and can interpret front-office policy to the men in ways that contradict its intent. Until sergeants, lieutenants, and captains are educated and trained to fulfill their function with expertise, there will be no appreciable improvement in the exercise of discretion on the street.

In short, until the structure of city government turns its attention and resources to the question of how to recruit, train, and supervise professional police officers with the self-assurance to earn the confidence of the communities they are serving, major segments of the public will move deeper into permanent conflict with the police. That condition in turn will produce a political climate that will reduce still further the chances of achieving the law enforcement goals that seem so widely shared.

The potential for a new kind of leadership is in the police agencies today. Given the right support it can be realized, and the depoliticization of the police will naturally follow. Police will not feel the need to organize to fight for political control when their professional interests are being served.

The burden for creating such a climate will have to be borne where it should have been all along—the civilian structure. It will be a long and arduous task because many years of neglect and indifference have bred suspicion and skepticism throughout law enforcement. The consequences of pursuing any other line of action, however, are emerging in Minneapolis. The police will control themselves. There will be less and less responsiveness to legitimate outside pressures, and the defensive, hostile character of the police culture, as it presently exists, will worsen.

NOTES

1. In testimony before the House Select Committee on Crime on July 30, 1969, Patrick Murphy, then of the Urban Institute and now commissioner of police in Detroit, Michigan, bluntly raised the question, "Do mayors recognize the complexities of police administration or share many common misconceptions about simplistic solutions?" (See Murphy, 1969: 5.)

2. See the letter from John Harrington, president of the Fraternal Order of Police to the Minneapolis *Tribune,* April 3, 1970, in which this point is clearly articulated.

3. See the President's Commission on Law Enforcement and Administration of Justice (1967) for a detailed prescription statement on the need for a restructuring of police agencies.

4. See Lohman (1967) for extended analysis of the implications of these facts.

5. See Kenneth Culp Davis (1969) for a full analysis of the role of individual policemen and administrative decision makers.

REFERENCES

DARNTON, J. (1969) "Color line a key police problem." New York Times (September 28).

DAVIS, K. C. (1969) Discretionary Justice: A Preliminary Inquiry. Baton Rouge: Louisiana State Univ. Press.

EDWARDS, G. (1968) The Police on the Urban Frontier. New York: Institute of Human Relations Press.

LOHMAN, J. D. (1967) "On law enforcement and the police: a commentary." Delivered at the American Association for the Advancement of Science, New York, December.

MURPHY, P. V. (1969) Testimony Before the House Select Committee on Crime, United States House of Representatives, July 30 (mimeo). Washington, D.C.: Urban Institute.

National Advisory Commission on Civil Disorders (1968) Report. New York: Bantam Books.

New York Times (1969) September 28.

President's Commission on Law Enforcement and Administration of Justice (1967) Task Force Report: The Police. Washington, D. C.: Government Printing Office.

SKOLNICK, J. H. (1969) The Politics of Protest. New York: Ballantine Books.

PART SIX

Law Enforcement and Social Research

A Selected Bibliography

Law Enforcement and Social Research

A Selected Bibliography

ABBOTT, D. W., L. H. GOLD, and E. T. ROGOWSKY (1969) Police, Politics, and Race: The New York City Referendum on Civilian Review. Cambridge, Mass.: Harvard Univ. Press.

ABERBACH, J. D. and J. L. WALKER (1970) "The attitudes of blacks and whites toward city services: implications for public policy," pp. 519-538 in J. P. Crecine (ed.) Financing the Metropolis: Public Policy in Urban Economies. Volume IV, Urban Affairs Annual Reviews. Beverly Hills: Sage Pubns.

ABERNATHY, G. M. (1962) "Police discretion and equal protection." South Carolina Law Q. 14 (Summer): 472-486.

ALDRICH, H. and A. J. REISS, Jr. (1970) "The effect of civil disorders on small business in the inner city." J. of Social Issues 26 (Winter): 187-206.

ALEX, N. (1969) Black in Blue: A Study of the Negro Policeman. New York: Appleton-Century-Crofts.

American Civil Liberties Union, Illinois Division (1959) Secret Detention by the Chicago Police. Glencoe, Ill.: Free Press.

Atlantic Monthly (1969) "The police and the rest of us." 223 (March): 74-135.

BANTON, M. (1964) The Policeman in the Community. New York: Basic Books.

BARRETT, E. L., Jr. (1962) "Police practices and the law: from arrest to release or charge." California Law Rev. 50 (March): 11-55.

BARTH, A. (1961) The Price of Liberty. New York: Viking.

BAYLEY, D. H. and H. MENDELSOHN (1969) Minorities and the Police: Confrontation in America. New York: Free Press.

BERKLEY, G. E. (1969) The Democratic Policeman. Boston: Beacon.

BIDERMAN, A. D. (1967) "Surveys of population samples for estimating crime incidence." Annals of Amer. Academy of Pol. and Social Sci. 374 (November): 16-33.

——— L. A. JOHNSON, J. McINTYRE, and A. W. WEIR (1967) Report on a Pilot Study in the District of Columbia on Victimization and Attitudes Toward Law Enforcement. Washington, D.C.: Government Printing Office.

BITTNER, E. (1967) "Policing skid row: a study of peace-keeping." Amer. Soc. Rev. 32 (October): 699-715.

BLACK, A. D. (1968) The People and the Police. New York: McGraw-Hill.

BLACK, D. J. (1970) "Production of crime rates." Amer. Soc. Rev. 35 (August): 733-748.

——— and A. J. REISS, Jr. (1967) "Patterns of behavior in police and citizen transactions," pp. 1-39 in Studies in Crime and Law Enforcement in Major Metropolitan Areas. Volume 2. Washington, D.C.: Government Printing Office.

——— (1970) "Police control of juveniles." Amer. Soc. Rev. 35 (February): 63-77.

BLUMBERG, A. S. (1967) Criminal Justice. Chicago: Quadrangle.

BORDUA, D. J. [ed.] (1967) The Police: Six Sociological Essays. New York: John Wiley.

——— and A. J. REISS, Jr. (1966) "Command, control, and charisma: reflections on police bureaucracy." Amer. J. of Sociology 72 (July): 68-76.

——— (1967) "Law enforcement," pp. 275-303 in P. F. Lazarsfeld et al. (eds.) The Uses of Sociology. New York: Basic Books.

BOUMA, D. H. (1969) Kids and Cops: A Study in Mutual Hostility. Grand Rapids, Mich.: William B. Eerdmans.

BURGER, W. E. (1964) "Who will watch the watchmen?" Amer. University Law Rev. 14 (December): 1-23.

CAMPBELL, A. and H. SCHUMAN (1968) "Racial attitudes in fifteen American cities," pp. 1-69 in Supplemental Studies for the National Advisory Commission on Civil Disorders. Washington, D.C.: Government Printing Office.

CAMPBELL, J. S., J. R. SAHID, and D. P. STANG (1969) Law and Order Reconsidered. Staff Report 10 to the National Commission on the Causes and Prevention of Violence. Washington, D.C.: Government Printing Office.

CHAPMAN, S. G. and T. E. ST. JOHNSTON (1962) The Police Heritage in England and America: A Developmental Survey. East Lansing, Mich.: Michigan State University.

CHEVIGNY, P. (1969) Police Power: Police Abuses in New York City. New York: Pantheon.

CLARK, J. P. (1965) "Isolation of the police: a comparison of the British and American situations." J. of Criminal Law, Criminology and Police Sci. 56 (Fall): 307-319.

COOK, W. (1967) "Policemen in society: which side are they on?" Berkeley J. of Sociology 12 (Summer): 117-129.

CRAY, E. (1967) The Big Blue Line. New York: Coward-McCann.

——— (1969) Law Enforcement: The Matter of Redress. Los Angeles: Institute of Modern Legal Thought.

——— (1966) "Annotated bibliography on police review boards." Law in Transition Q. 24 (Summer): 197-205.

CUMMING, E., I. CUMMING, and L. EDELL (1965) "Policeman as philosopher, guide and friend." Social Problems 12 (Winter): 276-286.

DERBYSHIRE, R. L. (1968) "Children's perceptions of the police: a comparative study of attitudes and attitude change." J. of Criminal Law, Criminology, and Police Sci. 59 (June): 183-190.

DOIG, J. W. [ed.] (1968) "A symposium: the police in a democratic society." Public Administration Rev. 28 (September-October): 393-430.

EDWARDS, G. (1968) The Police on the Urban Frontier. New York: Institute of Human Relations Press.

ENNIS, P. H. (1967) Criminal Victimization in the United States: A Report of a National Survey. Washington, D.C.: Government Printing Office.

——— (1967) "Crime, victims, and the police." Trans-action 4 (June): 36-44.

FICHTER, J. H. and B. JORDAN (1964) Police Handling of Arrestees. New Orleans: Loyola University of the South.

FOGELSON, R. M. (1968) "From resentment to confrontation: the police, the Negroes, and the outbreak of the nineteen-sixties riots." Pol. Sci. Q. 83 (June): 217-247.

FOOTE, C. (1956) "Vagrancy-type law and its administration." University of Pennsylvania Law Rev. 104: 603-650.

FOX, V. (1966) "Sociological and political aspects of police administration." Sociology and Social Research 51 (October): 39-48.

GARDINER, J. A. (1967) "Public attitudes toward gambling and corruption." Annals of Amer. Academy of Pol. and Social Sci. 374 (November): 123-134.

——— (1968) "Police enforcement of traffic laws: a comparative analysis," pp. 151-172 in J. Q. Wilson (ed.) City Politics and Public Policy. New York: John Wiley.

——— (1969) Traffic and the Police: Variations in Law-Enforcement Policy. Cambridge, Mass.: Harvard Univ. Press.

——— (1970) The Politics of Corruption: Organized Crime in an American City. New York: Russell Sage Foundation.

GOLDSTEIN, H. (1963) "Police discretion: the ideal versus the real." Public Administration Rev. 23 (September): 140-148.

GOLDSTEIN, J. (1960) "Police discretion not to invoke the criminal process: low-visibility decisions in the administration of justice." Yale Law J. 69 (March): 543-594.

Governor's Select Commission on Civil Disorder (1968) Report for Action. Trenton: State of New Jersey.

GRIMSHAW, A. D. (1963) "Actions of police and the military in American race riots." Phylon 24 (Fall): 271-289.

HAHN, H. (1969) "Philosophy of law and urban violence." Soundings 52 (Spring): 110-117.

——— and J. R. FEAGIN (1970) "Riot-precipitating police practices: attitudes in urban ghettos." Phylon 31 (Summer): 183-193.

HARRIS, R. (1969) The Fear of Crime. New York: Frederick A. Praeger.

HOLDEN, M., Jr. (1969) "The quality of urban order," pp. 431-454 in H. J. Schmandt and W. Bloomberg, Jr. (eds.) The Quality of Urban Life. Volume 3, Urban Affairs Annual Review. Beverly Hills: Sage Pubns.

HOLLADAY, R. E. (1962) "The police administrator: a politician?" J. of Criminal Law, Criminology, and Police Sci. 53 (December): 526-529.

INGERSOLL, J. E. (1964) "The police scandal syndrome." Crime and Delinquency 10 (July): 269-275.

JANOWITZ, M. (1968) Social Control of Escalated Riots. Chicago: University of Chicago Center for Policy Study.

KEPHART, W. M. (1957) Racial Factors and Urban Law Enforcement. Philadelphia: Univ. of Pennsylvania Press.

KEY, V. O., Jr. (1935) "Police graft." Amer. J. of Sociology 40 (March): 624-636.

KLONOSKI, J. R. and R. I. MENDELSOHN [eds.] (1970) The Politics of Local Justice. Boston: Little, Brown.

LA FAVE, W. R. (1962) "The police and nonenforcement of the laws: part I." Wisconsin Law Rev. (January): 104-137.

——— (1962) "The police and nonenforcement of the laws: part II." Wisconsin Law Rev. (March): 179-239.

——— (1965) Arrest: The Decision to Take a Suspect into Custody. Boston: Little, Brown.

LANDESCO, J. (1968) Organized Crime in Chicago. Chicago: Univ. of Chicago Press.

LANE, R. (1967) Policing the City: Boston, 1822-1885. Cambridge, Mass.: Harvard Univ. Press.

LEVY, B. (1968) "Cops in the ghetto: a problem of the police system." Amer. Behavioral Scientist 11 (March-April): 31-34.

LOHMAN, J. D. (1968) "Law enforcement and the police," pp. 359-372 in L. H. Masotti and D. R. Bowen (eds.) Riots and Rebellion: Civil Violence in the Urban Community. Beverly Hills: Sage Pubns.

——— and G. E. MISNER (1966) The Police and the Community. Washington, D. C.: Government Printing Office.

McDONALD, D. (1962) The Police: An Interview by Donald McDonald with William H. Parker. Santa Barbara, Calif.: Center for the Study of Democratic Institutions.

McINTYRE, D. M. (1967) Law Enforcement in the Metropolis. Chicago: American Bar Foundation.

MacNAMARA, D. E. J. (1950) "American police administration at mid-century." Public Administration Rev. 10 (Summer): 181-189.

MARX, G. T. (1967) Protest and Prejudice. New York: Harper & Row.

——— (1970) "Civil disorder and the agents of social control." J. of Social Issues 26 (Winter): 19-57.

MITCHELL, R. E. (1966) "Organization as a key to police effectiveness." Crime and Delinquency 11 (October): 344-353.

MENNINGER, K. (1968) The Crime of Punishment. New York: Viking.

National Advisory Commission on Civil Disorders (1968) Report. Washington, D.C.: Government Printing Office.

National Center on Police and Community Relations (1967) A National Survey on Police and Community Relations. Washington, D.C.: Government Printing Office.

National Commission on Law Observance and Enforcement (1931) Report on Lawlessness in Law Enforcement. Washington, D.C.: Government Printing Office.

NEWMAN, D. J. (1966) Conviction: The Determination of Guilt or Innocence Without Trial. Boston: Little, Brown.

NIEDERHOFFER, A. (1967) Behind the Shield: The Police in Urban Society. Garden City, N.Y.: Doubleday.

PACKER, H. L. (1964) "Two models of the criminal process." University of Pennsylvania Law Rev. 113 (November): 1-68.

PARNAS, R. I. (1967) "The police response to the domestic disturbance." Wisconsin Law Rev. 1967 (Fall): 914-960.

PARSONS, M. B. (1963) "The administration of police juvenile services in the metropolitan regions of the United States." J. of Criminal Law, Criminology, and Police Sci. 54 (March): 114-117.

PEABODY, R. L. (1963) "Authority relations in three organizations." Public Administration Rev. 23 (June): 87-92.

PILIAVIN, I. and S. BRIAR (1964) "Police encounters with juveniles." Amer. J. of Sociology 70 (September): 206-214.

PREISS, J. J. and H. J. EHRLICH (1966) An Examination of Role Theory: The Case of the State Police. Lincoln: Univ. of Nebraska Press.

President's Commission on Crime in the District of Columbia (1966) Report on the Metropolitan Police Department. Washington, D.C.: Government Printing Office.

President's Commission on law Enforcement and Administration of Justice (1967) The Challenge of Crime in a Free Society. Washington, D.C.: Government Printing Office.

——— (1967) Task Force Report: Crime and Its Impact—An Assessment. Washington, D.C.: Government Printing Office.

——— (1967) Task Force Report: The Police. Washington, D.C.: Government Printing Office.

——— (1967) Task Force Report: Science and Technology. Washington, D.C.: Government Printing Office.

"Program budgeting for police departments." (1967) Yale Law J. 76 (March): 822-833.

QUINNEY, R. (1964) "Crime in a political perspective." Amer. Behavioral Scientist 8 (December): 19-22.

RAINE, W. J. (1967) The Perception of Police Brutality in South Central Los Angeles. Los Angeles: UCLA Institute of Government and Public Affairs.

RANKIN, J. H. (1959) "Psychiatric screening of police recruits." Public Personnel Rev. 20 (July): 191-196.

REISS, A. J., Jr. (1967) "Public perceptions and recollections about crime, law enforcement, and criminal justice," pp. 1-114 in Studies in Crime and Law Enforcement in Major Metropolitan Areas. Volume 1. Washington, D.C.: Government Printing Office.

——— (1967) "Career orientations, job satisfaction, and the assessment of law enforcement problems by police officers," pp. 1-123 in Studies in Crime and Law Enforcement in Major Metropolitan Areas. Volume 2. Washington, D.C.: Government Printing Office.

——— (1968) "How common is police brutality?" Trans-action 5 (July-August): 10-20.

——— and D. J. BLACK (1967) "Interrogation and the criminal process." Annals of the Amer. Academy of Pol. and Social Sci. 374 (November): 47-57.

REMINGTON, F. J. (1965) "The role of police in a democratic society." J. of Criminal Law, Criminology, and Police Sci. 56 (September): 361-365.

——— and V. G. ROSENBLUM (1960) "The criminal law and the legislative process." University of Illinois Law Forum 1960 (Winter): 481-499.

ROSSI, P. H., R. A. BERK, D. P. BOESEL, B. K. EIDSON, and W. E. GROVES (1968) "Between white and black: the faces of American institutions in the ghetto," pp. 70-215 in Supplemental Studies for the National Advisory Commission on Civil Disorders. Washington, D.C.: Government Printing Office.

SKOLNIK, J. H. (1966) Justice Without Trial. New York: John Wiley.

——— (1969) The Politics of Protest. New York: Ballantine.

SMITH, A. B., B. LOCKE, and W. F. WALKER (1968) "Authoritarianism in police college and non-police college students." J. of Criminal Law, Criminology, and Police Sci. 59 (September): 440-443.

SOWLE, C. R. [ed.] (1962) Police Power and Individual Freedom: The Quest for Balance. Chicago: Aldine.

STERN, M. (1962) "What makes a policeman go wrong?" J. of Criminal Law, Criminology, and Police Sci. 53 (March): 97-101.

STINCHCOMBE, A. L. (1963) "Institutions of privacy in the determination of police administrative practice." Amer. J. of Sociology 69 (September): 150-160.

STODDARD, E. R. (1968) "The informal 'code' of police deviancy: a group approach to 'blue-coat crime.' " J. of Criminal Law, Criminology, and Police Sci. 59 (June): 201-213.

SWETT, D. H. (1969) "Cultural bias in the American legal system." Law and Society Rev. 4 (August): 79-110.

TOCH, H. H. and R. SCHULTE (1961) "Readiness to perceive violence as a result of police training." British J. of Psychology 52: 389-393.

THURSTONE, L. L. (1922) "The intelligence of policemen." J. of Personnel Research 1: 64-74.

TREBACK, A. S. (1964) The Rationing of Justice. New Brunswick, N.J.: Rutgers Univ. Press.

TURNER, W. W. (1968) The Police Establishment. New York: G. P. Putnam's.

VOLLMER, A. (1930) Report on the Police. United States National Committee on Law Observance and Enforcement. Washington, D.C.: Government Printing Office.

WASKOW, A. I. (1966) From Race Riot to Sit-in, 1919 and the 1960's. Garden City, N.Y.: Doubleday.

——— (1969) "Community control of the police." Trans-action 7 (December): 4-7.

WESTLEY, W. A. (1953) "Violence and the police." Amer. J. of Sociology 59 (July): 34-41.

——— (1956) "Secrecy and the police." Social Forces 34 (March): 254-257.

WILSON, J. Q. (1963) "The police and their problems: a theory." Public Policy 12: 189-216.

——— (1964) "Generational and ethnic differences among career police officers." Amer. J. of Sociology 64 (March): 522-528.

——— (1968) Varieties of Police Behavior. Cambridge, Mass.: Harvard Univ. Press.

——— (1968) "The police and the delinquent in two cities,"pp. 173-195 in J. Q. Wilson (ed.) City Politics and Public Policy. New York: John Wiley.

——— (1969) "The urban unease: community vs. city," pp. 455-472 in H. J. Schmandt and W. Bloomberg, Jr. (eds.) The Quality of Urban Life. Volume 3, Urban Affairs Annual Review. Beverly Hills: Sage Pubns.

WILSON, O. W. (1964) "Police authority in a free society." J. of Criminal Law, Criminology, and Police Sci. 54 (June): 175-177.

ZEITZ, L. (1965) "Survey of Negro attitudes toward law." Rutgers Law Rev. 19: 288-316.

The Authors

HOWARD ALDRICH is Assistant Professor of Organizational Behavior in the School of Industrial and Labor Relations at Cornell University. His interests include organization-environment theory and research on inter-organizational relations. **ALBERT J. REISS, Jr.** is Professor of Sociology and Professor, Institute of Social Sciences, Center for Urban Studies, Yale University. His recent work focuses on the social organization of crime and law enforcement in major metropolitan areas.

THOMAS E. BERCAL, who received his degree in industrial engineering, is currently employed by the Southeast Michigan Council of Governments. He was formerly a Research Associate at the Center for Urban Studies of Wayne State University.

RICHARD L. BLOCK is Assistant Professor of Sociology at Loyola University. He was a research assistant to Philip Ennis in the study of criminal victimization in the United States.

DAVID J. BORDUA is Professor of Sociology at the University of Illinois. He is the editor of *The Police: Six Sociological Essays* and the author of several articles and monographs concerning law enforcement. **EDWARD W. HAUREK** is Assistant Professor of Sociology at the University of Minnesota. His current research is a study of the relationship between the social backgrounds of adolescents and their educational and occupational aspirations.

ROBERT W. CLAWSON is now Assistant Professor of Political Science at Kent State University. During the spring of 1966 he was an exchange scholar at Moscow State University, faculty of law. His current research efforts center on Soviet political interest group activity. **DAVID L. NORRGARD,** now Assistant Director of the Municipal Reference Bureau, University of Minnesota, formerly was on the political science faculty at Kent State University. He served as a consultant to the President's Crime Commission and is the author of *Regional Law Enforcement: A Study of Intergovernmental Cooperation and Coordination.*

MARVIN J. CUMMINS is Associate Director of the Social Science Institute at Washington University (St. Louis). He was previously Assistant Professor of Sociology at the University of Oregon.

EUGENE EIDENBERG is Associate Professor of Political Science at the University of Minnesota. He is the co-author of *An Act of Congress.* **JOSEPH C. RIGERT** is an editorial writer for The Minneapolis Tribune, specializing in urban affairs. He was a staff writer for The Oregon Journal, The Associated Press and The Minneapolis Tribune before becoming an editorial writer in 1967. He also was a press secretary for two U.S. Congressmen.

JOE R. FEAGIN is Assistant Professor of Sociology at the University of California, Riverside. He is the author of several articles concerning race relations, poverty, and civil disorders.

W. EUGENE GROVES and **PETER H. ROSSI** are members of the Group for Research on Social Policy at The Johns Hopkins University where Groves is also receiving his Ph.D. and Rossi is Chairman of the Department of Social Relations and Professor of Sociology.

HARLAN HAHN is Professor of Political Science at the University of California, Riverside. He is the author of *Urban-Rural Conflict: The Politics of Change* and of a forthcoming book on urban law enforcement.

MARK H. HALLER is Associate Professor of History at Temple University. He is the author of *Eugenics: Hereditarian Attitudes in American Thought.* He has edited and written a new introduction for John Landesco's *Organized Crime in Chicago.* He also served as a consultant for the President's Commission on the Causes and Prevention of Violence.

ROBERT A. MENDELSOHN is a Staff Psychologist at Lafayette Clinic, Associate Professor of Psychology at Wayne State University, and coinvestigator for the social psychological study of Detroit's civil disturbance.

NEAL A. MILNER, Assistant Professor of Political Science at Grinnell College, is the author of *The Court and Local Law Enforcement: The Impact of Miranda*.

LEONARD SAVITZ is Professor of Sociology at Temple University. He is the author of *Dilemma in Criminology* and the co-author of *Sociology of Crime* and *Sociology of Correction and Punishment*.

JAMES LEO WALSH is Assistant Professor of Sociology at Oberlin College. He is the author of several articles concerning professional strivings among medical personnel.